Lincolnshire
COUNTY COUNCIL

COMMUNITIES, CULTURAL SERVICES
and ADULT EDUCATION

**This book should be returned on or before
the last date shown below.**

HP3

To renew or order library books please telephone 01522 782010
or visit www.linco'
You will require a Person:
Ask any member

'A riveting, rollicking read with man
Fareed Zakaria, editor
American World

Also by Michael Meyer

The Alexander Complex

THE YEAR
THAT CHANGED
THE WORLD

The Untold Story behind
the Fall of the Berlin Wall

MICHAEL MEYER

POCKET
BOOKS

LONDON • SYDNEY • NEW YORK • TORONTO

First published in Great Britain in 2009 by Simon & Schuster UK Ltd
This edition published by Pocket Books, 2010
An imprint of Simon & Schuster UK Ltd
A CBS COMPANY

1 3 5 7 9 10 8 6 4 2

Simon & Schuster UK Ltd
1st Floor
222 Gray's Inn Road
London
WC1X 8HB

www.simonandschuster.co.uk

Simon & Schuster Australia
Sydney

A CIP catalogue copy for this book is available
from the British Library.

ISBN: 978-1-84739-434-7

Designed by Erich Hobbing
Printed by CPI Cox & Wyman, Reading, Berkshire RG1 8EX

To MN

and those few who dared

CONTENTS

PREFACE

One fine day in early spring 1988, my phone rang.

"Mike," asked our chief of correspondents. "How would you like to go to Germany?"

I'd heard, some weeks ago, that the assignment had already gone to someone else. What happened?

"Changed his mind. Decided it was too risky."

In the news business, *too risky* means "bad for one's career." The reporter opting out concluded that Germany and Eastern Europe were too far off America's radar screen. Not much was happening. He feared he wouldn't get into the magazine.

I couldn't believe my good fortune. For fifty years, Europe had been frozen. Now a new man was in charge: Mikhail Gorbachev. Change was afoot. You could feel it. I remember, vividly, thinking I would have perhaps a year or two to see the old Europe, a part of the continent that had been cut off behind the Iron Curtain, as if under glass, before it all went away. In my youthful enthusiasm, I considered it an almost anthropological adventure, a chance of a lifetime.

"When do I leave?" I asked. As soon as you can was the reply. And so, in the summer of 1988, I became *Newsweek*'s bureau chief for Germany and Eastern Europe. It was like stepping onto a magic carpet, to be whisked away into a world of revolution—and revelation— beyond imagining.

Nineteen eighty-nine was a year of magnificent and unfathomable upheaval. Revolutions ignited across Eastern Europe, setting the stage for the collapse of the Soviet Union. I was an eyewitness to history. In Poland, I covered the renaissance of Solidarity. I was with

Vaclav Havel and other friends in Prague as they engineered the Velvet Revolution. I was the last American journalist to interview Nicolae Ceausescu and have free run of his tyrannized Romania. I airlifted into Bucharest with the German Luftwaffe during the fighting that deposed him and watched his execution in the company of the secret police who did him in.

The most epochal moment of that epochal year was November 9—the day the Berlin Wall came down. I watched it happen from the Eastern side of the border as the people of East Germany rose up and stormed the gates, ending four decades of communist dictatorship. I joined them as they danced atop the Wall and paraded through the streets, reveling in what was a new Berlin, the famous divided city suddenly divided no more. And like every American, I rejoiced. The Cold War was over. We won. Democracy was triumphant.

We saw this as our moment of vindication, a victory that justified all our struggles—four decades of Cold War confrontation, trillions of dollars spent on national defense, too many lives lost in shadowy wars far across the seas. And in most ways it was. Nineteen eighty-nine was a year that changed the world. The end of the Cold War moved us from a world of division and nuclear blackmail to one of new opportunity and unprecedented prosperity. It set the stage for our modern era: globalization, the triumph of free markets, the spread of democracy. It ushered in the great global economic boom, lifting billions out of poverty around the world and firmly establishing America as the one and only superpower.

And yet it was a dangerous triumph, chiefly because we claimed it for ourselves and scarcely bothered to understand how this great change really came to pass. I sensed that we weren't seeing the full story, even at the time. Today, I am sure of it. From the vantage point of two decades, and with a great deal of further research, I know now that our victory in the Cold War was not what it seemed. I have learned that it simply did not happen the way we think it did. Most painfully, the myths we spun around it have hurt the world and ourselves.

What are these myths, which we accept as truths?

First, The People. Most accounts of 1989 come down to a simple plotline: Eastern Europe's long-repressed citizens, frustrated by poverty and lack of freedom and inspired by our example, rose up en masse and overthrew their communist overlords. Well, yes and no. In some countries, that is pretty much what happened. But in others, there was nothing of the sort. The most interesting (and certainly most decisive) subplot in this year of revolution was the tale of a small band of East European buccaneers—a mere handful of five or six top Hungarian leaders, with little popular support—who set out to bring down communism, not only in their own country but across the East bloc. In a conspiracy worthy of the most contrived Cold War spy thriller, they deliberately took aim at the Berlin Wall—and more than any others, it was they who brought it down. Theirs is the great untold story of 1989.

A second myth concerns the role of history. We Americans tend to see the end of communism as somehow foreordained. The inherent flaws of communism brought about its collapse; it could not stand up to the example of the West. This is a tectonic view, history as the interplay of great and almost inevitable forces. Seen from the ground, however, it looked very different. If you were there the night the Berlin Wall fell, you knew that it came to pass, in the way it did, because of a freak accident, a small and utterly human blunder. The iconic imagery of jubilant East Berliners celebrating atop the Wall, pounding it with sledgehammers, in reality owes as much to happenstance as to culminating history.

A third myth is most dangerous: the idea of the United States as an emancipator, a liberator of repressive regimes. This crusading brand of American triumphalism in time became gospel among neoconservatives, including many in the administration of George W. Bush. For them, the revolutions of 1989 became the foundation of a new post–Cold War weltanschauung: the idea that all totalitarian regimes are similarly hollow at the core and will crumble with a shove from the outside. If its symbol is the Berlin Wall, coming down as Ronald Reagan famously bid it to do in a speech in Berlin in 1987, the operational model was Nicolae Ceausescu's Romania. "Once the wicked witch was dead," as Francis Fukuyama, the eminent political economist, has put it, "the munchkins would rise up and start singing joyously about their liberation."

It is true that instead of seeking to contain the former Soviet

Union, as previous administrations had done, the United States under Ronald Reagan chose to confront it. He challenged Mikhail Gorbachev not only to reform the Soviet system from within but to "tear down this wall." Yet other factors figured in this equation, not least a drop in oil prices from roughly $40 a barrel in 1980 to less than $10 a decade later, not to mention the Soviet leader's own actions. Even less well-known is Ronald Reagan's political evolution. From hardened cold war warrior, he softened both his rhetoric and his policies to the point where his administration became the very model of enlightened diplomatic engagement—the antithesis of hard-right confrontation.

Without question, the United States uniquely contributed to the end of the Cold War, from the Marshall Plan and the reconstruction of Europe, to containment, to our efforts to help create what today has become the European Union. But others "won" it, on their own (and our) behalf. *The Year That Changed the World* gives overdue credit to the true victors and the remarkable degree to which the upheavals of 1989 resulted less from mass revolution than from the careful planning and thoughtful work of a few farsighted and courageous individuals, as well as human error and the shortsightedness of others.

The purpose is not to debunk accepted history but to liberate it. Twenty years later, as a new generation arises with little or no memory of these epic events, the narrative deserves retelling. Told truthfully, it becomes if anything more dramatic. And who knows, perhaps along the way it might help us rethink the underpinnings of American foreign policy as we move into the second decade of a new century.

It's a straight line from the fantasy of 1989 to Saddam Hussein and Iraq, with all its aftershocks. America's disaster in the Middle East, it can be argued without overly stretching the point, grows from the hubris attending "our" victory in Eastern Europe. By logical extension, from past to present, all we have to do is confront the Evil One and, with a big push, the people will rise up and throw off their shackles. Drunk on pride and power, we got it terribly wrong. If America could be likened to an alcoholic on the mend, it is time to go back to the beginning, to see where and why we went awry, and to look at the world as it is.

PREFACE

I owe a great many people a great many thanks: to *Newsweek*, chiefly, for sending me to Europe, and to its often brilliant editors. Among them, the late Kenneth Auchincloss, my boss during those exciting days, and more recently Fareed Zakaria. One could not possibly hope for a more rewarding association. The American Academy in Berlin made this book possible, first by awarding the fellowship where I wrote an early draft, in 1999, and second, in helping to shape its themes. For this I am eternally grateful to Richard Holbrooke, Gary Smith and Everette Dennis. Friends, colleagues and loved ones played no less a role. Colin Robinson, who took the project under his wing at Scribner, was a most able editor. My wonderful wife, Suzanne, more than once saved me from scrapping the project. She was its most stalwart champion; this book would not exist without her. Others inspired me to undertake it in the first place and helped me to see much that I would otherwise not have. I do not know how to begin to repay such gifts.

THE YEAR
THAT CHANGED
THE WORLD

CHAPTER ONE

Genesis

Every great nation has its founding myths. Every true leader has a defining vision. Every person has his or her story, the narrative that gives shape and meaning to one's life. The problem begins when life and the narrative fall out of joint. The greater the disjuncture, the more fatal the problem.

George W. Bush idolized Ronald Reagan. From the outset he modeled his presidency upon him. His first inaugural deliberately echoed Reagan's patented blend of stirring rhetoric, moral clarity and iron conviction in basic principles. Advisers drew the comparison at every opportunity. "Reagan's son," they called him, and spoke reverently of how their man was impregnated with "Reagan's DNA."

Bush put the former president ahead of even Winston Churchill and Theodore Roosevelt—the "gold standard"—in his personal pantheon of heroes. Eulogizing him in 2004, he evoked a legacy he clearly saw as his own. "He acted to defend liberty wherever it was threatened. He called evil by its name." The famous Berlin Wall was the concrete symbol of communism and its hated masters. Among those who swung their hammers to bring it down, said Bush, there was no doubt: "The hardest blow had been struck by President Ronald Reagan."

As Bush saw it, Reagan's world was one of moral absolutes—right and wrong, black and white. As Reagan stood up to confront communist tyranny, so would he stand up to a more modern challenge. The "evil empire" became the new president's "war on terror," the "axis of evil." Yet the essential narrative of a grand struggle against an implacable enemy of freedom remained unchanged.

1

Standing aboard the USS *Lincoln* on May 1, 2003, Bush declared "mission accomplished" in Iraq, a triumph for liberty in the tradition of Roosevelt's Four Freedoms, the Truman Doctrine and "Ronald Reagan's challenge to an evil empire." In a 2005 speech to the National Endowment for Democracy (delivered in the Reagan Amphitheater), he spoke of how the fight against Islamic radicalism "resembles the struggle against communism in the last century." He drew a staccato series of comparisons. "Like the ideology of communism, our new enemy teaches that innocent individuals can be sacrificed. . . . Like the ideology of communism, our new enemy pursues totalitarian aims. . . . Like the ideology of communism, our new enemy is dismissive of free peoples."

On he went, evocations of the threat faced by Ronald Reagan coupled with invocations to answer "history's call" in shouldering today's "global campaign of freedom." To critics who considered the war in Iraq to be a mistake, Bush offered a retort grounded in a Reagan antecedent. In 1982, when the fortieth president told an audience at Westminster Palace in London that communism's days were numbered, opponents on both sides of the Atlantic ridiculed him as "simplistic and naive, even dangerous."

Again and again, as his political troubles deepened, Bush returned to precedent in answering those who attacked him and his policies. Less than a year before he left office, on a day in early February 2008, when his approval ratings were around 30 percent, he drew cheers at the American Conservative Union. When the Twin Towers fell, "we stood our ground," he declared. "We stood our ground" in Afghanistan and Iraq. "We stood our ground" for America as a "leading light, a guiding star, the greatest nation on the face of the Earth"—language inspired directly by Reagan. Then he concluded with the ultimate exculpation, as if he were a latter-day Saint Sebastian: "Ronald Reagan, too, was called a 'warmonger,' an 'amiable dunce,' an actor detached from reality. Yet within a few years after President Reagan left office, the Berlin Wall came down, the Evil Empire collapsed, the Cold War was won."

Everyone hears the echo. Everyone knows the reference. "Mr. Gorbachev, tear down this wall!"

A generation of speechwriters wish they had crafted that clarion call. A generation of statesmen wish they had uttered it, among them many who belittled it at the time. Rightly, it is included in collections of the century's great presidential addresses. Video clips of the speech can be watched on YouTube. For a generation of Americans, it has become a defining moment of the twentieth century, a turning point in the long struggle to win the Cold War.

This one line, the epochal phrase in the most memorable speech of a presidency, grew over the years to become the touchstone of the Reagan legacy, the man and his ideas distilled to their essence—his optimism, his faith, his willingness to confront the conventional order, his bedrock belief in American values, most of all freedom and democracy and the power of people to change their lives and the world for the better.

Reagan delivered it on a warm spring afternoon in the divided city of Berlin, June 12, 1987. Behind him rose the famed Brandenburg Gate, its arches and columns still blackened and pockmarked from the smoke and shrapnel of the last European battle of World War II. It was a dramatic proscenium for a bit of geopolitical theater. Snaking through the background, one hundred yards behind the dais where Reagan stood, was the Wall—the crude, blunt twelve-foot barrier of gray cement and barbed wire that divided East from West, the world of democratic freedom from that of totalitarian oppression, the literal embodiment of the Cold War.

A guard tower poked up from the death strip running behind the Wall. Armed East German border guards surveyed the scene through binoculars. Large sheets of bulletproof glass shielded the president from the rear. Unseen from the Western side, crowds of East Germans gathered to hear Reagan, hoping loudspeakers would project his voice across the divide. East German police pushed them back, the president was told. This in itself was a demonstration of all that Reagan hated about communism, and he punched out his words with angry force—a direct exhortation, delivered personally, to the Soviet leader Mikhail Gorbachev.

Reagan began slowly, speaking of other American presidents who had come to Berlin, John F. Kennedy and Jimmy Carter, honoring their duty to speak out against what he called "the scar" that split the city. He spoke of America's efforts to save Berlin after the war—aid under the Marshall Plan, the Berlin airlift of food and medicine when the Red Army cut supply lines to the West. Echoing the old Marlene Dietrich song, he joked that he kept a "suitcase" in Berlin—*Ich hab' noch einen Koffer in Berlin*—a metaphor of solidarity with this outpost of freedom so isolated behind enemy territory. And he spoke of the winds of change he knew to be blowing, coming from the East as glasnost and perestroika, openness and reform, authored by none other than Gorbachev himself.

Then, a little after 2 p.m., he made his move: "We hear from Moscow about a new openness." Could these hints of change be real? Is this talk to be believed or trusted? If so, said Reagan, fixing his jaw and speaking progressively more loudly, bluntly, hammering every word as if it were a nail, give us a sign that you are sincere—"the one sign . . . that would be unmistakable. General Secretary Gorbachev, if you seek peace, if you seek prosperity for the Soviet Union and Eastern Europe, if you seek liberalization: Come here to this gate! Mr. Gorbachev, open this gate! Mr. Gorbachev, tear down this wall!"

The crowds cheered. Some waved American flags, though most of these had been planted by the U.S. embassy. After it was done and the president had gone, along with the ten thousand or so West Berliners who had come to hear him, local TV carried highlights. Not many Germans watched. Few admired Reagan and a large majority actively disliked him, especially in liberal and often anti-American Berlin. Most far preferred Gorbachev, seen as the peacemaker, who would arrive a few weeks later to be mobbed like a rock star. (Gorbimania, they called it.) Major U.S. newspapers with correspondents in Europe, such as the *New York Times*, carried stories that ran in the back pages. And that was that until two years, four months, twenty-eight days and nine hours later—long after Reagan had left office—when the Berlin Wall actually came down.

Abruptly, it was as if word were deed. Ronald Reagan became not only a prophet, foreseeing what no one else had, but the prime mover in a stunning geopolitical transformation. Overnight, it seemed, the world changed. The Cold War was over. We won!

At least, this is the spin we Americans put on it. In recent years, particularly among U.S. conservatives, the Berlin Wall speech has taken on the talismanic weight of an ideological icon, both the symbol and founding idea of a new post–Cold War weltanschauung. As president, Reagan did what no one else had done before him: he confronted the enemy—and triumphed. He changed America's way of acting in the world, its sense of sheer possibility. Reagan had no patience with the old order. Gone was time-honored talk of "détente" and "containment" and "mutual nuclear deterrence." All that was for the ash heap of history. With his arms race and tough talk, he pushed the Soviet Union to the point of collapse, creating a new axiom of American foreign policy: stand tall and confront the enemy, as Reagan did that day in Berlin.

From this axiom flowed a contemporary corollary—that all dictatorial regimes are similarly hollow at the core and will crumble with a shove from the outside. All it takes is faith and a little Reagan spunk, backed by U.S. military power, and we can change the world. George W. Bush could thus say, dedicating a memorial in 2007 to an estimated 100 million victims of communism, that "evil is real and must be confronted." He could tell a graduating class of West Point cadets in 2006 that, as in the Cold War, America today must "confront" new dangers. Indeed, the word became one of the most popular verbs in his rhetorical arsenal. "We will confront threats . . . confront new adversaries . . . confront new enemies . . . and never back down, never give in, never accept anything less than complete victory." Again, the Reagan echo with a nod to Winston Churchill. Be resolute, and the enemy will blink. Goodness and light will triumph. The fall of the Berlin Wall serves as proof and inspiration.

There's only one problem—that of disjuncture, a confusion of cause and effect. What if it didn't happen quite that way?

Let us return to that fateful moment.

It was the night of November 9, 1989. The place: Checkpoint Charlie, the famous border crossing in the heart of Cold War Berlin.

The Wall loomed up, grim and forbidding. In the harsh yellow glare of the frontier's high-intensity arc lights, strewn round with barbed wire and tank traps, thousands of East Germans faced a thin line of Volkspolizei, the ubiquitous state police. People were gathering at all the checkpoints to the West, confused but exhilarated. They called out to one another and, increasingly, to the guards, who only moments before they feared. *"Sofort,"* they shouted. "Open up!!"

Emboldened by their numbers, they pushed within a few meters of the barricades, arguing with and even mocking the guards, who stood fiddling with their weapons. No one knew what to do. The crisis had materialized from nowhere. It was dangerous, for the police had no orders except to use deadly force to keep people from fleeing to the West. The crowds kept their good humor. But what if that changed, or if they tried to storm the gates? Would the police shoot?

They had begun gathering shortly after 7 p.m., four hours earlier. They came tentatively, huddled in small clusters some distance from the police, asking timid questions and holding out identity cards. But as their numbers grew—first by the dozens, then by the hundreds, finally by the thousands—they grew bolder. By 10 p.m. they had pushed to within a few paces of the guards faced off before them. And still they kept coming, channeling toward the checkpoint from three converging streets like tributary rivers building up behind a dam. The multitude of their voices shouted as one. "Open up! Open up!"

Past the police and their guard dogs, past the watchtower and the curling barbed wire of the infamous death strip, on the other side of the Wall, came an answering call from an equally boisterous mob of West Germans. "Come over! Come over!"

Blazing television lights suddenly flipped on from the West, silhouetting the Wall and the guards, intensifying the eerie scene. Inside his lighted, glass-walled command post, the captain of the East German border guard, a beefy guy with a square face and the dark bristly hair of a Doberman, stood dialing and re-dialing his telephone. For hours he vainly sought instructions. Clearly he was confused. Certainly he was frightened; the crowds had grown so fast, unlike anything he had ever seen, and now they pushed so close to the barriers that their breath, frosting in the night air, mingled with that of his increasingly anxious men.

Panicky calls flew from checkpoints up and down the Wall to the Interior Ministry, to no avail. Top officials tried to reach the members of the Politburo, but the leaders of the regime seemed to have disappeared. Once again the border guard put down his phone. He stood rock-still. No one had any answers; other border-control commanders were just as confused as he. Perhaps he had just been informed that the Bornholmerstrasse crossing, to the north, had moments ago opened its barriers, besieged by some twenty thousand people. Perhaps he came to his own decision. Maybe he was simply fed up.

Whatever the case, at 11:17 p.m., precisely, he shrugged his shoulders, as if to say, *Why not?*

"*Alles auf!*" he ordered. "Open up," and the gates swung wide.

A great roar rose out of the crowds as they surged forward. Suddenly, the Berlin Wall was no more. "*Die Mauer ist Weck,*" the people cried out as they celebrated atop it before the cameras throughout the night. "The Wall is gone!"

At that moment, history took an epic turn. A frontier that for five decades divided East from West was breached. Within the blink of an eye, it seemed, the Berlin Wall fell. The Cold War ended. Germans, suddenly, were once again Germans. Berliners were Berliners, no longer "East" nor "West."

Earlier in the evening, just after 6 p.m., another man had shrugged, in much the same manner as that beefy border guard. Gunter Schabowski, the portly spokesman for the new East German Politburo, installed just weeks earlier, stopped by the offices of the communist party boss, Egon Krenz, en route to the daily press briefing, a recent innovation designed to demonstrate the regime's new openness.

"Anything to announce?" Schabowski asked, casually.

Krenz shuffled through the papers on his desk, then passed Schabowski a two-page memo. "Take this," he said with a grin. "It will do us a power of good."

Schabowski scanned the memo while being driven from party headquarters. It seemed innocuous enough—just a short press release. At the news conference, he read it out as item four or five from a list of the various announcements. It had to do with passports. Every East German would now, for the first time, have a right to one.

For a nation locked so long behind the Iron Curtain, it was tremendous news. At the press conference, there was a sudden hush, followed by a ripple of whispers. Schabowski droned on. Then from the back of the room, as the cameras rolled, broadcasting live to the nation, a reporter shouted out a fateful question: "When does it take effect?"

Schabowski paused, looked up, suddenly confused. "What?"

The reporter repeated the question, his voice almost lost in a cacophony of shouts from others seeking similar clarification.

Schabowski scratched his head, mumbled to aides on either side. "Um, that's a technical question. I'm not sure." He perched his glasses on the end of his nose, shuffled through his papers, then looked up again . . . and shrugged.

"*Ab Sofort,*" he read aloud from what he saw written on the press release. Immediately. Without delay.

At this, the room erupted. Schabowski, we now know, didn't fully appreciate the significance of his announcement. He had been on vacation during the preceding days when the decision was taken; he was out of the loop. Krenz had handed him the memo, without further explanation; Schabowski simply read it off to the press.

For the reporters in the room, the impact was tremendous. At that very moment, thousands of East Germans were illegally fleeing the country, driving their sputtering two-stroke East German–made cars, the infamous Trabant, across the border to neighboring Czechoslovakia, and from there over the mountains to West Germany. Earlier that summer, hundreds of thousands of other East Germans had escaped via Hungary. Of all the ills of communism, as they saw it, the most onerous was that they could not travel beyond the Iron Curtain. Like anyone else, they, too, wanted to see the world. They, too, wanted to see the West. A passport represented their right to live free.

Thus the uproar in the pressroom. Amid the instantaneous hubbub of shouted questions, one rang sharp and clear. "Mr. Schabowski, what is going to happen with the Berlin Wall?" As if finally sensing danger, the ground shifting beneath his feet, Schabowski dodged. "It has been brought to my attention that it is seven p.m. I'm sorry. That has to be the last question. Thank you for your understanding." And off he went.

The damage had been done, however. *Sofort.* Immediately. Without delay. In fact, this was not at all what the regime had in mind. Yes, East Germans would be granted passports. Yes, they would be allowed to travel. But to use them, they would first have to apply for an exit visa, subject to the usual rules and regulations. And the fine print said they could do that only on the next day, November 10.

Certainly, the last thing Krenz intended was for his citizens to just get up and go. But East Germans didn't know that. They only knew what they heard on TV, which circulated like wildfire through the city. Thanks to Schabowski, they thought they were free. *Sofort.* By the tens of thousands they flocked to the crossing points to the West.

Strangely oblivious to the earthquake his words had caused, Schabowski headed home for dinner. Other senior officials went to the opera, or to the bowers of their mistresses. As East Germany's final, existential crisis fell upon it, the country's leadership was virtually incommunicado. Overwhelmed by the crowds, receiving no instructions from the military or party elite, border guards at the Wall were left to act on their own. Like Schabowski, the Checkpoint Charlie border guard shrugged—literally—and threw open the gates.

And so the Wall came down.

From afar, it was as Ronald Reagan decreed. But was it? Seen up close, on the ground, it looked very different from how we remember it.

No big international crisis set the stage for November 9, 1989. It did not spring from any great-power confrontation. There was no stirring rhetoric, no rattling of sabers, no politicians playing to the cameras. To Americans, particularly, this decisive moment of the Cold War came unexpectedly, seemingly out of the blue.

Only one TV anchorman was on the scene—Tom Brokaw of NBC. No Western leader was on hand to witness the event or greet the victims of so many years of communist oppression as they found their way, wide-eyed and bewildered, to freedom and the West. German chancellor Helmut Kohl was on a state visit to Poland. President George H. W. Bush learned of it from his national security adviser, Brent Scowcroft, who heard it on the news. Together, the two men went into the president's private study adjoining the Oval Office and turned on the TV. Gosh, Bush remarked to aides. "If the Soviets are going to let the communists fall in East Germany, they've got to be really serious—more serious than I realized."

As turning points in history go, this was pretty ad hoc. World War I ended with the ceremonial signing of an armistice in a railroad car in a forest near Compiègne. It was followed by the grand partition of the German and Austro-Hungarian empires in the Treaty of Versailles in

1919, a literal redrawing of the world's map. World War II ended with formal surrenders at Allied headquarters in Belgium and on the battleship *Missouri* in Tokyo Bay in 1945, signed by the representatives of a defeated emperor, in top hat and tails, flanked by ranks of their conquerors. By contrast, the Cold War ended with a spontaneous whoop, or more accurately a street party. Ordinary people, demanding change, took matters into their own hands. They brought down the Wall, not armies or world statesmen. And then they danced atop it.

Accident played an enormous role. Would the Berlin Wall have fallen, as dramatically as it did, were it not for Gunter Schabowski's bungle? It was the shrug that changed the world. And what of the commander of the East German border guard at Checkpoint Charlie? Another shrug, another bit of happenstance that through the ages has shaped history and decided the fates of men.

As for those famous four words of Ronald Reagan's—"tear down this wall"—they were nearly never uttered. Peter Robinson, a White House speechwriter, tells how Reagan planned to attend the annual summit of G7 industrialized nations in Venice. Then came a request from the German government to visit Berlin on the occasion of the city's 750th anniversary. Here was a chance to emulate Kennedy and speak at the Wall, suggested someone on the president's staff. Could Robinson please write up something to say on foreign policy?

Robinson spent a day and a half in Berlin gathering material. First he wrote, "Herr Gorbachev, bring down this wall." Then he considered playing to the local audience by having Reagan deliver the line in German: *"Herr Gorbachev, machen Sie dieses Tor auf."* (There's a quote for the ages.) Settling finally on the words we now know by heart, Robinson circulated the speech to the State Department and the National Security Council. "Both attempted to squelch it," he writes in his memoir, *How Ronald Reagan Changed My Life*. The draft was "naïve," they said. It would raise "false hopes." It was "clumsy" and "needlessly provocative." It would make the president look like a "crude and anticommunist cowboy." The ranking diplomat in Berlin, John Kornblum, eventually to become ambassador to Germany, was particularly dismissive and offered what he considered to be a far superior substitute: "One day, this ugly wall will disappear." And one day, perhaps, pigs will fly, Robinson thought to himself.

In all, the speech went through seven drafts. Each time the policy experts elided the offending line. The fight raged all the way to Berlin, when Reagan resolved the flap with Kenneth Duberstein, his deputy chief of staff, en route to the Wall in the presidential limo.

"So, Ken. I am the president?"

"Yes, sir."

"Well, Ken," said Reagan with a laugh. "Let's just leave that line in."

The rest, as they say, is history—of a sort. For nothing, here, supports what has come to be conventional wisdom about Reagan's Berlin speech: that it was a defiant challenge, a ringing expression of a U.S. policy of confrontation that would lead not only to victory in the Cold War but beyond. To the contrary, Ronald Reagan would have been appalled at the uses to which his words have been put. The truth is that, in 1987, he faced a new phenomenon—a challenge to which confrontation, he came to conclude over time, was no answer. That was the ascent of Mikhail Gorbachev as general secretary of the communist party of the Soviet Union on March 11, 1985.

Gorbachev hit the Soviet landscape like a giant meteor from outer space, transforming everything on impact. He was that rarest and most powerful force in history: the singularity, the wild card, what scientists call an exogenous variable, the unprecedented element that changes all theories and throws off all calculations and, with them, changes the world as it is known.

Aside from a certain softness around the eyes, Gorbachev looked little different from his old-guard predecessors. Gray-suited and stockily built, the son of peasant farmers in Stavropol in remote southern Russia, he had risen through the ranks of the party by virtue of bureaucratic smarts and hard work. Only a sharp sense of humor, a certain outspokenness and the birthmark on his forehead, looking nothing so much as a large bird-dropping, seemed to distinguish him from the communist pack. And yet, this new Soviet man came to office full of indignation and a passion for change. At fifty-four, he was the youngest general secretary, promoted by his mentor, head of the KGB secret police, Yuri Andropov. Like Andropov, he saw the flaws of the Soviet system: an economy that was stalled, that soaked up money for military use but left little for civilian expenditures, a society that was sinking ever deeper into backwardness and stagnation. Unlike

Andropov, he was determined to do something about it. He saw the nuclear disaster at Chernobyl, in early 1986, precisely for what it was: an indictment of the Soviet system, poisonous and broken and a threat to all humanity. It had to be changed, he knew. He was convinced that it could be reformed. "We cannot go on like this," he told his wife, Raisa, walking in their garden long before Chernobyl's radioactive plume began to reach across Europe. "We cannot go on like this."

Within weeks of taking office, the new Russian leader introduced the world to those twin revolutionary concepts that he would become famous for, and to which Ronald Reagan alluded in his Berlin speech—glasnost and perestroika. He called for an era of "new political thinking," at home and abroad. He fired the Soviet Union's traditional face to the West, Foreign Minister Andrey Gromyko, the dour hard-liner popularly known as Mr. Nyet, and replaced him with the charismatic Eduard Shevardnadze. Gorbachev began reaching out to Europe and the United States, cultivating personal ties with Western leaders. Famously, Margaret Thatcher pronounced him a man she could "do business with." He struck up a friendship with Helmut Kohl and began speaking of how Russia belonged in what he called the "common house of Europe." Most important, he began telling leaders of the Soviet satellite nations of Eastern Europe that their future resided with themselves. Just as he would seek to reform Russia from within, so too should they work to reform their own societies. How they would do it was for them to choose, without interference from Moscow.

Reagan's speech in Berlin came at a critical moment in his own relations with the new Soviet leader. He first met Gorbachev in Geneva, in November 1985, where they discussed nuclear disarmament in a media-friendly "fireside chat." They continued the conversation at their second famous summit in Reykjavik, in October 1986, where in an extraordinary meeting of minds the two men came close to a deal to abolish nuclear weapons. By the time of his Berlin Wall speech, Reagan was well along in changing his thinking about Gorbachev. The president had read his recently published book, *Perestroika: New Thinking for Our Country and the World.* "It was as damning as anything written about communism in the West," said Reagan. Meanwhile, negotiations for a third summit were far advanced. On December 8, 1987, Gorbachev and Reagan met in Washington to sign a treaty rather cumbersomely known as the Intermediate Nuclear Forces accord, or INF. Dramatically, it did away with an entire class of nuclear weapons as Soviet SS20s and U.S. cruise and Pershing missiles were removed from Europe.

Hard-liners in the U.S. national security establishment were aghast. Defense Secretary Caspar Weinberger, backed by his special adviser Richard Perle, among others, viscerally opposed Reagan's talk of disarmament and instead pushed hard for an escalation of military spending. As the hawks saw it, Reagan was in danger of going soft on communism. And they were right. Like Thatcher, Reagan had concluded that Gorbachev was trustworthy, that he could "do business" with him. But he had a problem: within the right wing of his party, all this was heresy.

As Reagan sought to change the climate of U.S.-Soviet relations, then, he had to find a way to neutralize opposition within his administration, just as Gorbachev himself had to negotiate a delicate and often perilous path among the factions of his own government. The Berlin Wall speech gave Reagan cover, notes James Mann, author of *Rise of the Vulcans*, a definitive portrait of George W. Bush's foreign policy team. To the hard-liners, it would sound like a traditional anticommunist speech of defiance and Cold War confrontation, which of course is why the State Department and the National Security Council tried so hard to get those four words out.

In fact, the speech was a remarkably nuanced balancing act. It managed to acknowledge how far the Soviet Union had come, while underscoring how far it had to go. Yet what many Americans heard only as a challenge was also an invitation—an invitation to engage, to continue further down the road the two men had come, a holding out of a hand, an offering to meet halfway. Certainly that's how the men standing at Reagan's side heard it that day; Berlin mayor Eberhard Diepgen said so at the time. Today's buzz phrase for this sort of diplomacy had not yet been coined: *soft power*. But that's what it was— a conviction, in the heart of the ultimate cold warrior, this consummate idealist, that cooperation and compromise and faith in the power of America's example would go further than militarist confrontation in making a better world. Reagan knew this, even if his disciples did not.

Within half a year, he had jettisoned the easy rhetoric of the "evil empire." That May, he visited Moscow, chatting with ordinary Russians in Red Square and delivering a talk to the students of Moscow University. Reagan clearly sensed a dawning of a new era. Nor was the symbol of Ronald Reagan in Moscow, hosted by a man calling for change in the Kremlin, lost on the people of Europe, especially those who had the misfortune to live on the wrong side of the Wall. They heard the real message, coming from both sides: accommodation, not confrontation. And that gave them hope and the courage to act.

The history of the revolutions in Eastern Europe was not written in Washington. It had little to do with American military might. It had far more to do with the rise of Gorbachev, coupled with the economic collapse of the Soviet system and the glaring contrast to the dynamism of Western Europe. The preparedness of East European leaders, with the exception of those of Romania, to accept peaceful change was critical. So was the role of sheer accident and happenstance, as we shall see. Above all, it had everything to do with people, individually and collectively, on the ground, deciding for themselves to tear down that Wall.

This is the story of how they did it, shorn of mythology.

CHAPTER TWO

The Wall

Arriving in Berlin, I would do what I always did: drop my luggage at the hotel and hail a taxi toward the East. I went to touch the Wall, to lay hands upon it. It didn't matter how many times I had done it before, or how many times I would do so again. It was my lodestone, my centering point, my story as a journalist covering Germany and the East bloc.

Nothing has ever been so freighted with symbolism, ideology and history. The Wall was World War II, the Cold War, the Iron Curtain, the high tide of totalitarianism and communist dictatorship, the frontier of democracy. You could feel it, smell it, run your hands over it, look across it. On the one side, us. On the other, them.

It didn't matter what direction you took. Berlin was an island; all paths led to the Wall. Usually I went down Bismarck Strasse, past the Siegessäule, the winged column celebrating Prussia's victory in the 1871 war against France, to the Reichstag. The Wall cut a few feet behind the old parliament, still blackened and pockmarked from flying debris from the war. A dozen crosses memorialized a few who died there trying to escape. An East German patrol boat, with spotlights and heavy machine guns, idled on the far shore of the River Spree. Only a few weeks before my first visit, a young man was gunned down near the spot and left to bleed to death where he lay.

Usually I would walk south, along the Wall past the Brandenburg Gate, across the muddy and eerily empty lots around Potsdamer Platz, the heart of old Berlin, once crowded with hotels and department stores and so busy in the 1920s that it received Europe's first traffic light. Hitler's bunker lay there in the death strip, a swelling breast of earth easily glimpsed from a spectator platform, illuminated by harsh security lights at night and girded with antitank traps. Farther along was Wilhelm Strasse and the weed-grown rubble of the Nazi SS headquarters, then after a series of sharp zigs and zags down abandoned and often broken streets came Checkpoint Charlie. YOU ARE LEAVING THE AMERICAN SECTOR a large sign warned in English, French and Russian, beyond which the green-uniformed Vopos—Volkspolizei— of the German Democratic Republic waited behind their barriers and barbed wire. The view stretched all the way to Moscow.

Ronald Reagan spoke for many, but it was hard to imagine the world without the Wall. Perhaps it was the touching. The Wall was so obdurate and outwardly solid. Its blunt, crude force, so hostile to movement, heart and spirit, had become a fact of life—regrettable and tragic, to be sure, but there, like cancer or the reality of evil in the world.

In Berlin, the Wall was felt everywhere, even when not in sight. It haunts the city to this day, twenty years later. Eerie remnants remain, catching one unawares: a stretch of Wall here, a watch-tower there, vacant lots where the death strip passed, a thin line of paving stones inlaid in the streets of the city's center, marked with bronze plates: BERLIN MAUER: 1961–1989. In the forested parts of Berlin, away from the now trendy Mitte, or city center, you may notice a steady march of pines through stands of birch and elder. The Wall's scar has been replanted. Dig in the sandy soil, and you find broken pieces of its distinctive concrete. The Wall abides like a phantom limb, a void that cannot be forgotten.

There is a misplaced sentimentality to these memories, a sort of Cold War romance, a thrill for a certain kind of tourist. Berliners for the most part simply lived with it, incongruous and sinister as it was. To live with something is to become oblivious. Mothers pushed their prams along it. In the western half of the city, artists painted it, at least for a time. But generally people turned their backs on it, except when seeking empty spaces to park their cars.

The Wall went up on August 13, 1961. The communist party leader of the time, Walter Ulbricht, saw it as the solution to his single most embarrassing problem: the flight of East Germans to the West, who were at the time leaving at the rate of some one thousand people a day. Historians know that the Allies could have prevented its construction and perhaps, thereby, changed history. Soldiers erecting the barrier—at first no more than a few strands of barbed wire—were not supplied with ammunition; Russian tank crews were ordered to withdraw if confronted. But the pugnacious Soviet premier Nikita S. Khrushchev, the man who threatened to "bury" the West and banged his shoe on the podium at the United Nations, knew what he was doing. At a small and jovial dinner party the night before, he tipped a small gathering of top Russian military leaders to his plans, clearly savoring the moment. "We're going to close Berlin," he crowed with his trademark gap-toothed grin. "We'll just put up serpentine barbed wire and the West will stand there, like dumb sheep." And it did, fearing a fight that might have gone nuclear.

Over the years, stone slabs and masonry replaced the barbed wire. A second parallel wall went up, one hundred yards farther in. Houses in between were demolished, creating a no-man's-land that became known as the death strip. Much of it was covered with raked gravel or turned earth, making it easy to track would-be escapees; it was mined and booby-trapped. Border guards patrolled along an inner track, often accompanied by attack dogs; others watched from any of 302 towers. Almost until the end, their orders were to shoot to kill, on sight. Reports vary, but as many as 192 people died trying to escape over the Wall; roughly a thousand were killed trying to flee over the far longer East German border.

It worked as Ulbricht hoped: between 1949 and 1962, 2.5 million East Germans fled. Between 1962 and 1989, that number fell to about five thousand. Overnight, the forty-two thousand square miles of the German Democratic Republic became a prison. Transportation and communication links were cut. Bustling streets and lively sidewalks in the heart of metropolitan Berlin suddenly became abandoned dead ends. Sewers, tramlines and power grids were blocked or cut. Families were broken, friendships severed. Children lost parents or grandparents. On official maps, the western half of the city was blotted out— figuratively erased from the world of the living. The city, particularly in the East, settled into a grim sadness, a long sleep from which its troubled citizens scarcely dared dream they would ever awake.

Only Berliners called it the Wall. Elsewhere, it was the "fence," or the "border," a three-hundred-mile swath through the heart of Germany. By 1989, the East Germans had removed their mines and remote-control machine guns. Even so, it was a formidable barrier: a twelve-foot-high mesh fence that could not be climbed without grappling hooks; an antivehicle trench to keep people from crashing through in cars; armed patrols with dogs; concrete watch-towers and machine-gun bunkers every few hundred yards; a three-mile security zone inside the border, where East Germans could live and travel only with special permits. Here and there it opened—guardedly—to admit a railway or highway. But for the most part it marched ahead unchanging and featureless, cutting through forests, zigzagging up sheer mountainsides, slicing through fields, streams and towns.

Early in my assignment, as late autumn turned into winter, I traveled along the divide at odd intervals over a few weeks, from the Baltic Sea in the north, where gray East German gunboats floated off a sandy beach, ready to shoot anyone who might try to swim to freedom, to the Czech border near Bavaria in the south. The idea was to search out the cracks that I supposed must be there, to intuit a coming revolution. But I found little evidence. Wherever I went, the Wall was simply there.

Driving in the countryside, down lanes of oaks lining the road, through verdant meadows and rolling green hills, you would unexpectedly come across it and stop, as if jolted by electricity. Along the border near the central West German town of Philippsthal, just north of the famous Fulda Gap where NATO forces fighting what they called the "next war" would try to stop invading Soviet armies rolling toward Frankfurt and the English Channel, the road wound along a pleasant river lined with willows. Boys fished on one bank. On the other, a gray wall suddenly loomed up, laced with barbed wire and studded by watch-towers. Soldiers peered through binoculars. Around a bend, the wall cut across the road; the older, bigger part of town was off-limits. You could only turn around and go back. If you lingered, a guard emerged to snap your photo. You were in the files of the East German security police.

Farther down the highway, in Rohringshof, a town renowned for its picturesque half-timbered barns and medieval houses, the Wall snaked through a cement plant. Once a single complex, there were now instead two huge cones of cement dust, two big conveyors, and two identical smokestacks. One belched choking clouds of dust (on the Eastern side); the other (on the West German side) emitted a more modest, environmentally conscious plume. Farther north, near the university city of Göttingen, developers had built a new golf course at Bad Sooden, only a long slice from the border. In neighboring Wanfried, the border split the local train station. The town's ancient baroque church with its cemetery was caught in the security zone between East and West. "When there is a funeral or a wedding, I sometimes get to see my relatives," said a West German farmer, standing on a hillock looking down upon the church below. "I wave, but we have not talked in twenty years. Perhaps we never shall. We are getting old." (In fact, he would speak to them, face-to-face and against all expectation, in a matter of mere months.) The road leading to the frontier was perfectly maintained. It stopped at the fence, lost in weeds and fallen leaves. But the electric lines ran on. The owner of the local power plant had friends and relatives in the East, and he supplied them even at a loss.

I expected people to be oppressed by such macabre proximity. But no. They accommodated themselves to it. Mainly it was outsiders who found it intrusive or malign. "The border is a fact. It's there, and we live with it," said Anita Geldbach, a tailor in a small shop along a cobbled street in Göttingen. Near the Czech border, to the south, a tank road cut through the forest on the East German side of the border, ending just feet from the parking lot of a local supermarket in the West. No one gave it a thought. All along the frontier, kids played soccer and adults went camping in the shadow of the watch-towers of the East. Few saw much of a threat.

Looking through my notebooks from the trip, so many years later, I am struck by the difference in reactions between Americans and those Germans living in the immediate shadow of the Cold War. "War? You mean like an invasion?" asked Gisela Sieland, a housewife in the little town of Altenburschla, surprised that I would ask whether she worried about a Soviet invasion. She seemed baffled at my suggestion that NATO and the Warsaw Pact could come into conflict, even though she resided at ground zero. "We don't feel the least fear," said Ulle Winter, a student at Göttingen University working part-time at a student pub, as she served a beer. "We have the utmost confidence in Gorbachev. The Americans might as well pack up their stuff and leave." I encountered this virtually everywhere: the sense that the border had become something almost natural, that the Wall would, and perhaps should, endure. "After all," Ulle added, wiping the counter clear, "we created the two Germanys. We Germans made the war."

It is almost impossible to comprehend the full dimension and consequence of the Cold War. For future generations, it will define the twentieth century. It dwarfs any other event, from the First and Second World Wars to the invention of the computer, modern telecommunications and the democratization of Wall Street. Since 1945, writes the author Martin Walker, "the history of the Cold War has been the history of the world."

It was the first truly global conflict, sucking in geographies and drawing battle lines between allies and adversaries that even World War II did not. It pitted two utterly alien political and economic systems, do or die, one against the other. There were few genuinely neutral parties, save Swiss bankers and some neolithic tribes in the remnants of the Amazon forest. Almost every nation and people were drawn in or touched by it. Americans fought in Vietnam and Korea, Laos and Cambodia. So did Turks, Algerians and Chinese. Cubans fought in Angola; Saudis battled Russians in Afghanistan. Proxy wars raged in Latin America and sub-Saharan Africa. We raced to close imagined "missile gaps," beat the Russians to the moon. Weapons manufactured for World War III in Europe were sold across the world, spawning regional arms races, wars and political upheavals. Ethnic and nationalist conflicts assumed geostrategic significance: India and Pakistan, China and Taiwan, Ethiopia and Somalia. Geographies became blocs, tinted blue or red, free and unfree. A bizarre constellation of places resonated fearsomely with even the youngest schoolchildren, Russian and American, Asian as well as European: Saigon. Hanoi. Seoul. Pyongyang. Kabul. Katanga. Tehran. Phnom Penh. Budapest. Prague. Warsaw. Salvador. Santiago. Honduras. Guatemala. Berlin.

The Cold War was a uniquely total war, not in movements of armies but in its social and economic effects. Dwight Eisenhower warned against a "military-industrial complex," with its vast army, intelligence apparatus and defense industries mobilized for a war that would wipe out human civilization. For the better part of five decades it absorbed anywhere from a quarter to a half of all U.S. government spending and 10 percent of the nation's GNP. The Cold War shaped America, in ways not always obvious. The interstate highway system was originally built to speed military logistics from one part of the country to the other. Today's Internet, with all its transformative effect on commerce and daily life, began as a military communications network designed to withstand a Soviet nuclear strike. The federal loans that generations of young Americans have relied upon for college began with the National Defense Education Act of 1958, a crash program launched after Sputnik to win the "brain race" against the Soviets. The California dream rode the tides of defense spending pouring into the state, swelling its population from 5 million before the Cold War began to more than 30 million by the time it ended. A whole new economic order evolved within the Cold War's shadow: Bretton Woods. The World Bank and International Monetary Fund. The United Nations. The U.S. Agency for International Development. The Marshall Plan, which helped rebuild postwar Europe. Postwar investment in Japan and the network of international trade and security organizations that spanned the globe, from SEATO to NATO to the Warsaw Pact, Cominterm and the Common Market cum European Union. All were creatures of the Cold War.

It usurped Western culture, which in turn diffused throughout the world. In American schools of the 1950s and early 1960s, kids "ducked and tucked" under their desks against atomic blasts. When they grew up, they explored the trade-offs between guns and butter in Economics 101. They were fluent in the lexicon of confrontation: *containment, mutually assured destruction*, the *domino theory*. Everyone knew about the nuclear button, the "hotline" between Washington and Moscow, the briefcase, aka the football, the satchel of nuclear codes that to this day accompanies the president everywhere. The Cold War was hip: James Bond, *The Third Man*, Graham Greene, John le Carré, Tom Clancy. It was the stuff of pop-culture thrillers and avant-garde films: *Z, State of Siege, Dr. Strangelove.* It wasn't enough to be merely American. The best and the brightest were all-American—patriots, not pinkos. The Cold War was counterculture, too. The Generation Gap. The antiwar activists of the Vietnam era. Rock 'n' roll grew up as a protest song against the Cold War.

We told ourselves that we won it. But it is equally fair to say that we also lost it, or at least shared amply in the loss. Clearly and simply, the Cold War was a catastrophe. Seldom in history had a conflict lasted so long, swept up so much of the world and cost so dearly. Within a few decades, as living memory dies, the Cold War will seem as distant as the Thirty Years' War. We will read about it as ancient history, much as we read about the battles of the kings and princes of 1648. We will forget that this greatest of the world's conflicts came at a commensurate cost, perhaps because we perceive ourselves to be the uncompromised victors and have never had to fully reckon the magnitude of the expense: how much treasure we expended, how economies were distorted, how we ourselves and our societies were changed by a half century's obsession. Our view is Churchill's, not Gorbachev's, when in truth it should be both.

Some have attempted an accounting, a Cold War "butcher's bill," if you will. Focusing purely on defense expenditures, the Brookings Institution in 1998 performed a so-called Nuclear Audit. Since atomic weapons constituted the backbone of Cold War deterrence and absorbed the lion's share of resources for military research, it was thought that the amount of money devoted to them would serve as a revealing index of the nation's sacrifice. By that reckoning, the United States between 1940 and 1996 spent $5.8 trillion (in constant 1995 dollars) on nuclear weapons and infrastructure. How much is that? According to Brookings, a stack of a billion $1 bills would rise about eighty miles. A trillion would tower 79,000 miles. As for nearly 6 trillion—the stack would reach the moon, encircle it and reach roughly a quarter of the way back. Put another way, the researchers estimated, the amount would paper every state east of the Mississippi, with enough left over to cover half the American West, including Texas. Put yet another way, it exceeds the amount of all outstanding mortgages on all homes and buildings in the country. It is roughly half of U.S. GDP—the amount Americans spend every year on everything from chewing gum and iPods to second homes in Vail. If you throw in military spending in the round—unfair, yes, but only partly since the Cold War inflated all defense spending, establishing a base that governs today—that total would balloon to $51.6 trillion, according to Brookings.

How to even begin to count the human cost? The Korean War claimed the lives of 32,629 American soldiers and approximately 3 million Korean civilians. One of every ten Americans who served in Vietnam became a casualty: 58,148 died and 304,000 were wounded. An estimated 1.2 million Vietnamese were killed over seven years of fighting. Half a million people died in Angola's twenty-seven-year civil war, waged among factions variously backed by the Soviets or the United States. The decade-long civil war in El Salvador, waged between Cold War proxies—leftist guerrillas versus a U.S.-backed military junta and its infamous "death squads"—claimed 75,000 dead. A similar conflict raged in neighboring Guatemala from 1960 to 1996, taking some 200,000 lives. Such numbers pale next to the 30 million Chinese who died in Mao's Cultural Revolution, or the million or so who perished in Pol Pot's Cambodian genocide, or the 30 million who died in Stalin's wars and purges. These events, too, grew out of the Cold War and are part of its dark heritage.

The symbol of all this was the Berlin Wall, the grim icon to half a century of human misery, oppression, struggle and hope.

For most Germans, as for most others, 1989 came out of the blue. That winter, on the cusp of the year that would change the world, there seemed almost no impetus for change. Only the most romantic West Germans dreamed of a day when the Wall might fall. Certainly Chancellor Helmut Kohl did not, nor any of his advisers that I spoke to. Neither did his foreign minister, Hans-Dietrich Genscher, for all his talk of *Ostpolitik*, who, in an interview with *Newsweek* at the time, dismissed Thatcher's and Reagan's harder-line advisers as "people who stick to the old enemy images and act as if nothing has changed or could ever change."

Virtually no one even spoke (except rhetorically in the most hazy future tense) of *Wiedervereinigung*, or reunification. Politicians might steadfastly refuse to recognize Germany's division, at least officially.

Yet most Germans were perfectly at ease with it. Everywhere, there was a cocoonlike sense of self-sufficiency, a basic contentment with the idea of two Germanys and a resistance to the continued pretense that there was only one. West Germans described themselves as just that—West Germans, or "Europeans," hardly German at all. Polls documented this sense of estrangement. In 1983, 43 percent of German students under the age of twenty-one described their titular East German brethren as *Ausländer*, or foreigners. In the summer of 1985, Allensbach researchers asked how long people thought the Berlin Wall would stand. The average response: thirty-four years. Amid the tens of thousands of documents released by the government Office on Intra-German Affairs concerning Deutsche Einheit, 1989–90, there was almost no discussion or evidence of planning for eventual unification. The topic was not verboten; it simply seemed . . . irrelevant.

I brought this up one night in February in a smoky bar in Kreuzberg, then West Berlin's bohemian district. A framed photo from the 1950s showed the establishment's patrons, East and West Berliners, casually sharing a beer over the little picket fence that then demarcated the border. A glossy bit of nostalgia, scoffed the member of the Berlin parliament who had brought me to the place. "We may talk about reunification," he said, "but that doesn't mean we want it." Foreigners from Russia and elsewhere in Eastern Europe, many of them ethnic Germans who had paid their way out of captivity or been bought out by the West German government to the tune of some $10,000 a head, were flooding into Germany—three hundred thousand in 1988 alone. Imagine what it would be like without the Wall? The lawmaker shuddered at the thought.

In the East, meanwhile, life went on. Crossing over, I always felt as though I were entering a parallel universe—familiar in its essential lineaments, with cars and streetlights and ordinary people going about their ordinary lives, yet somehow dimmer, drearier, shabbier and indefinably oppressive. At Checkpoint Charlie, there was always the same tedious routine, sometimes lasting hours. You would join a long queue, shuffling slowly forward. East German guards rummaged through every paper, wrote down every telephone number. What would I be doing? Who would I be seeing? Drivers leaving East

Berlin were ordered to open the trunk and hood of their car; guards inserted a probe into the gas tank to ensure that it contained only gasoline and not would-be escapees. Before the war, Berlin was always famous for its Berliner *Luft*, its fresh and invigorating air. Once in the East, that sense of lightness would instantly vanish. The air suddenly felt heavier, constricting. East Berliners referred to it as "sticky," something that clung to you, vaguely menacing.

This was the effect of a police state. The German Democratic Republic under its leader for life Erich Honecker, the man who oversaw the actual erection of the Wall and who wanted to be known to his people as Papi, however deadly his instincts, was the most rigidly controlled, totalitarian state in the East bloc with the possible exception of Nicolae Ceausescu's Romania. The secret police, the infamous Stasi, were ubiquitous. They could be your neighbors, your friends, even your family. Citizens were seduced, suborned, blackmailed and coerced into working for them. If you fell sick, vital medication might be withheld until you cooperated by informing on those you worked with or knew in private. If you wished to travel abroad, attend university or be promoted, you made a compact with the devil: collaborate, or pay the price. "The Stasi targeted everyone," writes Alexandra Richie in her aptly titled *Faust's Metropolis: A History of Berlin*, from miners and waitresses to Intourist guides, musicians and kindergarten teachers. Files were kept on more than 6 million people. The regime's infamous Order No. 2, introduced by Stasi chief Erich Mielke in 1985 after Gorbachev came to power, directed the secret police to "prevent, discover and combat" all underground political activity using all means. Dissidents, critics and even mere moaners, Richie notes, were "checked, followed and documented in files which were regularly updated" in a campaign of "total information." By its own official count, the regime at the end of its life had 97,000 employees and 173,000 informers. In a nation of 17 million, that translates to one in every sixty-three people working for state security. No wonder the air felt sticky. No wonder politics was taboo as a topic of conversation. No wonder no one trusted anyone—fathers or sons, mothers or daughters, lovers.

From time to time, I would go to a small private restaurant named Papillon, one of a handful in East Berlin, where I would casually talk to locals. One evening I met a trio of young musicians, a pair of young men and a girl. They spoke quietly with bowed heads, as if fearing to be overheard. "We don't have feelings of nationalism," said one of the men, echoing his compatriots in the West. "Why not two nations? It works fine." His biggest regret was not the presumed impossibility of unification, nor even necessarily East Germany's low living standards. He chaffed at his inability to travel, as if the country's leaders sincerely believed their world would collapse if citizens were allowed to move freely. This truly irked him, to the point of deep alienation. Would he come back if he was allowed to visit the West? "Of course," he replied. "I only want to see it, not live there. This is my home." Then two men sat down at the next table and lit cigarettes, and the atmosphere changed. "Socialism must be preserved," the young man said abruptly, speaking suddenly more loudly. And for the first time the girl opened her mouth. "Honecker is right," she exclaimed, also rather too loudly. The men at the next table looked at us, ignoring the waitress who asked if she could serve them, and my companions got up and left.

Winds of change may have been blowing from Moscow, but the German Democratic Republic was not about to bend. Its leaders, the ruling Politburo of the Socialist Unity Party of Germany, had grown white-haired and inflexible, convinced of the rightness of their path and determined to hold power. Popularly they were known as the *Alt-Herren Riege*, the team of old men. Honecker was seventy-six as the year began; Mielke was over eighty. They knew the party line and cleaved to it uncompromisingly. Unification with the Federal Republic was an "impossibility," Honecker would declaim again and again. "Socialism and capitalism are like fire and water."

Yet deep within, Honecker was fearful. He knew that East Germany's command economy was feeble and growing weaker. The sputtering two-stroke Trabant automobile, made of plastic and belching plumes of exhaust as it bounced flimsily across the communist landscape, bore testimony to reality: the GDR was not on an economic plane with Spain, an only slightly less efficient model of traditional German industry than the Federal Republic, as we journalists often wrote. It was a basket case. Shortages of basic goods were endemic and people lived in suppressed despair and deprivation.

The other thing Honecker feared was Mikhail Gorbachev. East Germans had cheered when he last visited Berlin. "Gorbi, Gorbi," they called out. "The people made it clear," writes Peter Wyden in his masterful history, *Wall*. "They longed for the fresh air he was breathing into communism." They, too, wanted change. Honecker and his men could sense it. They saw it when East Berliners tried to approach the Wall to hear Ronald Reagan speak in 1987, and again a few months later when they again approached the Wall to overhear a performance on the Western side by the rock band Genesis. They could see it in the jokes East Germans told.

The Volkspolizei were favorite targets, as in: Two Stasi agents on a surveillance mission grew bored. Said one, "Hey, what are you thinking about?" Replied the other, "Oh, nothing special—the same as you." First agent: "In that case you're under arrest!"

The people made fun of the shortages of basic foods, and especially luxuries such as bananas: "How do you use a banana as a compass? Place it atop the Berlin Wall. East is where a bite has been taken out of it."

Political jokes took on a particularly hard edge: Honecker meets Mao and asks, "How many political opponents do you have in China?" The Chinese leader answers, "I estimate seventeen million." To which Honecker replies, "Oh, that's pretty much the same here," which of course was the entire population of East Germany.

The 2007 Oscar-winning movie *Das Leben der Anderen* (The Lives of Others) featured an especially sharp jab at Honecker and communism in general:

Early one morning, Honecker arrives at his office and opens his window. He sees the sun and says, "Good morning, dear sun!"

The sun replies, "Good morning, dear Erich!"

Honecker begins his work, then, at noon, looks out the window and exclaims, "Good afternoon, dear sun!" And the sun replies, "Good afternoon, dear Erich!"

In the evening, Honecker calls it a day and goes once more to the window. "Good evening, dear sun!" But the sun is silent, so Honecker says again, "Good evening, dear sun! What is the matter with you?"

The sun replies, "Kiss my ass. I'm in the West now."

This was the mood across the East bloc as 1989 began. It may have been hard to see from the West, but in the East the signs were unmistakable. The climate was changing, a thaw was breaking up the frozen landscape. Gorbachev was in Moscow. In Poland, there was movement. The famous trade union of yesteryear, Solidarity, was showing signs of renewed life. In Prague, with a wary eye to the east, communist hard-liners were trying to read the winds and talking cautiously about "reform," like the Soviet leader, even if they did not really mean it. In all the communist realm, Hungary was the place to watch. It was there that the first real spark of revolution was lit—not by its people, in the form of a popular uprising, but rather by a small band of pirates, numbering no more than half a dozen, who decided to light the fuse on a powder keg that would blow up the communist world.

Among them was a man few Americans have ever heard of. His name: Miklos Nemeth, Hungary's Harvard-educated prime minister. Working secretly with a few Western allies, chiefly in the West German chancellery, Nemeth and his small crew of communist subversives consciously set out to bring down the Iron Curtain that separated Hungary from the West. Their goal, as he put it, was to "join Europe" and restore their country to the ranks of the modern world. To do so, he knew he had to destroy the whole communist system. The means they chose, and the cunning and courage with which they executed their intricate plan, was one of the great subterfuges in the annals of diplomatic history—on the order of the legendary Operation Fortitude, and the tale of Britain's gambit to fool Hitler into thinking the Allied invasion of 1944 would come near Calais rather than the beaches of Normandy, effectively winning World War II.

This is the untold story of 1989.

CHAPTER THREE

Democracy on the Danube

That was the thing about the man. He sat there so imperturbably, so genial and seemingly genuine. It was impossible not to like him, hard not to trust him. But could you? After all, he was the justice minister of the People's Republic of Hungary. By virtue of his title, he was the ultimate enforcer in Hungary's communist regime, charged with jailing dissidents and hounding would-be democrats—a principal in the country's vast secret police and security apparatus.

Yet here he was, this friendly bear, a onetime law professor with florid cheeks and curly graying hair, talking animatedly about James Madison and the Federalist Papers and sounding every bit like a Hungarian Thomas Jefferson. A new prime minister had brought him into the government, just a few weeks earlier, and already he was elbow-deep in paperwork, he said, authoring a new national constitution. "We must guarantee the rights of the individual against the state," he declared with forceful energy. Free speech, free association and free property are "inalienable rights." And that wasn't all from this card-carrying commie. "Our goal is to create a parliamentary democracy," he went on, identical to those in Western Europe.

You mean free elections, I asked, incredulous.

"Absolutely."

How long would this take—for real democracy?

"Oh," he said breezily. "One to three years."

And if the communists lose?

He didn't even hesitate. "We step down."

At this, I laughed. Across Eastern Europe, so many "reformers" were spouting such talk of "openness" and "change," echoing their patron in Moscow, Mikhail Gorbachev, chanting his mantra of glasnost and perestroika. But if Gorbachev seemed to mean it, the leaders of his Warsaw Pact satellite nations did not. These Hungarians appeared more sincere than most but this, I felt, was going too far.

Kalman Kulcsar frowned at my evident skepticism. "You don't believe me, Mr. Meyer?" He leaned over in his leather swivel chair and slid open a drawer of his carved wooden desk, pulled out a small booklet and waved it over his head. "What do you think this is?" It was a copy of the U.S. Constitution and Bill of Rights. "Mark my words," the minister said, emphasizing each word with unsettling force. "Within nine months, this will be ours."

He was wrong. It would be all of ten months. Still, it was a dramatic moment. Here in Budapest, unnoticed by the outside world, communists had become . . . anticommunists. My god, I thought. This is for real. And that was when I discovered that something I'd always taken as a figure of speech was, in fact, a physical phenomenon. Quite literally, the hairs on the back of my neck stood up.

By night, it would be easy to mistake the Hungarian parliament for the symbol of democracy it was meant to be. Bright with lights reflecting on the waters of the Danube, it's an unabashed imitation of the British Houses of Parliament, except for one significant detail. By design, it's precisely one meter longer and one meter wider than its inspiration. The architectural allusion was apt in late 1988. It was at once an ironic symbol of Hungary's historic aspirations and a reminder of its lesser attainments.

Not for long, though.

I had come to Budapest to investigate reports that after four decades under communism the first tender shoots of democracy were pushing up along the Danube. The city was in the grip of a December blizzard. But beneath the deep freeze, a political spring was indeed germinating.

Just a month before, in November, a small group of communist reformers had come to power. Kalman Kulcsar was but one of a number of Hungarian leaders who were saying (and doing) the most uncommunist things. Within the last few months, they had opened a stock market—a temple to the antipodal capitalist faith. They passed new laws encouraging private enterprise, slashed subsidies for state-owned enterprises, abandoned communist-style price-fixing in favor of a free market. The cost of food, fuel and housing would henceforth be determined by supply and demand, they told the people, well aware of how painful that transition could be. Hello, Keynes. Goodbye, Marx?

It quickly became apparent that this revolution—for that was what it had already become—went far beyond the marketplace. Six months earlier, just before his first state visit to the United States in July, the thuggish chief of the Hungarian Socialist Workers Party, a former printing engineer named Karoly Grosz, sat down with *Newsweek*. Contemptuously he dismissed all talk of democracy and what, within opposition circles, was being discussed as the potential for "multiparty rule." Anything but the classic dictatorship of the proletariat, meaning him and his Socialist Party henchmen, he said, was "an historic impossibility." He declined even hypothetically to discuss sharing power or offering a role in government to opposing political parties. Yet that was precisely what Hungary's new government, appointed and duly installed by Grosz and his communists, was working to do.

Eager to stamp their more human face on the old order, they had just taken a step that no other East European regime dared—to create a real opposition to their own rule. This came in the form of a new law, enacted soon after the reformers took office, allowing the country's first independent political parties to organize. They could not officially recognize these groups as bona fide "parties," at least not yet. That would violate the ironclad principle of Marxist Leninism: that there could be only one party—the socialist or communist party—whose destiny it was to guide the nation in all important matters. So they played games with names. They called them "clubs," "movements" or "alternative organizations." At a time when signs of a thawing in the Cold War were yet faint, this was a remarkable, even radical development.

Suddenly, the entire country was in ferment. Budapest's cafés buzzed with the D-word, *democracy*. You could virtually see the internal rift emerging—the young reformers on one side, the old guard on the other, each girding for a struggle that would unfold with astonishing speed. In September, a populist group called the Hungarian Democratic Forum (which within the year would go on to form Hungary's first postcommunist government) set itself up as a "democratic spiritual-political movement." Other groups soon followed, among them the League of Young Democrats (a student association better known as Fidesz) and the Alliance for Free Democrats, an organization of trade unions. All would go on, in future years, to dominate Hungary's political scene. Meanwhile, censorship was eased. A robustly free press began to emerge. Underground samizdat publications came into the open. The few dissidents who deserved the name either went mainstream by joining one of the parties or were ignored, both by people in the street and the authorities who once persecuted them. Dissent against what, you might ask, or whom?

How do you dissent, really, from someone like Miklos Nemeth, the man who put so much of this in motion. He was no Lech Walesa, Poland's archetypal charismatic leader, the hero of Solidarity, who in 1980 became famous in America and the world for leaping over the fence in the Gdansk shipyard and brandishing a fist in the face of Soviet authorities. No, Nemeth was the quiet man, a technocrat, a trained economist who spent a year at Harvard Business School and played tennis with the U.S. ambassador. He was only forty years old when the communist party appointed him prime minister on November 24, 1988. Sober-suited and bankerly, his mild manner masked inner toughness. His was a life-or-death situation. Hungary's economy was a shambles. The country's finances were in crisis. Everything was falling apart. His job was to step in and save the day—and his own career. To do so, he knew that mere "reform" would not be enough. He would have to dismantle the entire communist system.

He did not say as much when I first met him, less than a month after taking office. Perhaps he was too mindful of the dangers and all that could go wrong. Sitting at a long, dark oak conference table in his offices in the Gothic-style parliament building, flanked by half a dozen aides, he did not look like a man who would change the world. In our three-hour meeting, he dabbed perspiration from his brow with a white handkerchief and lapsed often into the opaque, excessively careful language of the high communist official. There was nothing communist about his message, however. When he said something that he especially wanted to be heard, he delivered it crisply with a quick, direct look that meant *Listen up*.

These clubs, these new political groups, I asked, could they eventually become bona fide American- or European-style political parties? "That is one of our greatest ambitions," Nemeth replied.

For as long as it had existed, the communist party had insisted on its so-called "leading role" in society—meaning unchallenged power. Would he be prepared to give it up, as Kalman Kulcsar claimed?

"In two years I could imagine a situation where the head of government would not necessarily be a member of the Politburo," Nemeth said, carefully but with unmistakable meaning.

This talk about creating capitalism on the Danube. Economists say that would mean putting one hundred thousand people out of work, perhaps three times as many. Wouldn't that be a big blow in a "workers' paradise" such as Hungary?

Nemeth offered a tight smile. "We are going to live through some painful years, yes. But in five years I would hope that Hungary will have become a market economy, with room for entrepreneurs and where people can have more hope for the future."

Moscow might have something to say about that, I noted. Would a setback for Mikhail Gorbachev in Russia overturn the applecart of reforms here in Hungary? Might the Russians even intervene, as in 1956?

"Gorbachev has taken the lid off a boiling pot," replied the young prime minister. "No doubt the steam is painful, but change is irreversible."

Thanks to Radio Free Europe, that quote would echo throughout the Soviet bloc. It also earned Nemeth a stern dressing-down from his titular boss, Karoly Grosz. But if Nemeth in his modest way provoked Grosz's ire, imagine the emotions inspired by another, brasher and even more outspoken member of his new government.

Imre Pozsgay was Nemeth's alter ego and most important ally, as outgoing as Nemeth was restrained. Popularly known as "Hungary's Gorbachev," he had spent much of the past decade in the political wilderness, a sort of in-house dissident with a gift for threading the minefield between those who sought radical reform and those who would go slower. When he was on the outs, Pozsgay taught political sociology at the University of Budapest and hosted a popular TV show on foreign affairs. When he was in, he was the perfect official interlocutor for Hungary's intelligentsia, able to segue flawlessly from Marx and Engels to Milton Friedman. In late 1988, Pozsgay was very much in— a minister of state, a senior member of the all-powerful ruling Politburo and a beacon for anyone within the regime who wanted change.

Of all the Hungarians I met that December, he was the most boldly free-speaking, often breathtakingly so. "Communism does not work," he told me bluntly on our first meeting, as soon as we had sat down. "It has come to the end of its days. It is an obstacle to progress in all fields—political, social and economic. We must start again, from zero." Rumpled and roly-poly, with the deceptively distracted air of a university professor, he had an instinct for the jugular—in his case, history.

In Hungary, as everywhere, the communists had rewritten it. In the winter of 1988 and early 1989, the country was haunted by the ghost of 1956. That's when Hungarian freedom fighters rose up against their Stalinist masters in a revolt that transfixed the world. For weeks they battled in the streets of Budapest against Soviet tanks dispatched by Moscow to crush them. An estimated twenty-five hundred people died and two hundred thousand fled into exile. Waves of arrests followed, and public discussion of the events was banned for the next three decades. Then along came Imre Pozsgay. For months, he had used the considerable authority of his office to push for a review of the official record. The party line was that the revolt had been a foreign conspiracy, plotted and provoked by Western counter-revolutionary traitors. The premier of the time, Imre Nagy, had been arrested and executed, along with others of his ilk.

With single-minded obsession, Pozsgay pushed for a revision of this twisted account. "We must come to terms with our history," he told me, relating how he was setting up a commission to study the matter. Every Hungarian knew the truth, he said. The tension was between truth and power. Was 1956 a counterrevolution, as Hungary's communist party would have it—that is, was it something to be crushed? Or was it what Pozsgay described as a "popular uprising"?

The first implies justification. The second connotes treason against the people, a debt yet to be paid. *J'accuse*, in other words.

As Pozsgay saw it, Hungary's communist rulers were guilty of mass murder. They had unlawfully suppressed a popular nationalist rebellion against the tyranny of foreign occupation and Soviet dictatorship. Therefore they had no right to continued rule. Pozsgay said all this so calmly, so dispassionately, that it was possible to imagine that he was discussing some academic matter, a point of obscure historical interpretation. In fact, it was a threat, a virtual declaration of war: Pozsgay against his party, the vision of an independent Hungary versus the vassal state of Moscow. His insistence on the historical truth challenged, to its face, the current regime's very right to exist.

Bidding good-bye, he suggested I buy a copy of a new magazine that had recently begun to publish. It had an interview with him concerning 1956. It's important, he said, but added that was probably not why I would like it. Every newsstand should have it . . . unless it was sold out.

He said all this with a cryptic smile, belying his deadly purpose, and I soon learned why. The magazine was called *Reform*, fittingly, an "independent democratic newsmagazine." In a country where most publications were still gray, text-heavy homages to communist party doctrine and the doings of its nomenklatura elite, *Reform* was an eye-catcher. This particular issue featured a coy pictorial, "The Best Breasts of Budapest." There they were, in unbrassiered Technicolor splendor, a declaration of Hungarian liberty. Socialism with a human face, indeed. But guess what? "It's not the breasts that sell," the magazine's publisher insisted. "It's the politics." Along with hip offerings on pop culture and shopping sprees to Vienna, the issue also included, as Pozsgay promised, a startlingly provocative article on 1956, denouncing the Soviet invasion and pointing a finger directly at the ruling communist party for colluding in it.

How remarkable: in Hungary, at that moment, political truth could outsell sex.

Poland usually gets credit for leading Eastern Europe's revolutions. Solidarity, Lech Walesa, the communist regime's declaration of martial law in 1981—the saga of 1989 would not have happened without

Poland's decades-long push for change. Yet in the winter of late 1988, Hungary emerged as the chief catalyst for change in the East.

Looking back, two decades later, three facts stand out. First, outside the bloc few people noticed how fast and fundamentally Hungary was changing, or asked what that might portend, both for Hungary and (more important) for the future of communism itself. Perhaps the country was simply too small, too marginal, to count in the grand scheme of the Cold War. More likely, the rest of the world was locked in its own way of seeing. To most of us, the Iron Curtain had stood for so long, obdurate and forbidding, that it had become part of the geopolitical landscape, an accepted feature of Cold War life.

Second, these changes did not happen the way we expected. Policy types tended to think in terms of the Polish "model," with its code words for resistance and suppression. Change, if and when, was supposed to come as a sustained "push" from "below." It would be organized by a popularly based "opposition" such as Solidarity. That's what was familiar to us in the West. Communism was about oppression, keeping the masses down. A few tragic heroes resisted, asserting their human right to speak out and live freely against the overwhelming power of the state. We honored them as "dissidents"—Andrei Sakharov in Russia, Vaclav Havel in Czechoslovakia. Yet the reality in Budapest, at least, was very different. Hungary was remarkable for the absence of a major "push" from below. You could count its classic dissidents on one hand. Its impetus, instead, was a strong "pull" from "above" and "within." The puller-in-chief, if you will, was Nemeth, allied closely with Pozsgay, Kulcsar and a very few others.

These people did not emerge from nowhere. Through the 1980s, a cadre of "reform socialists" had been working their way up through the communist party and government bureaucracy. They were young—mostly in their thirties and forties—and tended to be well-educated, highly trained professionals in law, economics and the social sciences. They also shared a strong commitment to change. Though all were communist party members in good standing, they agreed that the system no longer worked. State mismanagement was slowly destroying the famous "goulash" economy that, a decade or so ago, had been the envy of the East bloc. Political life had atrophied. Progress seemed paralyzed. Not only did the party's old guard resist needed reforms, so did ordinary people. The question for this new generation of leaders was how to break the impasse. By 1984, before Gorbachev had arrived on the scene or anyone had heard of glasnost and perestroika, this group of internal critics had come to virtually dominate public debate over Hungary's future.

And what a debate it was. Hemmed in by resistance to change, they leaned increasingly toward drastic solutions. The famous "big bangs" of an abrupt embrace of capitalism—enacted in Poland and other places after 1989—were first bruited in Hungary by these regime reformers. They talked about creating a new political culture, used phrases such as *deep democracy* or *socialist pluralism*, and posed challenging questions: how to create genuine participatory government, such that ordinary people had a say and (therefore) a stake in changes to come. Why should parliament only meet eight days a year? they asked. Why shouldn't Hungary have free elections, supervised by international observers? They spoke about restoring the rule of law, rather than the fiat of the communist party. Above all, they speculated about how to make government both effective and accountable. As they saw it, a regime's legitimacy should rest on performance, how well it did its job. An incompetent government that couldn't deliver on its promises—that flouted the implicit social contract between a state and its people, that impoverished its citizens—should be tossed out. The only issue was how.

Nemeth and his government emerged from this dynamic. Indeed, he and his allies were in its vanguard. Yet it's important to recognize a remarkable feature about Hungary's reform debate: not only was it largely internal, without much involvement from more conventional dissidents, but it was marked by an extraordinary unanimity between the younger liberals and more old-guard conservatives. All saw the need for change. Only after Nemeth became prime minister did the two sides irreconcilably part ways, and we shall soon see why.

A third point. At the time, it was easy to be awed by Hungary's daring, particularly for a young correspondent new to the region. I didn't learn until years later how hard the work was, or how dangerous. That summer, before Nemeth and his corps took power, sharp disagreements had broken out within the party about where Hungary was going, and how. If some in the regime wanted sweeping change, like Nemeth and Pozsgay, others wanted it confined to economics, keeping a tight check on politics—the Chinese model, if you will. Chief among them was party boss Karoly Grosz. Around the time I met Nemeth, in late November, the general secretary delivered a speech to the communist rank and file warning of the prospect of "White terror." The new prime minister had scarcely been in office a week, yet conservatives were already alarmed. From their point of view, these young Turks were moving too far, too fast. They were out of control. They were breaking all the rules. An end to censorship, letting newspapers report whatever they wanted? The talk of free markets and an end to state industry? The very idea that elections could be held and the results honored—that the communist party could be thrust from power? It was unthinkable, a recipe for social disorder. They must be stopped. We must resist "counterrevolutionary enemies," Grosz told the cheering faithful. "Anarchy and chaos" threatened. The next day, another Politburo hard-liner, Janos Berecz, told a conference of coal miners that Hungary was in the grip of a "revolutionary crisis."

Precisely what Grosz and other hard-liners intended is not clear, even now, but it appears to have involved the threat of force—perhaps by strong-arm miners, traditional government allies, coupled with Hungary's riot police and workers' militias. Nemeth, at least, did not mistake the message. "From that point on, we knew," he told me. "It was them or us." By early January, these concerns had grown to the point that the U.S. and Soviet ambassadors each paid highly publicized visits to Grosz and senior Hungarian security officials to warn them against the "likely consequences" of violence, according to Rudolf Tokes in his definitive history, *Hungary's Negotiated Revolution*. These plots came to naught, Tokes believes, because the interior minister of the time, Istvan Horvath, threatened to expose them. Yet it was a clear sign of the risks that Nemeth and his fledgling government were running, and a measure of the schism that split the Hungarian leadership. As Tokes puts it, the party's "fundamentalist hard core" was composed of "desperate and dangerous people who, if given the chance, might have turned the clock back."

What stayed their hand? In a word, uncertainty. At this delicate moment, no one had an answer to the ultimate question: what would

Moscow do? In late December, Gorbachev delivered a speech to the United Nations, announcing that by the end of the following year the Soviet Union would unilaterally withdraw a quarter million men and some ten thousand tanks, artillery and aircraft from Eastern Europe. He aimed to spark a breakthrough on stalled talks with the United States on reducing conventional forces in Europe and in doing so dropped this nugget: "It is obvious that the use or threat of force cannot be an instrument of foreign policy."

Many in the West, particularly, saw this as an implicit renunciation of the infamous Brezhnev doctrine justifying Soviet intervention in such cases as the 1968 Prague Spring. The problem was that, in typical Soviet fashion, Gorbachev did not say it directly. The leaders of Eastern Europe were left to interpret his remarks, to figure it out on their own. On the one hand, these communist regimes possessed ample power to crack down, if they chose. On the other, they expected Gorbachev to change his tune and come riding to the rescue if faced with a bona fide anticommunist revolution, as Charles Gati notes in *The Bloc That Failed*. Amid the confusion and uncertainty, they waited.

Across the Atlantic, America also waited, all but oblivious to the drama beginning to take shape in Europe. It had been a distracting year, full of revolutionary developments. For the first time ever, in 1988, music CDs outsold vinyl. Prozac was introduced as an antidepressant. At the summer Olympics in Seoul, gold medal sprinter Ben Johnson was caught using steroids after setting a world record in the 100-meter dash. Robin Givens filed for divorce from boxer Mike Tyson. The Reverend Jimmy Swaggart was exposed as having a liking for prostitutes. Soviet forces began to withdraw from Afghanistan. In the skies over Lockerbie, Scotland, a bomb allegedly planted by Libyan terrorists exploded aboard Pan Am flight 103, killing 271 people from twenty-one countries and setting the stage for U.S. military retaliation.

Most important, a new president had just been elected. George H. W. Bush, vice president under Ronald Reagan, defeated Massachusetts governor Michael Dukakis in a campaign distinguished less by the quality of its debate over foreign policy and U.S.-Soviet relations than by silly photographs of the Democratic candidate riding ill at ease in an M1 Abrams tank and a flap over the furlough of a convicted-killer-turned-rapist named Willie Horton. As happens every four years, all but the most pressing issues got lost in the consuming obsession with gaining the White House.

As the new administration planned its transition, attention turned first to filling jobs, and only secondly to policy. If the incoming team might logically have been expected to build on the momentum of their predecessors in the Reagan administration, particularly in relations with Mikhail Gorbachev and the Soviet bloc, it was not to be. The newly designated secretary of state, James Baker, made that crystal clear. "There was a deliberate pause when President Bush succeeded President Reagan—in all foreign policy, not just matters involving the United States and the Soviet Union," he told CNN. "We had a new team," he added, including a new national security adviser, Brent Scowcroft, and his deputy, Condoleezza Rice. These "new players" were determined to put their "own stamp" on foreign policy, said Baker. In fact, he expected the "real action" to be in Asia, according to an aide, rather than "old hat" Europe where nothing much would change.

The president-elect did not even try to conceal his skepticism about Gorbachev. Reagan had introduced them during the final days of his presidency. "I know what people are telling you now that you have won the election," Gorbachev told the new U.S. leader over lunch on Governors Island. "You've got to go slow, you've got to be careful, you've got to review. That you can't trust us, that we're doing all this for show." But he was not doing this for show, the Russian leader told Bush, looking him square in the eye. "You'll see soon enough. I'm not going to undermine you or surprise you or take advantage of you. I'm doing this because I need to. I'm doing this because there's a revolution taking place in my country. I started it. And they all applauded me in 1986 when I did it and now they don't like it so much. But it's going to be a revolution nonetheless." Yet that is exactly what Bush did: go slow, review. Like Scowcroft, in particular, he did not trust the Soviet leader the way Reagan had come to. "Everyone looked favorably on glasnost and perestroika," Bush said years later in an interview with CNN, "but I thought it was prudent to take some time to reevaluate the situation."

Incredibly, this "pause" would become a freeze lasting nearly six months through what would prove to be some of the most dramatic developments in the twentieth century.

As 1989 began, then, Miklos Nemeth and his fellow revolutionaries quietly went about their business, largely alone, unnoticed and without allies in what would be a bitter and potentially fatal struggle for power. Nemeth was under no illusions about the depth of Hungary's crisis, nor why he had been tapped as prime minister. He was being set up. He was to be the communists' fall guy, the man whom the people would blame when the economy completely crumbled.

Grosz and other party leaders feared they could not arrest Hungary's economic slide—30 percent inflation, the highest per capita foreign debt in Europe, falling living standards and wages. Few Hungarian families could make ends meet without working two or even three jobs. Resentment was growing. So that May, at a fractious party conference, they looked around for a potential scapegoat to become prime minister. Nemeth, then head of the party economics department, was their choice. "I was the innocuous compromise candidate," he would tell me years later, recounting the story of his surprising rise and expected fall—a man who could be counted on to make no waves. Let Nemeth try these "reforms," their thinking went. "If he fails, we can blame him. As for me, I would be kicked out and painted as a young and energetic expert—who failed. Politically, I would be dead."

Nemeth figured he had six months. Every move he made during this time had a single objective: to loosen the grip of the party on his government. "Nothing was more important." Without breaking free of the party, he could not push economic reform. Without promoting democracy and a more pluralist society, he could not break free of the party. And so it was. Those exciting conversations with Nemeth and Kulcsar, the talk of democracy and a bill of rights inspired by Madison and Jefferson: it was perfectly genuine, but it was also realpolitik—a means to an end in a brutal tug-of-war for power. How this battle was fought, in coming months, would decide the future of communism in Hungary and set the stage, by late summer, for more dramatic events—the dissolution of the German Democratic Republic and the collapse of communism throughout Eastern Europe.

I wasn't conscious of any of this at the time I flew back to Bonn, the sleepy city on the Rhine that was then Germany's capital, where I lived with my young family. More subliminally, though, I wonder. Just before New Year's, I did a late-night radio show somewhere in the United States, one of those midnight-to-dawn broadcasts where time stands still and the audience is anyone driving long distances through the darkness. We talked for nearly two hours: what was happening in Moscow, in Eastern Europe, what the new year might bring. I spoke about Hungary, the nobility of what I saw, my own feelings of a deep upwelling promise, how something was in the air in the East that we in the West hadn't yet sensed. Maybe it was the transport of the moment. Perhaps it was living for the first time in such a haunted land as Germany. The Rhine flowed past our house in the silent darkness, history entered in. I went so far as to say that the Wall might soon come down, possibly by next Christmas!

Was it a moment of clarity and insight, or a fantasy that somehow came to pass? Whatever, even I did not believe it in the morning.

CHAPTER FOUR

A Miraculous Conversion

General Wojciech Jaruzelski was famous for his dark sunglasses and ramrod-stiff bearing. He was the infamous Polish strongman who declared martial law in Poland on December 13, 1981. He had crushed the Solidarity trade union, rising up in the summer of 1980 to challenge communist rule, and jailed its leaders. Yet in the early winter of 1989, he correctly sensed the change in political climate and knew what to do.

Like Hungary, Poland was in crisis. Like Hungary, it was chiefly economic. And like Hungary, this crisis was largely invisible, borne quietly by the people but nonetheless fissile, an explosion waiting to happen. Just as Hungary's communists sought to shift blame for the country's problems to someone else—Miklos Nemeth and his reformist government—so did Poland's rulers. In extremis, they took a bold and unprecedented step. They decided to make common cause with their mortal enemy, Solidarity. The man who led them to do so, whose brainchild it was, would be none other than the Polish Antichrist, the poster boy of communist oppression, at least as seen in the West, Wojciech Witold Jaruzelski.

What demons swirled in that poor man's head. What a Shakespearean psychodrama consumed him. It was as if the past were repeating itself, returning to haunt him. He could choose his role: Hamlet or Lear. Whether one or the other, he almost certainly sensed, his personal destiny would not end well.

That spring, strikes had broken out in the coal fields of southern Poland. They continued sporadically but with growing fervor through the summer. To the consternation of the government,

43

protesting workers called for a return of Solidarity, banned since the imposition of martial law seven years before. *Solidarnosc* had always drawn its strength from the nation's rough-and-tumble miners, steelworkers and machinists. Here, once again, they were marching and chanting a slogan from yore that sent shivers through the regime: "There is no liberty without Solidarity!" Jaruzelski clearly heard the echo. Wage freezes and government price hikes had triggered the latest unrest, but he knew it reflected the deeper and more generalized anger of economic desperation. He knew, too, that it presented him with a choice, almost identical to one he had to make so many years before—the choice that had tormented him and cast him as a traitor. As leader of the nation, head of the communist party, should he act to preserve an increasingly untenable status quo, most likely requiring force? Or should he try something new?

In 1981, Jaruzelski's choice had been force. He justified the decision as a lesser evil. It was either impose martial law and restore order on Russia's border or risk a Soviet invasion and occupation. To his mind, he was a patriot who had done what he had to do to save his country. How could his countrymen, even the world, not understand? Bidding those who would judge him to put themselves in his shoes, he described the world as he saw it. Solidarity was about to call a general strike. The economy was on its knees. Civil unrest threatened. "Emotions were explosive and spiraling," he would explain in later years. "The petrol had been spilled."

He did not seem a man reconciled to his decision. In 1982, when U.S. defense secretary Caspar Weinberger branded him "a Russian in Polish uniform," Jaruzelski lashed out irrationally. He announced that Poland would impose "sanctions" on the United States. Cultural ties were terminated and American scholars sent home. Never mind that Poland, notwithstanding two years of U.S. sanctions, was economically afloat only thanks to Western loans and trade credits. Yet Weinberger had it right. More than any other East European leader, Jaruzelski owed his existence to Moscow. When the Soviets organized Polish units during World War II, he enlisted. He fought with the Russians in Berlin. He became a spy for the Kremlin within the Polish military as early as 1946, helping to suppress anticommunist insurgents in southern Poland. In 1968, after becoming defense minister, he was heavily involved in an anti-Semitic "cleansing" of the Polish army. (Perhaps not coincidentally, many of the most freethinking and reform-minded of Poland's military were Jewish.) He led the Polish contingent that put down Prague Spring in 1968. In 1970, he helped organize the execution of striking workers during an uprising in Gdansk, Gdynia and Szczecin. And named communist party secretary and prime minister in early 1981, he essentially declared war on his own nation.

Translated literally, that declaration of martial law—*stan wojenny*—meant "state of war." Critics scoff at the notion that Jaruzelski acted to avoid a Soviet invasion. Documents released from Kremlin archives after the collapse of the Soviet Union, they say, suggest the Soviets had no intention of invading and that Jaruzelski acted to preserve the communist party and its power, pure and simple. And yet, was it really so simple? As Jaruzelski later recounted it, his was a "devil's choice." He was torn between the "anvil" of internal conflict, arising from the challenge of Solidarity, and the "hammer" of Russian intervention. "I spent weeks prior to taking the decision on martial law as in some horrible nightmare. I entertained thoughts of suicide." What tipped him to use force, he explained, were the unmistakable signals from Moscow. Under the pretext of holding maneuvers, they had stationed twenty divisions of the Red Army on Poland's eastern border. Leonid Brezhnev, the Russian leader, telephoned Jaruzelski repeatedly, urging him to "take the decisive measures you intend to use against the counterrevolution"—almost precisely the same message, in tone, that Moscow had delivered to Alexander Dubcek in 1968, prior to the invasion that ended Prague Spring. And so, Jaruzelski acted.

By 1989, however, circumstances were very different. There was no external threat, real or imagined. Meeting in Moscow in 1986, Mikhail Gorbachev had told Jaruzelski that, henceforth, Poland's problems were its own to solve. Then came the Soviet leader's speech to the UN, in December 1988, and his implicit repudiation of the Brezhnev Doctrine. Others might have doubted his sincerity, but not Jaruzelski. He knew the Russians. After all, he was their man. The handwriting was on the wall. Instantly, he knew that it was time to deal.

With the same decisiveness he displayed in crushing Solidarity in 1981, he this time embraced it. In late August, even as the miners' strike was petering out in the face of public apathy, Jaruzelski announced a "brave turnaround." From now on, Solidarity would be a part of Poland's future. Talks would begin to determine its proper role in helping to solve the nation's problems, particularly economic. A "Round Table," he called it. Though stopping short of proposing that the trade union be officially resurrected—and legally recognized—Jaruzelski suggested something that would soon prove far more dramatic. Taking a leaf from Hungary, he floated the possibility of allowing "opposition groups," such as Solidarity, to participate for the first time in parliamentary elections that spring, just a few months away. Perhaps, he intimated generously, an opposition leader would even be allowed to join the government.

The communist party rank and file were shocked. Yet Jaruzelski paid little heed. He was all steel and iron resolve, as determined on his present course as he was in his last, in the black days of 1981. Stand with me in charting a new course for Poland, one that acknowledges Solidarity, he told party leaders at a confrontational meeting of the ruling Central Committee in January, or he would resign. Though few recognized it, inside the country or without, Poland at that moment passed a tipping point—Jaruzelski's unwittingly radical "brave turnaround." He could have played Lear and drenched himself and his nation in blood once again. But this time, as he himself later described it, he chose Hamlet.

True to the role, he was a study in ambiguity. He both acted, decisively, and held back. He was visionary—and blind. He was torn between his own past and his country's future, between a dubious morality and just action. He almost certainly did not foresee where his course would lead and seemed driven as much by intuition (if not hope) as by political calculation. Confiding in almost no one, he was unknown. Was he motivated chiefly by expedience, once again doing what needed to be done to preserve socialism and the party's prerogatives, as critics presupposed? Or was it something deeper and more subliminal, a banishing of ghosts, whereby Jaruzelski, ashamed of his choice nearly eight years earlier, was now determined to make amends, to act justly and accept the consequences—to let the cards fall as they may? The answer may be too buried within Jaruzelski's psyche for even him to know.

In any event, he got what he wanted from the Central Committee by a single vote. Thus began Wojciech Jaruzelski's slow, lonely path of self-redemption—and Poland's 1989 revolution.

A cold drizzle fell on the fifty or so demonstrators gathered forlornly, it seemed, outside a baroque palace in Warsaw. Everything was gray: the smog-ridden air, the begrimed buildings and broken pavement, the people in their drab, worn clothes and clunky East bloc shoes.

It was all the more depressing given the momentousness of what was going on inside. It was February 6, 1989. For the first time since 1981, Polish authorities were meeting with Solidarity. The loyalists gathered in the rain dreamed of legalizing their movement and recasting Poland's political system. Judging by their numbers, that seemed a frail hope. Yet pictures of the opening of this famous Round Table, with its great bouquet of flowers in the middle, became the talk of Eastern Europe. For there, face-to-face, former political prisoners sat conversing politely with their former jailers about their common future.

Foremost among them was Lech Walesa, the electrician who scaled the fence around the Gdansk shipyard in 1980, founded Solidarity and was jailed by the very men who now faced him. He was awarded the 1983 Nobel Peace Prize, a salute to the spirit of human liberty as well as to the tenacity of the man himself. And while the communist leaders seated around the table did not know it yet, they would before too long be addressing him as "Mr. President." There was also Tadeusz Mazowiecki, a journalist, human rights lawyer and Solidarity activist who had spent more time in prison under the communists than any other figure in the opposition. Within seven months, to the astonishment of himself and his partners, communist and opposition alike, he would become the first popularly elected prime minister in Eastern Europe since World War II. There was Bronislaw Geremek, a gentle and bearded professor of medieval literature, Solidarity's chief tactician, a future foreign minister and president of the Organization of European Security and Cooperation who would within a decade become responsible, among other things, for orchestrating NATO's intervention in Kosovo. And alongside them, in turn, were a dozen other activists who would shortly replace the men, communist leaders all, who considered themselves the powers at this august occasion and many of whom, even now, scarcely deigned speak to anyone outside their ruling clique. Among them was the communists' chief interlocutor, Czeslaw Kiszczak, head of the Polish secret police and minister of interior during the years of martial law, the onetime nemesis of virtually all those surrounding him.

This bizarre moment, so rich with irony, would set the tone for changes elsewhere in Eastern Europe. When push came to shove in East Germany, Hungary and Czechoslovakia, communists and anti-communists would call for talks on the Polish model. But only in Poland were they actually decisive, both in terms of their outcome and their bona fides as a genuine, give-and-take negotiation. This was made easier because both communists and opposition recognized that sheer economic necessity compelled them to work together. It helped, too, that neither side had any idea of the magnitude of what they stood to gain or lose.

I had been flying in and out of Poland since September. Eight years of martial law had brought nothing but hardship. In a proud nation that had long considered itself to be *West* European, a third of the population now lived in poverty. Inflation stood at 60 percent annually but was accelerating toward 500 percent, according to the latest indexes. The country was not only slipping further behind Western Europe but also, humiliatingly, its own East bloc neighbors. The British historian Timothy Garton Ash, traveling in Poland during the time of the strikes, asked the demonstrators faced off against the police what they hoped to achieve. The memorable reply: "Forty years of socialism, and there's still no toilet paper!"

Walking the streets of Warsaw, it was impossible to miss the cadres of "garbage can people," as one underground newspaper called them—scavengers who went about scrounging for scraps of food and clothing. In glaring contrast were the "banana people," so named because they could afford to buy fruit. These wealthy few, usually the sons, daughters and spouses of the communist elite, could go to the special shops where, for a stiff premium in hard currency, they could pretty much buy any luxury or necessity they desired: toilet paper, women's stockings, TVs, imported tea, coffee.

Everyone else lived essentially as hunter-gatherers. They carried plastic bags wherever they went. If a line formed, they joined it, waiting patiently for whatever was for sale, making the rounds of shops where they might enjoy a personal relationship with the proprietor, who would put goodies away for them in return for whatever similar favor they might be able to offer. On the very day the Round Table convened, I stood waiting in line at a state bank to open a new account for the *Newsweek* bureau. Suddenly, every clerk in the place jumped up and ran out the door. Why? Downstairs on the street, someone was selling oranges. Hundreds of people stood in the bank queue for the next hour, shifting wearily from foot to foot until the clerks slowly filed back in, each clutching several precious oranges. The likes of us—indeed, the bank itself—had no choice but to wait for the employees to finish their private business. We didn't dare sacrifice our place in line.

Welcome to Poland, 1989. Danuta Zagrodzka was Poland's spokeswoman for human rights. She shrugged at my tale of the oranges. As far as she was concerned, privations such as that were no more than a trivial inconvenience. They represented only the smallest tip of the iceberg of a far more general abuse of individual freedom—the right to a modicum of dignity and comfort. I had gone to talk with her about political prisoners in Poland, a big issue in the United States. She shrugged at that, too. Conditions were not good in Polish prisons, she readily conceded. Cells designed for three people held nine. Toilets didn't work. There was lots of thuggery. Then she offered a novel defense of Poland's human rights record. "The truth is that there are no longer any political prisoners in Poland," she said, explaining that there were instead only degrees of deprivation—for all Poles, in prison or out. With that, she pulled a thick folder off a shelf. "What do you want to know? I have all the facts." And without prodding, she began to read.

Inflation and prices for everyday goods? Her latest figures pegged it at 60 to 80 percent, ten times higher than a year ago. According to the Central Statistics Office, the annual cost of living in Poland had increased by 55 percent more than incomes over the first half of the 1980s. The average Pole, she reported, worked half an hour to afford a loaf of bread, four hours for a chocolate bar. Outside the major cities, only 45 percent of Poles had running water; three-quarters had no indoor toilet. Consumer goods such as refrigerators were getting harder and harder to find. People seeking to buy one from a state store might have to wait anywhere from a month to three months. So that they would not have to stand in line all day, every day, for weeks or months, people would form "line committees," with designated officers responsible for maintaining everyone's place in the queue and fending off interlopers who might try to force ahead of them. During a lull in a Round Table briefing, one Polish journalist told of a Warsaw television store that recently announced it would begin accepting down payments for TVs, starting the next Monday. A line formed the preceding Friday. At opening time, fifteen thousand people were waiting for the privilege of paying nearly $1,300—a year's average wages—for a no-frills set they would be lucky to receive in a few months' time. "This is life by attrition," he said. "After a time, you begin to feel that everything around you is crumbling."

Young Poles were especially desperate. Most had no homes of their own; in some parts of Poland, it could take twenty to thirty years to reach the top of the waiting list for an apartment. The wait for a telephone or a car could take ten to fifteen years. "Everyday life has been destroyed. The streets are broken. It's dirty. Buildings are falling down and are never repaired. People are tired and worn to their bones," Danuta went on. Let's see, she said, consulting her notes one last time. "Oh, yes, Poles spend, on average, one-quarter of their waking day waiting in queues." She closed her folder and added with only a trace of humor, "I can say these things because I am the smiling face of the establishment."

It would have been easy, under such circumstances, to portray Poles and their government as totally at odds. But that would be too simple. As Danuta said, she was the smiling face of the establishment—a senior communist official making no bones about her frustration with the system, not even bothering to pretend that it worked, and displaying immense sympathy for "the people" it was slowly crushing. In Poland by this time, Solidarity had become far more than a mere trade union movement, a political opposition. It was, increasingly, a way of life, a movement shared not merely among the ruled but, to a surprising degree, by their rulers.

The author Janine Wedel captured this phenomenon in her memoir of the time, *The Private Poland*. Solidarity, she wrote, stood for renewal in social, economic and political life. Its name was a social injunction, a call to "help each other." Its most common manifestation was the intricate network of personal ties that all Poles relied on to get what they needed in life—food, medicines, the latest books and magazines, anything that could not efficiently be delivered by Poland's broken demand-but-no-supply economy. More abstractly, it became a shorthand for the Polish sense of morality, even honor. It was hardly unknown for communist officials to help the friends and family of jailed Solidarity activists, often at considerable danger to themselves.

Yet martial law indeed drew some sharp social lines. Those deemed to be collaborators, who colluded in its imposition, became an unacceptable "them." Wedel tells of a well-known actor, head of the communist party committee at a major Polish theater, who in 1981 went on the evening news to express his official support for Jaruzelski and his government. Ever after, when he appeared onstage, the audience would begin applauding—and not stop until he withdrew, unable to deliver his lines. A famous career was ruined. Similarly, a noted author endorsed martial law. Soon after, people began stacking copies of his books on the sidewalk in front of his apartment building. They were "returning" them. Members of the political opposition would isolate "traitors," refusing to shake hands with an academic, say, known to associate too closely with the government. When a nineteen-year-old boy died after being beaten by police, tens of thousands of Poles showed up at the funeral to protest. Hundreds of thousands marched at the funeral of a murdered pro-Solidarity priest, Father Jerzy Popieluszko, in 1984. And so it was again in 1989 when another clerical activist, Father Stefan Niedzielak, was found dead just days after Poland's communist leaders offered to recognize Solidarity. Many interpreted the killing as a message to the resurgent opposition: go slow, or else.

Perhaps it was only a matter of time before something happened. That previous spring, when the strikes first broke out in the south around Nowa Huta and Katowice and workers began demanding the restoration of Solidarity, I was visiting Poland for the first time.

The party's short, fat, bald and supremely funny spokesman, Jerzy Urban, invited me to lunch. He was full of contemptuous dismissiveness. "Solidarity is dead," he assured me. As for that Lech Walesa . . . a wave of his hand, fat pinkie held delicately aloft as he sipped a luncheon liquor. He was merely a "private citizen," not someone to reckon with, a "drunk," a "misfit," a "buffoon." Yet it turned out to be "that Walesa" the communists would have to reckon with as 1989 began. "We must kick out the jerks who have brought us to beggary," he had told strikers the previous summer. Street demonstrators soon took up a catchy slogan: "Hang the communists." It had a ring, and no doubt helped focus minds within the regime.

Poland's Round Table, beginning that cheerless February day, would stretch over four months of tortured negotiation. Every other week or so, I would fly in to see what was happening. From afar, it looked to be little. Progress stumbled on one critical point: Solidarity insisted that it be legally recognized as a union; otherwise, there would be no Round Table. The government was no less adamant. The workers Solidarity sought to organize comprised the backbone of the United Communist Workers' Party. At the Lenin Shipyard in Gdansk, Solidarity's birthplace, thirty-five hundred of four thousand workers said they would join Solidarity if given the choice. "We would be committing suicide," a senior communist party official confided over drinks late one night, just as the talks were getting going. "Recognizing Solidarity would mean the end of the communist party in Poland."

I nicknamed this man Kat, partly for the feline pleasure he took in drawing a cloak of mystery around what he knew and how he knew it. He was one of the few sources I found who could accurately and honestly describe what was happening within the party. "Consider these the views of a party official who feels he has wasted his life," he told me in one of our first conversations, asking not to be identified. Beware, he advised. The talks between Solidarity and the government might look peaceable and encouraging, but only from the outside. From his vantage point, atop the bureaucracy that ran state media, the situation looked nasty. A dangerous act of political theater was playing out. Jaruzelski worried about the economy and rising social tensions. He wanted to change the regime's cast of characters and address the problems. But he could not do so without alienating the party. Even with the backing of the army, he would not want to risk a split that would diminish his authority. As Kat saw it, swirling his scotch, legalizing Solidarity could lead to "civil war" within the regime.

I mentioned this conversation to Bronislaw Geremek, the scholarly medievalist who over these months emerged as the chief strategist behind Solidarity's rebirth. Bearded and bespectacled, as soft and gentle in manner as his patched and well-worn sweaters, Geremek was the epitome of the East European intellectual. This day, he sat in his book-lined study in a gray apartment block on a narrow backstreet in what remained of Warsaw's Old Town. I didn't call ahead, even in those changing times, because I preferred not to alert the secret police. Geremek nodded at the talk of "civil war." Solidarity sought only one thing from the talks: legal recognition. The government was willing to offer everything but this, he explained. "They talk of 'deep changes' in our politics and economy. They tell us the opposition might be represented in parliament or the government. They offer changes in the tax law to encourage private enterprise and speak of a new 'law of association,' whatever might be meant by that. But on the issue of Solidarity, they say, 'We can't do this right now.' From our perspective, this is the number one priority. Because it goes to the heart of democracy and the nation's social and economic troubles." Failure to reach what Geremek called a new "social contract" could lead to more than a war within the party. It could easily touch off a social "explosion."

The novelist Tom Wolfe, in his 1980s bestseller *Bonfire of the Vanities*, anointed one Reverend Bacon as the man who controlled "the steam" in New York, twisting a social safety valve to release pent-up pressure when racial relations approached the bursting point, or notching them up when he wanted to make a political point. In Poland in early 1989, that role fell to General Jaruzelski. As the talks between Solidarity and the government dragged on inconclusively, he would break the impasse. The Round Table had been his idea. He brought the two sides together. He faced down communist hard-liners threatening to bolt the party at that stormy January meeting of the Central Committee. Ultimately, he would push them to success. Those who led Solidarity would later admit that they "owed" Jaruzelski. Jacek Kuron, a union organizer who spent seven years in jail and would go on to become minister of labor, put it bluntly: "Jaruzelski was the one who saw it just wasn't working anymore, not just communism but the whole system. He was big enough to see it."

That Jaruzelski should reach out to the hated Solidarity, at a moment when he saw Poland threatened every bit as much as in 1981, was as much an act of courage as it was pragmatism or expedience. Neither he nor the opposition knew where the talks might lead. And it's striking how modestly each side defined their goals. At what would be a fateful watershed, Solidarity sought little more than recognition of its right to exist; beyond that, it would accept what it could get. The government may have hoped for a partner in culpability. If there was no glory in socialism, party leaders reasoned, at least they could spread the blame of failure by giving the opposition a modest voice in power. But Jaruzelski also hoped that Solidarity could help smooth the road through some tough economic belt-tightening that he was wise enough to foresee as necessary.

Only the true believers, the hardest of hard-liners, appear to have seen the threat as it was—the end of communism in Poland. Change began in Poland as it would across much of Eastern Europe, with a combination of blindness and expedience. The old guard knew their weakness and tried to remedy it. Yet they seemed to think they could control change, get out in front and lead. Seldom did they recognize the force of the events they set in motion.

CHAPTER FIVE

Parallel Universes

By tradition, any new head of state in the East bloc traveled first to Moscow. Not Miklos Nemeth. He went to Vienna, then Warsaw. "Hungarians got the message," he said—a "small sign" that the country's future lay to the west, not east.

As spring approached, however, Nemeth felt he could defer a visit no longer. Hungary's reforms were entering a crucial—and worrisome—phase. He would soon announce that free elections would be held, possibly before the end of the year. Kalman Kulcsar, his justice minister, was finishing the new constitution, with full guarantees of free speech and private property. It wasn't just socialism with a human face. It was . . . a human face, period.

Nemeth wanted to make sure he was not going too far, or too fast. Only one person could answer that question. So Nemeth wrote to Mikhail Gorbachev, asking for a meeting in the first week of March. His timing was influenced by another factor. Communist party secretary Karoly Grosz planned to see Gorbachev, as well. That visit was scheduled for March 23–24. Nemeth told Gorbachev that, as Hungary's head of state, he too should be meeting with the Soviet leader and, in recognition of diplomatic protocol, should be first. Privately he feared that Grosz would undermine both him and his government's reforms by casting them as a threat to the party's continued hold on power—which would, in fact, be precisely what happened.

Nemeth had requested an hour's audience. Instead, he was offered twenty minutes. "Gorbachev and I were alone, each with an aide." Describing his plans for democracy in Hungary, and why he thought it necessary, Nemeth told Gorbachev plainly what the consequences could be—a popular vote that might drive the communists from office. How would Moscow react, he wanted to know.

Gorbachev was taken aback. The longer the two men spoke, the more agitated Gorbachev became. "He was very angry," Nemeth recalled years later. "'I do not agree with this "Hungarian way,"' Gorbachev said. 'The proper path is to go back to the roots of Leninism.'" He sternly urged Nemeth to follow the guidance of his boss, the correct-thinking General Secretary Grosz, who opposed any course that might undermine the authority and leading role of the communist party.

Now it was Nemeth's turn to be shocked. He had expected to find a fellow reformer, a sympathetic ear, even an ally in his fight against Grosz and others who resisted too-rapid change. But no. "I realized, very strongly at this moment, that Gorbachev was a socialist to his core. He outlined for me how socialism could find its way again, by going back to the time before Stalin. I felt completely the opposite and said so. When I told him we were considering elections, and not merely talking to the opposition, he was especially angered." It was a blow against socialism, Gorbachev argued heatedly, a violation of the party's right to create a just society. You couldn't just leave that to chance, for the people to decide.

Nemeth remembers feeling physically sick. He feared that all he had been working toward was about to crumble. How could he possibly go ahead without Gorbachev's blessing? Images of Soviet troops in Budapest flickered through his head. At the very least, Moscow's resistance to his policies would mean the end of his own career. For a fleeting moment, Nemeth wondered whether he might even be thrown in jail. Then, abruptly, Gorbachev changed his tone. "But of course, comrade," he said, "you are responsible, not me." Hungary's direction was for Hungarians to decide, not Moscow.

Suddenly, the immense pressure lifted. Nemeth pressed the point, posing again the elemental question. "I asked him specifically, 'If we set a date for an election and are voted out, would you intervene as in 1956?'" Without a hint of hesitation, Gorbachev answered, "Nyet." Then he paused and, with a ghost of a smile, added a telling caveat: "At least, not as long as I am sitting in this chair."

This no was of immense importance to Nemeth. "It meant we

could go ahead. It opened the way for everything that would follow," he said, from the creation of a democratic Hungary to, ultimately, the fall of the Berlin Wall. This brief encounter with Gorbachev, coming with the first breath of spring after a long winter, would prove to be a hidden but decisive turning point in the end of the Cold War.

Yet Nemeth was not finished. Having accomplished his chief mission, he dropped a second bomb, in some ways even bigger than the first. He told Gorbachev that he wanted to pull Hungary out of the Warsaw Pact, the Soviet military alliance established as a counterweight to NATO.

In late December, shortly before Christmas, Nemeth had been summoned to a secret meeting at the Hungarian Defense Ministry. Karoly Grosz informed him that, as the country's new prime minister, he had to review and sign some papers. "So I went. Never will I forget that terrible day." Military security guards met Nemeth at the gate and escorted him into the bowels of the building. A small group of senior officials awaited him, including the commanding general of Soviet forces in Hungary. There he was briefed on the threat from the West. "NATO plans to invade from Italy," he was informed. Maps showed the likely movements of Allied and Warsaw Pact forces. Nemeth's personal command bunker was, coincidentally, located in his native village in eastern Hungary. "Then came the really secret part," according to Nemeth. "I was informed that nuclear warheads were stored in Hungary," secured in bunkers in the forests around Lake Balaton, where he loved to sail. After signing some documents and a statement agreeing not to disclose the information, he left.

Nemeth was stunned. Moscow had always denied the presence of nuclear weapons in Hungary, but they were there in "quite substantial numbers." Nemeth broke his pledge of secrecy immediately, telling his wife and two key advisers, one of them Defense Minister Ferenc Karpati. Even then, Nemeth had planned to inform Gorbachev that he wanted Soviet troops withdrawn from Hungary. Now he included Russia's nuclear weapons in the request. Gorbachev blinked. "I will get back to you," he said, giving no hint of what he would decide. Both men understood that they were talking about a staggering development, as yet unimaginable in the West.

Nemeth left the Kremlin for the airport, his feelings weirdly mixed. Elation coupled with relief, yet he felt a deep trepidation. He and his reformers had come a long way. They had just negotiated a passage that many among them had dreaded. But that only set the stage for greater dangers ahead. In the end, a meeting that was to last twenty minutes had stretched to nearly three hours.

If Miklos Nemeth's visit to Moscow cracked the edifice that was the Soviet bloc, another fissure opened a few weeks later in Poland, far more visibly. To the surprise of almost everyone, the Polish Round Table ended on April 7 with a historic pact. At a glittery ceremony in Warsaw's seventeenth-century Namiestnikowski Palace, the two sides toasted one another with vodka and champagne. Both got more than they bargained for. Neither knew it.

Solidarity had dreamed of regaining its legal standing, seven years after being outlawed under martial law. It came away not only with that, but also with the right to compete in Poland's next parliamentary elections, just two months away. For Poles, this was breathtaking—the country's first free elections since World War II. To be sure, *free* was a qualified term. Under the deal, Solidarity could contest only a third of the seats in the Sejm, the lower house of the national legislature; the remaining two-thirds were reserved for the communists. A new upper house, the Senate, was to be created, though its role would be confined to reviewing legislation proposed by the lower house. Key posts such as the Defense and Interior ministries would be kept by the communists, as well as the presidency—presumably Jaruzelski, who announced at the conclusion of the talks that Poland was "on the road to becoming a socialist parliamentary democracy."

Evidently he believed it. Nothing suggests Jaruzelski had the least doubt that the party would retain power—that is, he chose to emphasize the "socialist" before "parliamentary" when it came to democracy. Perhaps he was seduced by his political experts' polls, purporting to show that Solidarity's popularity was declining as his own was rising. More likely, he simply couldn't imagine a different outcome. These elections would be like any other communist vote, he not illogically presumed: the results foreordained, the people grateful to participate and show their support for their government's leadership, which after all had only their best interests at heart. Not even the nation's dyspeptic post-1981 mood, nor the economic hard times, appeared to shake his confidence.

The party rank and file did not share his optimism, Kat among them. As the Round Table progressed, his mood steadily deteriorated. "Socialism in Poland is being dismantled," he complained bitterly late one night, smoking cigarette after cigarette. He was full of dark foreboding. The party was colluding in its own demise, he said. Jaruzelski and his men deluded themselves if they thought they could control events they were about to unleash. Kat had just learned with astonishment that the government itself had proposed that Solidarity field candidates for the June election. The opposition hadn't even asked for it. Talk about an instinct for self-destruction! "What a spectacle," he declared, shaking his head in perplexity and contempt.

He guessed that, in a genuinely free election, the party would be lucky to retain a majority in Parliament. At a recent briefing for top communist officials, the government negotiator, Czeslaw Kiszczak, had been hooted down. "Attitudes within the party were hostile," he reported. "The old guard, especially, asked, 'Why do this? We risk sacrificing all our privileges, without any gain.' " Even party liberals felt they were being dragged along against their will and own best interests. Hard-liners were angry enough, Kat believed, that they might try to oust Jaruzelski—a "traitor," this time, to their cause.

As the Round Table neared its conclusion, I invited Solidarity's chief strategist in the talks, Bronislaw Geremek, for dinner at the Victoria Hotel in central Warsaw, facing the gargantuan square where Poland's communist elite staged their annual May Day parades. Ever the academic, in his mothy tweed jacket and well-worn sweater, he could not have afforded on his own to eat in such an establishment. Yet there he was, having just helped engineer one of the most extraordinary diplomatic coups in modern European history.

Like Jaruzelski, he too was full of confidence. It did not matter whether the communist party liked the deal or not. "The army is the true power in Poland," he said. "Jaruzelski will deliver. The conventional wisdom that the party would step in to prevent an erosion of its power is wrong." Of course, he added, the general would be named president. Though elated at all that Solidarity had won, Geremek did not foresee a dramatic change in Poland's political landscape, let alone a rapid transition to democracy. The June elections would merely be a prelude to fully free elections four years later. It would be a decade, he suggested, before Poland might actually see a noncommunist government.

Never did he imagine it would be four months.

On January 20, 1989, George H. W. Bush was sworn in as the forty-first president of the United States. Shortly after taking office, he ordered a strategic review of U.S.-Soviet relations. It arrived on the president's desk in mid-March, not long after Miklos Nemeth's secret Moscow summit.

Brent Scowcroft, the new national security adviser, was unimpressed. "Disappointing," he called it, a bland interagency overview, cobbled together from cursory CIA reports and State Department memos. Its fatal flaw in his eyes, however, was that it represented "continuity," as one of his senior deputies would describe it. There was too much of the old administration, and too little of the new. Scowcroft and Secretary of State James Baker wanted a complete break, not some Reagan-Bush hybrid. Scowcroft set the review aside and began working instead with a "think piece" on Gorbachev's intentions and policies, drawn up by an energetic and smart young protégée on the NSC named Condoleezza Rice.

Rice's revealing memo laid out a strategy for "coping with Gorbachev," as Scowcroft put it, premised on the "need to underscore the credibility of NATO's nuclear deterrent" and a deep wariness about Soviet intentions. The new national security team saw the Soviet leader as a "propagandist," seeking to lull the United States into a false sense of security. Ronald Reagan was too popular to publicly repudiate, but the incoming administration believed that the former president had gone too far in his rapprochement with Moscow. Reagan trusted Gorbachev too much. It was time to dial back. Reagan's more ambitious disarmament initiatives were put on hold. The new defense secretary, Dick Cheney, pushed for tougher policies of confrontation to "test" the Russian leader, coupled with increases in U.S. military spending to counter what he presented as an escalating rather than a diminishing Soviet threat. A sudden East-West chill set in.

I found this troubling, even from afar. It was as if the movie *Back to the Future*, the sequel to which was then being filmed, were playing out in geopolitics. On the ground, I saw Nemeth dismantling communism in Hungary. Here was Poland, on the brink of democratic elections. Gorbachev was everywhere, the hero of a newly vigorous Europe. Yet in Washington a new administration took power with a frame of reference best summed up as Cold War Lite. This seemed especially ironic given that the main theme of the transition, as Bush himself described it, was to "dream big dreams" and see the world fresh. The beflummoxed outgoing secretary of state, George Shultz, leaving office in January, wrote in his memoir, "It was as if the Bush administration did not understand or accept that the Cold War was over."

This skepticism ran deep. Scowcroft and his team were well aware of events in Hungary and Poland. They noted, for instance, the publication in Moscow of a long newspaper article praising Lech Walesa, a clear signal that the Kremlin approved of the course Jaruzelski was charting. The successful conclusion of the Round Table, with its promise of elections, was recognized as a breakthrough. But Scowcroft, in particular, advocated caution. He was a military man and a dyed-in-the-wool conservative. He had seen previous eras of détente turn sour, and he worried that Gorbachev's strategy was to fool the United States into lowering its military guard in Europe, toward whatever unforeseen end. "I was suspicious of Gorbachev's motives and skeptical of his prospects," he wrote in his memoir with George Bush, *A World Transformed*. Gorbachev's goal was to revitalize the Soviet Union so as to "better compete" with the West. "To me," said Scowcroft, "this made Gorbachev potentially more dangerous than his predecessors, each of whom, through some aggressive move, had saved the West from the dangers of its own wishful thinking."

Others in the administration were no less wary. Never mind that, in April, George Kennan, dean of American Sovietologists and the original author of America's bedrock strategy of containment, told the Senate Foreign Relations Committee that the Soviet Union no longer posed a threat. Never mind that Margaret Thatcher declared the Cold War to be over. James Baker would suggest that "Gorbachev's strategy was premised on splitting the alliance and undercutting us in Western Europe." Hard-liners within the Defense Department, led by Cheney and a phalanx of aides who would become famous in a later

Bush administration—among them Paul Wolfowitz, Richard Perle and I. Lewis "Scooter" Libby—argued against more moderate State Department officials who saw the changes gathering force in the East bloc as an opportunity for closer engagement. Cheney was especially virulent in his suspicions, all but calling Gorbachev an impostor and a "fraud." Giving too much credence to Gorbachev's "new thinking," he told CNN in late April, exposed the United States to the risk, indeed the likelihood, that he would fail and be replaced by someone "far more hostile" to the United States.

U.S. intelligence analyses did little to reshape the discussion. A CIA National Intelligence Estimate dated November 23, 1988, focused on the Soviet Union's deteriorating economic situation, accurately suggesting that internal reforms offered scant prospect of solving the country's growing troubles. But in reference to developments elsewhere in the bloc, it projected rather tamely that "attempts at political reform in the USSR are likely to generate pressure on East European countries for similar reforms"—neglecting to note that changes there were already running well ahead of anything happening in Moscow. A second intelligence estimate a month later, focusing specifically on Soviet policy toward Eastern Europe, concluded that Gorbachev's "agenda" for the region had "increased the potential for instability." Any changes would most likely be "evolutionary," however, leading to "greater diversity" but far short of radical transformation. "In extremis," the CIA judged, "there is no reason to doubt [Gorbachev's] willingness to intervene to preserve party rule and decisive Soviet influence in the region."

The agency would stick by this view in a National Intelligence Estimate dated as late as November 18, 1989, even as Eastern Europe slipped ever more out of communist control and after the Wall itself had toppled. Indeed, the closest it came to calling events right came in a dissent to that document written by Deputy Director for Intelligence John Helgerson. Presciently, it argued that Gorbachev would avoid a crackdown in the East but would "progressively lose control of events" and be forced to give up his "still authoritarian vision in favor of a truly democratic one."

For both the intelligence community and the White House, the ruling assumption through most of 1989 was that Moscow still called the shots in Eastern Europe, despite all Gorbachev was saying and doing. More than once, the Soviet leader implicitly—and, as time went on, increasingly explicitly—renounced the interventionist Brezhnev Doctrine. His chief advisers, Alexander Yakovlev and Oleg Bogomolov, unequivocally said as much in face-to-face meetings with senior U.S. and European officials. There were Gorbachev's assurances to Miklos Nemeth, who promptly relayed them to his tennis partner, Ambassador Mark Palmer, who sent them on to Washington. In Poland, Czeslaw Kiszczak, chairing the government side in the Round Table talks, relayed the essence of Gorbachev's message to Jaruzelski to Solidarity's negotiators, who quickly told the Americans. Meanwhile, classified cables flooded into the White House and State Department from the likes of the U.S. ambassador in Moscow, Jack Matlock, flatly describing the Brezhnev Doctrine as "dead" and casting Gorbachev as a bona fide "revolutionary" who represented a historic opportunity for the United States to reshape relations with the Soviet Union.

Years later, Rice would admit that the new administration, focusing on Gorbachev's troop withdrawals and the implications for U.S. nuclear doctrine, had missed the bigger picture entirely. "I missed completely, really, the revocation of the Brezhnev Doctrine." All the while, communism continued to crumble, increasingly visibly as the spring went on. Yet none of it quite seemed to sink in. As the Solidarity activist Adam Michnik would bitingly put it, America at this decisive moment was "sleepwalking through history."

CHAPTER SIX

The Hungarian Connection

May 1, 1989. East Berlin. An aging Erich Honecker, seventy-seven, stood atop the reviewing stand for the annual May Day parade, flanked by his top Politburo henchmen. To his left was one of the most feared men in the East bloc, the murderous Erich Mielke, minister of state security, head of the ubiquitous East German secret police. To his right, the toothy Egon Krenz, general secretary of the Central Committee, and not far away, Gunter Schabowski, first secretary of the Berlin communist party.

Both Krenz and Schabowski would soon be plotting against him, though it would scarcely matter. The real threat, invisible as yet, lay shaping far away, hundreds of miles to the south. But on this day there was no sign of intrigue. The sun was shining. A warm breeze, a sign of an early spring, tousled Honecker's fluffy, grandfatherly white hair. Outwardly he was the very image of the revered leader, a benign First Comrade, doting on children and beloved by his people, the citizens of the German Democratic Republic.

Every religion has its symbols. They give voice and shape to faith. When violated, especially if deliberately, it is not merely a desecration. It is a challenge to orthodoxy, a heresy, even treason. Among the believers of communist Europe, few symbols were dearer than May Day. Those who did not grow up during the Cold War will not remember the tanks, missile launchers and armies of troops parading each spring through Red Square. Atop Lenin's Tomb, generations of Soviet leaders paid homage to these emblems of socialist might. The satraps of Moscow's colonies celebrated no less fervently. Within the East bloc, this was not merely a commemoration of the 1917 revolution. It was a legitimation of their rule. As wine and wafers are to Christians, May Day was to communist officialdom.

This particular May Day in Berlin was special. It was a Jubilee year, marking the East German regime's fortieth anniversary in power. The annual parade was thus even more colossal than usual. Banners flew, bands played. The youth of the communist party, the Freie Deutsche Jugend, saluted smartly as they marched proudly by, cheered by thousands mustered by fiat for the occasion. Honecker and his men waved back, warm in the sun, basking in the display, secure in their cocoon of power. Could it be two years since Honecker had triumphantly returned from his first state visit to the West German Federal Republic, a de facto recognition of himself and his nation that he had yearned for over decades? To him, it seemed only yesterday.

Erich Honecker built the Wall, behind which he ruled as master. His predecessor, Walter Ulbricht, ordered it. But Honecker personally oversaw its construction and was its guarantor. Every year, East German border police shot a handful of citizens who dared to try to escape—"wall-jumpers," malcontents. *Die Mauer bleibt noch hundert Jahre,* " Honecker had declared in January, marking the beginning of this auspicious year. "The Wall will last another hundred years." Nothing on his political horizon clouded his prospects. To the east, Mikhail Gorbachev might be championing change. Poland and Hungary were chasing their aberrant path to socialism. But the GDR itself had never seemed so outwardly solid. There was no hint that this day, this very day, would be its high-water mark. Nothing in the cloudless skies over Honecker's head suggested the tempest that would soon engulf him. Indeed, he scarcely saw that first mortal blow as it fell. It came as a bolt out of the blue.

Shift to Budapest, four hundred miles distant. As Erich Honecker luxuriated in the welcoming spring sun, Karoly Grosz trudged through a sullen rain. Nor was there a parade. Change was afoot, and communist party officials decided they had best put on a fresh face.

Instead of the traditional May Day ceremony, as in East Berlin, they opted for a People's Picnic. At a nearby park, a vast feast awaited—food and drink, balloons and tents, ready to receive tens of thousands of guests. The rain was not to blame that only a thousand showed up, mostly aging party stalwarts and their damp and unsmiling spouses. Across town, a rally by Hungary's new opposition political parties drew more than one hundred thousand people. Their banners proclaimed DOWN WITH COMMUNISM!

There were student groups, ecology groups, artist groups, new political groups of every description, each with its own tent lining the paths of a city park, all busily signing up members and discussing programs for change. Jazz bands played; people danced in the mud. "The communists are finished," shouted one political organizer who would go on to become a leader of his country. Not long ago he would have been arrested. Today, he was the young face of Hungary's future.

The party's humiliation was plain. It was a public desecration, a frontal challenge to orthodoxy and to communism itself. And it was so deliberate. Not a single senior official in Nemeth's government bothered to attend, save for the prime minister himself, who felt obliged. "That was the day of my humiliation," he remembers. He stood there as Grosz spoke to the party faithful, furiously attacking Nemeth and his government's policies and all but charging him with treason to the socialist cause.

"This may be your day," Nemeth told Grosz icily, as they went their separate ways. "But my day is not far off."

This was no idle threat. For Nemeth had a plan: not merely to reform communism, but to bring it down—not only in Hungary but across the whole East bloc. Grosz had no inkling, of course. But he would, and soon. In fact, Nemeth would deliver his first, finely calculated blow the next day.

On the morning of May 2, 1989, the Hungarian government announced that, for reasons of fiscal economy, it would "no longer maintain" the electrified security barrier running the length of its western border with Austria. The thing was an expensive "anachronism," Nemeth informed his cabinet. His choice of language was deliberately bureaucratic, designed to veil his true intent. But his actions plainly spoke louder than his words. Within hours, a photo destined to become famous flashed over the international newswires: Hungarian soldiers cutting down a stretch of barbed-wire fence at the Austrian-Hungarian border.

Let us pause, here, and think about that. A hole in the Iron Curtain. For the communist world, this was the equivalent of Martin Luther hammering Protestantism to the doors of the Catholic Church. It was like *Sputnik*, rousing America to the reality of a space race, or the urban riots of the sixties that awoke the nation to the depth of its racial divide. The image of Hungary snipping holes in the barrier separating East from West sent a profound tremor through East Berlin. "What are those Hungarians up to!" Honecker shouted at his assembled ministers, gathered the next morning, May 3, for the weekly meeting of the Politburo. But he knew very well what they were "up to." He recognized the danger.

He realized East German tourists would soon begin their summer travels. Hungary was a favorite destination. Locked behind the Iron Curtain, as they were, Budapest and the countryside around Lake Balaton was the closest ordinary East Europeans could come to paradise. With its unique brand of "goulash economics," leavening Marxist industrial policy with a measure of free enterprise, Hungary offered the trappings of prosperity missing virtually everywhere else—nice restaurants and cafés, ample food and groceries, good wine, pleasant camping and a (comparatively) lively capital city.

Neither Honecker nor anyone else at the top of his government needed to be briefed on the likely scenario to come. It was a nightmare straight from 1961, the reason the Berlin Wall had been built in the first place: to stop communism's unhappy citizens from voting with their feet. If Hungary's border to the West was open, those East German tourists, numbering in the hundreds of thousands, might not come back home. They would merrily go south to Hungary on "vacation," then turn right, cross the border, and end up in Austria or West Germany. For Honecker, that would represent an existential crisis, a fatal blow to his legitimacy and consequently to his rule. It could even bring down the whole house of cards that was the GDR.

Furious, Honecker stormed into the Politburo without even a hello and demanded a full report, immediately. "Call your counterpart in Hungary," he instructed Defense Minister Heinz Kessler. "This border is their responsibility!"

Kessler left the meeting. Half an hour later, he returned. He had just spoken to Ferenc Karpati. "This is just those radicals," the Hungarian defense minister told him. He said that he didn't agree with the decision, either, but there was no cause for alarm. "The border will still be patrolled. There is no possibility of East German citizens leaking out through a hole in the fence."

Nemeth also remembered Kessler's call. He and Karpati discussed how to reply. "Tell them it's a symbolic act," Nemeth suggested. "Tell them it is a question of money, as I told Gorbi. And by the way, tell them I consider that fence to be a barbarism. Tell them we intend to tear it down!"

Karpati was aghast, until he realized Nemeth was joking. Neither he nor the defense minister would have said any such thing. "We were much more diplomatic," Nemeth recalled, laughing. "We assured him we would not let East Germans flee across the border, and that the frontier would still be patrolled. But as I say, that was the diplomatic answer."

The East Germans did not believe this explanation, not for a moment. Gunter Schabowski, the Berlin party chief who had stood in the sun on that reviewing platform just two days before, was among those attending the meeting. The jarring thing, what stood out, he recalled, was not merely what Hungary had done, but its manner. It was clearly sabotage, almost insolently so. "There was no warning, that was the thing," he told me. "Here was Hungary, a member of the Warsaw Pact, a tiny member, going off on its own and doing something that challenged the very existence of the bloc, that was so opposed to its ideology. It was a very dangerous situation, quite obviously. It was the first concrete sign of the breakup of the bloc. And if there were no bloc, where would that leave us?"

Around the cabinet table, Schabowski recalled, there was a long silence. The question on everyone's mind was left unanswered, not even discussed. One can only imagine what passed through their minds. Was this the fatal moment when they instinctively knew the jig was up, perhaps like Hitler learning that morning in June 1944 that the Allies had invaded Normandy, not Calais as expected?

The meeting broke up. Though inwardly seething, the East German leader pronounced himself satisfied with Hungary's explanation. Who could disagree? "After all," Schabowski noted, "he was the one who built the Wall." It seemed surreal that May Day could have been only the day before yesterday. How abruptly Honecker's cocoon of sunshine and security had been pricked.

All this was precisely as the Hungarians intended. Nemeth and his men had been plotting just this scenario for the better part of two years, first among themselves and later, secretly, with the West German Federal Republic. And so began an intimate choreography. For on that day, May 2, they delivered the first of a series of strategic blows that would knock the Iron Curtain into the trash bin of history.

The script—and we can call it that—was crafted for maximum publicity. It kicked off with a press conference, well attended by several hundred foreign journalists alerted in advance and transported from Budapest to the border crossing at Hegyeshalom, the gateway on the main highway to Vienna. There, Hungarian authorities announced with high ceremony before the international TV cameras that, henceforth, the electronic alarm and surveillance system along the frontier would be switched off. An officer ostentatiously pulled a lever in a circuit box and, lo, it was so. Then guards got to work with outsize wire cutters. The photo instantly flashed around the world: Hungarian soldiers taking down large sections of barbed wire and carting them away.

The symbolism had many layers. Most obvious, it was a declaration that, as far as Hungary was concerned, the Cold War was over. The future lay to the west. It was time for Hungarians to live normally, without artificial geopolitical divides. Beyond that, according to Nemeth, "it was a test of Moscow's tolerance, especially Gorbachev's." What would he do? How angry would he be? Would he wake up and take a hard look at all that was going on in Hungary and realize, to his dismay, that events were spinning out of control? With a bit of encouragement from Moscow, Hungary's hard-liners would only too willingly put down Budapest's experiment with democracy. But to his surprise, Nemeth got no complaint. "I met the Russian ambassador ten times after the event and not once did it come up."

Nemeth saw this, too, as a sign.

Here, beneath the surface, is a consummate tale of Cold War intrigue. Nemeth had not blindsided Gorbachev. He had told him on his visit to Moscow in March that he planned to dismantle the border. But he had not told the whole truth.

During their meeting, Gorbachev spent an immense amount of time talking about money—how there wasn't any. Oil prices had plunged, from a high around $40 a barrel in the spring of 1980 to less than $9 in 1988, falling by 50 percent in 1986 alone, Gorbachev's first year in power. Russian production fell as well, partly because Moscow could not afford to invest in new capacity and exploration. Export revenues were down even more, eaten up by interest on heavy foreign borrowing. Rejuvenating the Soviet economy—Gorbachev's cherished perestroika—was proving far more difficult than he expected. The Soviets required massive investment in new industrial technology, all of which had to be imported from the West and paid for with increasingly scarce hard currency. Growth rates fell to a third of what they were in the mid-1970s under Brezhnev. Much-in-demand consumer goods became more expensive and harder than ever to find; per capita consumer income shrank by two-thirds or more as food prices doubled. The CIA's National Intelligence Estimate of November 1988 had it right in one respect: Gorbachev faced severe economic challenges, possibly beyond his ability to solve.

No one was more aware of this than Nemeth. After all, he was in charge of the government's economic reform team before becoming prime minister. Now he moved to take advantage of Gorbachev's dilemma. Hungary faced equally serious financial constraints, he told the Soviet leader during his March visit. "Comrade General Secretary, we can no longer afford to maintain the frontier barrier," Nemeth said, describing it as outdated and falling apart. "Rabbits were always setting off the alarms." He gave a figure—astronomical, by East bloc standards—for renovation costs. Much of that expense would be in foreign currency, he added, because Russia had ceased manufacturing the stainless-steel fencing that would be required, which meant that replacements would have to be imported from the West. "I told Gorbachev, 'I won't spend a forint to fix that fence. It's a Warsaw Pact fence. They should pay for it.' Gorbachev replied, 'No way. The funding is not there.' "

In relating all this, Nemeth paused for a moment, looking bemused. Then he continued, with a sly smile, "This is only what we told Gorbachev. We Hungarians had very different reasons for opening the border." Subtly, Nemeth had tapped on the door of the Kremlin castle, offering a Trojan horse.

For the past several months, Nemeth and his foreign minister, Gyula Horn, had secretly been conferring with the Austrians and West Germans. In late April, as the Hungarians were preparing their May Day surprise, Nemeth telephoned Chancellor Kohl's key foreign policy aide, Horst Teltschik. "He called me at home and asked if he could come to Bonn immediately. He said it was very urgent," Teltschik told me a decade later, speaking in his director's office at BMW in Munich. Taking great care not to be detected, Teltschik himself drove to a private airport near Cologne to pick up the Hungarian conspirators and took them to meet Chancellor Kohl—not at the chancellery, but at his private home. Nemeth told the Germans that he intended to cut the border fence within the next few days. He told them why he was doing it, at just this moment. He wanted ample time, he said, for word to get out before the annual onslaught of vacationing East Germans arrived in Hungary. He feared that the Warsaw Pact would retaliate, perhaps by cutting off supplies of energy or imposing economic sanctions.

"Will you support us?" Nemeth asked Kohl. According to Teltschik, the German chancellor's response was unhesitating. "We offered him any support he needed. The amount of money was not important. We wanted him to be sure he felt he was on the right side, economically." Significantly, this took place on Kohl's initiative alone. German foreign minister Hans-Dietrich Genscher was not informed.

It was not the first such contact, nor would it be the last. To understand the revolution in Hungary, and how the Berlin Wall came down, it is critical to understand West Germany's role. Teltschik was the point man. Curly-haired and almost elfin, easygoing and quick to laugh, youthful despite his forty-nine years, he could easily be mistaken as "just another aide" among the legions serving Kohl. In fact, he was a rarity: a serious, long-range thinker, a doer like Kohl himself and a believer in the power of the few to accomplish the work of many. Most important, having worked for Kohl since 1972, he enjoyed the chancellor's complete trust.

Teltschik had been in contact with the reformers around Nemeth since the mid-1980s, when one of their number, Istvan Horvath, the ambassador to Germany, came to his office in Bonn. "He was so out-spoken, so radical, that in the beginning I distrusted him," said Teltschik of that first meeting. "What does he want? For a commu-nist, he was so . . . different. I learned, later, that I could trust him, as well as the others."

Teltschik quietly visited Budapest in late 1987, when he first met Nemeth. He kept up his contacts as Nemeth rose through the ranks to become the communist party's chief economist. Officially, Teltschik told me, their meetings were all business—economic reform and negotiating the terms of a billion-mark credit that the Hungarian government sought from Deutsche Bank. Unofficially, the conversation was how to bring decisive change to the GDR.

In the summer of 1988, Teltschik approached Gorbachev to get Nemeth appointed prime minister. He was exactly the sort of "new man" that was needed, he told the Soviet leader. Nemeth could help bring about the economic reforms that could revive the economies of the East bloc. Teltschik said the same to Karoly Grosz. Nemeth was "clean," Teltschik added, untainted by the internecine political infight-ing that compromised other candidates for the job. Coincidence or not, Nemeth was appointed prime minister on November 24.

By then, the bolder of Hungary's reformers were already telling Teltschik that Grosz "wasn't working out." The communist party chief shared Nemeth's desire to retool Hungary's economy—but only that. Economic reform, yes; social reform, no. In their frustration, Nemeth and his small group of allies again approached Kohl through Teltschik. "They felt they had to take over themselves," Teltschik recalled. Once again, the Germans' answer was the same. "We sup-ported them very closely," Teltschik told me. "It was a deal: we will help you, if you will help us," whenever and however the need arose.

Throughout that summer and fall and into the spring of 1989, Teltschik and the Hungarians shuttled back and forth between Bonn and Budapest. Everything was done in the utmost secrecy. During one trip, Kohl's adviser encountered a delegation of high-ranking Soviet Politburo members strolling through a park in downtown Budapest. "It was a very funny situation. They were there to see what was happening, trying to figure out what they could learn. And there

I was, meeting with the same people, talking about how to undermine the system!

"Fortunately," said Teltschik with a laugh, "they did not recognize me." Nor would they recognize his hand in their downfall, so well concealed, until long after it was too late.

Three months into his presidency, George H. W. Bush faced his first European crisis. It had little to do with recent events in Hungary or Poland. Indeed, those seemed not to fully register on the new administration's radar. No, this crisis centered on Germany and one of the sacred cows of the Cold War—nuclear deterrence.

A pair of Germany's most senior officials bore the brunt of Washington's dissatisfaction when they arrived at the State Department on the morning of April 24. It was a beautiful spring day; daffodils bloomed in the gardens. But inside, the reception was glacial. For fifteen minutes they were conspicuously kept waiting—no small breach of diplomatic nicety, considering that the visitors were Foreign Minister Hans-Dietrich Genscher and Defense Minister Gerhard Stoltenberg. Nor was there the usual grin-and-grip photo op for the newspapers. With a perfunctory handshake, Secretary of State James A. Baker III icily cut to the chase: "We are deeply disappointed in your attitude."

With all that was happening in the East bloc, from Poland to Hungary to Russia itself, the issue in dispute might have seemed arcane, if not outright anachronistic. Washington wanted to upgrade its arsenal of short-range nuclear weapons in Europe—the missiles, bombs and artillery shells that constituted the North Atlantic Treaty Organization's main deterrent against Soviet aggression. Specifically, it sought to modernize and deploy a new generation of Lance missiles, with a range of 280 miles rather than 70. A crucial NATO summit was coming up toward the end of May. A decision had to be made, and the Germans were resisting.

Genscher hadn't wanted to come to Washington. He had been pushed to do so, against his better judgment, by Chancellor Kohl. The conversation he was now caught up in was purposeless, as he saw it. Even this most diplomatic of diplomats was hard-pressed to conceal his impatience. Genscher believed the whole modernization debate was moot, out of touch with the times—"eerily unreal," he recalled it in his memoirs, given the changes under way in Europe and the Soviet Union.

Back home in Germany, the country's energetic antiwar left had seized upon the nuclear issue to attack Kohl and his government. Opinion polls told it all. A survey by the Allensbach Institute showed that 79 percent of Germans wanted all nukes withdrawn from Europe; 44 percent favored a withdrawal from NATO. Increasingly, the alliance was seen as a throwback, a vestige of an era fast receding into history. Germans were tired of hosting three hundred thousand foreign troops. They were tired of jets flying low over their houses, tired of American soldiers crawling through their flower beds on "maneuvers," tired of the Cold War. It's over, they were saying. Why is all this necessary? The only people who didn't seem to understand were those who made the decisions, politicians in gray suits talking nukes.

When I visited one of Kohl's senior foreign policy advisers, the man reminded me of Gorbachev's frustration in trying to get through to President Reagan's hard-line advisers, to impress upon them that times had changed. With the exception of Secretary of State George Shultz, who was able to separate reality from ideology—and, ironically, Reagan himself—Gorbachev had complained about the U.S. administration's "caveman mentality." They were so wedded to their Cold War point of view as to be slow or even unable to grasp the significance of what he represented, a chance for peace and a breakthrough. Kohl's adviser himself shrugged, confessing that he largely shared Gorbachev's view. Pushing for more nukes in Europe at a time when "Gorbi" was taking Germany by storm? "Wake up, boys," he said. "Smell the coffee brewing." As far as Germans were concerned, Gorbachev was the peacemaker, the man of the future. Americans with their nukes were seen as dinosaurs, retrogrades, warmongers.

None of this made much impression on the president's men. Baker listened politely but coolly. Defense Secretary Dick Cheney abruptly got up and left in the middle of the meeting—rudely, Genscher felt—to make a speech on this very topic at the National Defense University. "We must not fall into this dangerous trap," Cheney told his audience. "One of the Kremlin's primary goals remains the denuclearization of Europe."

The Germans departed, wondering whether the Americans lived in a different universe. Behind their backs, the Bush team talked of them as sellouts. Genscher was "devious," suspected of conniving to pull Germany out of the Western camp and negotiate a "separate peace" with the Soviets. Kohl, they agreed, was in a "panic," playing politics and wooing the left in a tight reelection race. Condoleezza Rice decried Gorbachev's "propaganda" and cast about for ways to "demonstrate American leadership." Little real consideration was given to the Germans' chief concern: that Europe's political climate was changing so fast as to make any agreement obsolete almost before the ink was dry.

In retrospect, that April 24 meeting in Washington was a window on a more profound problem, with implications far beyond nukes. That was a question of mind-set: the inability to break free of a Cold War view of the world, even as the system was about to come unglued.

I remember thinking this at the time, as if those of us on the ground in Europe inhabited one world and Washington another. Toward the end of winter, I visited the U.S. Army's Eleventh Armored Cavalry Regiment in Fulda, the center of NATO's most forward defensive line. The highway I was driving dropped down from the Thuringian mountains, then cut north across a rolling, wooded plain. A tourist would see pretty fields, streams and rustic farmhouses. A soldier saw the killing fields of the famous Fulda Gap. Hannibal passed this way. So did Napoleon and Patton. So might the Russians, in theory, as their armored battalions "knifed" (such were the words usually employed to describe the Russian threat to the West, even then) across the border in a run for Frankfurt, the financial hub of Europe, just sixty miles away, and beyond that the English Channel. "This is the NFL," growled Colonel John Abrams, who commanded the sector. "We stop 'em here or not at all."

It was all hugely theatrical. Abrams was the son of the Vietnam general; his tanks were Abrams tanks. We boarded a helicopter for a tour of the intra-German frontier, hugging the ground and swooping just over the treetops as if in combat. "The Fulda Gap is the shortest distance to the Rhine," Abrams shouted over the din of the chopper's rotors. "It is the most perfect tank battlefield in the world." It was also one of the toughest, if your forty-six hundred men were outgunned three or four to one. Abrams scanned the open, rolling terrain. In his mind's eye, he watched as hundreds of Soviet tanks churned through the neatly tilled fields. He pointed out the enfilades, valleys and forests where his units, operating in small platoons, would lie in wait. Here, just over the lip of this ridge, his tanks could dig in. There, from the edge of that woods, antitank guns could savage the Soviet flank. Just back from the immediate front, behind those hills, helicopter gunships like the one we were in could pop up, launch their missiles, then duck back down before enemy gunners found them.

In the face of Abrams's confidence that NATO could repel a Soviet invasion, I mentioned a conversation with one of his West German counterparts, a Bundeswehr commander stationed nearby. "All these weapons; all this training. It will, of course, kill mostly Germans," he had told me. Could NATO stop the Russians? "Yes," he replied. "But we would lose a third of the territory of the Federal Republic," not to mention most of the German army. Abrams blinked when he heard this. "He said that? No wonder they're talking with Gorbachev."

It seemed surreal, those preparations for what Abrams and his men routinely referred to as "the next war." But it testified to the force of the status quo, the Cold War as a system with its own momentum. Inertia was a state of mind, a way of seeing. Psychologists are fond of saying we underestimate the force of habit. For forty-five years, we lived in the habit of East versus West, them and us, communism and democracy. So many years later, it's not so hard to see how many of us missed what was happening, all the small ways in which the world was changing. Everything—economics, public attitudes, military strategy, our very way of living and being—argued for what was and would seemingly always be. Almost nothing cried out for change.

As Hungary punched a hole in the Iron Curtain, and with Poland just a week from its first free and democratic elections since World War II, the allies at the last minute patched together a face-saving compromise resolving America's "Europe crisis." The Europeans agreed to "consider" an eventual and incremental deployment of the new missiles, *should circumstances dictate*—a formulation fuzzy enough to satisfy everyone. The White House could claim it had not bent to public pressure and had successfully defended the future of NATO and America's leadership. Bush was able to go on to what aides called a "triumphant" May 26 summit in Brussels, where he called for a "Europe whole and free" and declared, Reaganesquely, "Let the Wall be next!"

As for those Lance missiles? Nothing came of them, needless to say. They were defunct, relics of a history that had already moved on.

CHAPTER SEVEN

High Noon

Pfft! Pfft! Pfft! What's that sound? Democracy in action.

Solidarity's election campaign featured a poster of a gun-slinging Gary Cooper as the sheriff in the classic western *High Noon*. It was June 4, 1989—reckoning day in Dodge City East. The polls had only been open an hour or so, but to journalists covering the story it was already obvious that Solidarity would win by a landslide. Yet neither the opposition nor the communists knew. The previous evening, flying in from Prague, I'd met Solidarity campaigners at the depressing Hotel Europejski. "We're like students before an exam," one said, nervously wondering whether they would pass. As for the communists, they still spoke about doing at least respectably.

Lambs to the slaughter. Let us visit the abattoir.

On this bright Sunday morning, a tentative spring had turned to summer. The grass ran long and wild in the parks. Clouds lounged carefree in a vast blue sky. People dressed for church, and on the way they stopped at the polls. Patiently, they queued to register and receive their ballots. Patiently, they entered the voting booths and carefully drew the curtains. Others sat at long tables, elbow to elbow with friends or neighbors. Younger ones squatted cross-legged on the floor. Amid the murmurings and shuffling of feet, the room was quiet but for that insistent sound. *Pfft! Pfft! Pfft!* It was the sound of pens and pencils being drawn across paper, fast and decisively.

At their dying day, all but finished and out of steam, Poland's communists mustered the strength for one last perversity, a final crowning act of unwitting but utter self-humiliation. They devised an electoral system whereby Poles would not vote for candidates of their choice. Instead, they would cross out those they did not like. Which is to say, each and every communist.

Everywhere you looked, the people were excising them from their lives. Here, at long last, was Poland's long-awaited popular uprising. Revolution by deletion! The pen, at last mightier than the sword, became a weapon of glorious retribution, wielded with style. Some voters slashed their ballots boldly, decapitating the old regime with flourishing strokes, like a charge of Polish cavalry, sabers drawn and glinting in the sun. *Pfft! Pfft!* Whole pages of communists were x-ed with disemboweling slashes. Others savored the moment, deleting slowly, perhaps puffing a cigarette as they paused over this or that name, not so much considering their choice as pleasuring in this or that special deletion. Oh, yes, he jailed my cousin. *Pfft!* Oh, that sponging apparatchik, living high on our penury. *Pfft!* Such delicious irony. Such sweet revenge. *Pfft! Pfft! Pfft!*

Here and there, a fair-minded few appreciated that communists such as General Czeslaw Kiszczak and others had made this day possible. They were working to reform the system. "I voted for a few of them," said a woman in a chic fur coat and stylish hat. (I had her pegged as a communist for sure.) Said another, "I voted for one communist for every three candidates for Solidarity. That seemed fair." Others might have felt as she did, but no matter. Forget rewards. Forget fairness. "Poles hate this regime. They're dead!" one unusually farsighted U.S. diplomat told me a day or two before, and he was right.

By the next day, the results were in. Out went Kiszczak. Out went everybody. Solidarity swept all but one seat in the newly created Senate, and that went to an independent. They won each and every contest for which they were eligible in the Sejm. (Under the Round Table agreement, two-thirds of these House seats were reserved for the communists and affiliated parties.) Worse, Solidarity humiliated a "national list" of thirty-five top government candidates. These party-backed VIPs ran unopposed but needed 50 percent of the vote to stay in parliament: ministers of defense, interior, foreign affairs, the head of the party. All but two went down. Afterward, with some justification, communist candidates complained that they would have lost to a monkey, had it run on the opposition's ticket. Even mainstream party loyalists supported Solidarity. Districts where the communists were expected to do well went to the opposition: army bases, government enclaves, even security headquarters. At the Polish embassy in Mongolia, diplomats cast thirty absentee ballots; all went to Solidarity. Its victory was so complete, so utterly overwhelming, that the communists retained only a slender majority in Parliament—and that only thanks to the way the deal was tilted in the party's favor. Prime Minister Mieczyslaw Rakowski and his entire cabinet faced the extraordinary prospect of being . . . booted out! The party even lacked the votes to elect General Jaruzelski president.

My source within the party's upper echelons, the man I had nicknamed Kat, was shocked. "Never in our darkest nightmares did anyone predict such a shameful rout," he spluttered, gulping whiskeys and shaking his head in astonishment. It was late Monday night, a day after the vote. That afternoon, at 3 p.m., Jaruzelski summoned top government officials and party leaders to his office. He had spoken to Mikhail Gorbachev. "Our defeat is total," he told them. "A political solution will have to be found." By that he meant no violence. The communists would have to live with the result.

Outsiders could see it coming, even if most insiders had not. During the weeks running up to the election, I traveled the Polish countryside, following the campaign. One Sunday in the rural hamlet of Bodzanow, a few hours' drive from Warsaw toward the Russian border, I listened as a parish priest concluded his Sunday mass with an unusual announcement. "The candidates from Solidarity are waiting outside to talk with you, and you will now go and hear them." The congregation dutifully filed out, mostly peasant farmers in baggy black pants and vests and floppy caps with gnarled hands and weathered faces, to hear four Solidarity candidates tear into the communist system. They nodded, accepting campaign brochures and sample ballots with a tip of their hats. "They don't need much convincing," said one organizer, a Solidarity activist from the capital. Almost as an aside, he noted that such conservative communities as Bodzanow were the backbone support of the communist party. Back in Warsaw, billboards outside St. Anne's Church were plastered with Solidarity's posters. "Vote for the candidate with the deepest Christian values," the priest instructed his flock. He might as well have said, "Throw the godless commies out."

Solidarity's campaign was full of zest. In Warsaw, snappy jingles introduced the candidates on radio and TV. Buses, billboards and shop windows were papered with posters and jaunty red-and-white Solidarity banners. All the candidates had their photos taken with Lech Walesa. They smiled forth from every kiosk, billboard, wall and flat surface in the city. Union organizers passed out Solidarity lapel pins, organized fund-raising concerts and canvassed for support outside churches and on street corners. Walesa himself was ubiquitous. "Ride the Solidarity tank to freedom," he exhorted voters.

The communist party, by contrast, was invisible. In all of Warsaw, it seemed, only a couple of government candidates had bothered to put up campaign posters. In Kraków, Poland's second-largest city, the party's electioneering went little further than publishing the candidates' résumés in the newspapers. Some did not even campaign. Most counted on the party's media monopoly to carry their message—a serious miscalculation, since the messages tended to be duds: "Vote for Leszek, a good communist." The official state-controlled news media wasn't much better, judging from this typical newswire report: Interior Minister Czeslaw Kiszczak, the chief government negotiator at the recent Round Table and a candidate for the Sejm, drew a "group of several dozen people" to a big party rally in the eastern part of the country. Visiting the Stomil tire factory in Kraków, I discovered just how exciting a rally of "several dozen" could be. As I eyed the meager crowd, mostly elderly, an old man rose to speak. "We're sick of seeing Solidarity posters all over town," he complained, leaning on his cane. "Where is our campaign? The party seems to be cowering with fear." At the government press office, a spokeswoman offered her opinion: "Well, they have decided they do not need to do anything special." Certainly, they never had to in the past.

The campaign soon became more than a campaign. It took on the feeling of tectonic movement, a change of climate that penetrated deep into society. The cautious repression that so dominated Polish life suddenly lifted, which struck me vividly one afternoon in Kraków. Two months earlier, before the Round Table, inflammatory antigovernment rhetoric could land a man in jail. Yet there, in the center of the old town's Market Square, a speaker for the Confederation of an Independent Poland, a radical independent party, stood amidst a crowd of several hundred people and breathed political fire. "We want to remove the communists from power," he shouted. "They waste everything. If the West lends them money, they will use it to buy cattle prods." He paused to look at three policemen lounging on a park bench across the square—and turned up the volume on his megaphone.

The carnival that was the Polish election should have been a spectacle that commanded world attention, especially in America. Here was democracy, bursting forth with tremendous vitality in a communist nation that was a linchpin of the Soviet bloc. America had championed Solidarity for more than a decade. Lech Walesa was a household name. How was it, then, that these dramatic events failed to spark a realization that change was on the march in Eastern Europe, that the Cold War world was profoundly and quickly changing?

The answer was Tiananmen Square. The massacre of demonstrating students in China—with its dramatic TV footage of rumbling tanks, riot police firing tear gas, screams, shots and bodies in the streets—occurred on the same day as the Polish election. June 4 also brought news of the death, at eighty-nine, of Ayatollah Ruholla Khomeini, the father of the Iranian Revolution. The imagery from China, coupled with the fanatical turmoil of Khomeini's funeral, thrust Poland's political transformation to the background of the news. "After that," one Bush aide later told me, "it was almost impossible to focus on anything else. It was Tiananmen, Tiananmen, Tiananmen. And then Iran. Eastern Europe? Yes, it was on the radar. But not really."

In retrospect, this made Poland's election all the more remarkable. First, the communists abided by the results. If hard-liners were looking for an excuse to crack down and preserve their power, they had all the cover they needed in Tiananmen. At Solidarity headquarters that evening, there was champagne and celebration but also fear. "This is the worst thing that could have happened," an editor of Solidarity's weekly *Election Gazette* told me as the scale of the government's defeat became apparent. He worried that an angry regime might yet lash out, as China had just done.

Second, not only did the communists abide by the result, but they ran a clean ballot. There was no evidence of vote-rigging, ballot-box stuffing or the political gamesmanship normally associated with communist elections where official candidates would routinely be elected with pluralities of 98 percent. This, as much as anything, testified to the determination of Poland's leadership to change. And so, on that black Monday evening, the official communist party spokesman went on TV, sitting next to a top Solidarity official, not only to concede defeat but to call for calm and good grace from a reluctant rank and file. Czeslaw Kiszczak, the man who had once personally jailed Walesa, even called his friend "Lech" to offer his "hearty congratulations." From then on they worked in partnership to complete a transition, later in the summer, to a Solidarity government—the first noncommunist government in Eastern Europe's postwar history.

Perhaps only Poles could fully appreciate the irony. Preceding political transitions had almost invariably been marked by bitter strife: alternating cycles of liberalization followed by bloody repression, workers' protests met with security-police crackdowns. Yet at the moment of Solidarity's glory, Walesa himself called it a triumph of "evolution over revolution." Poles' brave history of challenging dictatorship in the end came to sitting down with the enemy, talking out a deal, then voting. It was precisely the reverse of how outsiders usually remember it. First came negotiation, then democracy—and only afterward revolution.

Third, Solidarity's peaceful victory became a lesson for the rest of Eastern Europe. For anticommunists everywhere, it was like drinking a large draft of courage. Thanks to Poland, what had only days earlier been thought impossible was, suddenly, possible.

A spring fever gripped Budapest, too. On June 16, 1989, Hungary buried a man and, in doing so, held a funeral for communism. Truth conquered power.

Thirty-one years before, the hero of the infamous 1956 Hungarian Revolution, Imre Nagy, was hanged as a traitor to his country. One year earlier, activists marking the anniversary were beaten by police. This day, he would be given a state funeral. Church bells tolled across the land.

The shameful story is legend. Imre Nagy had sought to give socialism a human face. Soviet tanks rolled in and ten thousand Hungarians died. Lured from their haven in the Yugoslav embassy with a written promise of safe passage from the man who had deposed them, Janos Kadar, Nagy and other leaders of the uprising were abducted by Russian secret police, interrogated, tortured, kept in solitary confinement and, after a mockery of a show trial, hanged as "counterrevolutionaries." Nagy was buried in an unmarked grave. For thirty years, the whereabouts was an official secret. But Hungarians knew: plot 301, tucked away in a remote and overgrown corner of a cemetery on the far outskirts of the city. They also knew how Kadar and his communists had lied—lied about their role in Nagy's death, about their collusion with the Soviets in suppressing the rebellion, in rewriting history to cover up their infamy.

For Hungarians, it was a powerful memory, all the more so for being repressed. This, too, the country's reformers would play to brilliant advantage. They did not organize Nagy's reburial; that was the work of a small group of relatives and courageous activists known as the Committee for Historical Justice. But they gave their permission. Miklos Nemeth and Imre Pozsgay, especially, offered protection and help. As they saw it, Nagy's rehabilitation—culminating in the hero's reburial he deserved—was a means of discrediting the current regime, the very system they themselves sought to bring down.

Pozsgay had worked for the better part of a year, in fact, to rewrite official history and, at long last, represent 1956 for what it was—a nationalist uprising against communist oppression, a plea for membership in the wider democratic Europe to which by culture and tradition Hungary belonged. In February, his special committee made it official. No longer would 1956 be considered a "counterrevolution," as Moscow's ideologists insisted. It was, instead, a "popular uprising." Nagy and his aides were victims of a "show trial." Pozsgay went so far as to call the 1917 Bolshevik revolution a "mistake." The true patriots of 1956, he said, were Nagy and his reformers—and, by association in 1989, themselves. The villains were Kadar and his stooges—and, again by association, communist party general secretary Karoly Grosz and his old guard. It was, in effect, a repudiation of communism and the entire postwar history of Hungary.

This historic day thus became a war of symbols—a clash of opposing faiths, as bitter as any wars of religion and as deadly. Standing amid the crowds at the ceremony, I remember making a mental catalog of all that was going on behind the triumphal scene. The proscenium, the mise-en-scène, was the steps of the National Gallery of Art on Heroes' Square, its great columns swathed in black. Green, red and white national flags hung between, each with a hole in the center: farewell, hammer and sickle. Was it an homage to the 1956 revolutionaries, who cut their flags this way? Or was it an acknowledgment that today's reformers were taking up the struggle, this time to win? Gathered as witnesses, a sort of Greek chorus, were some two hundred thousand people. On the ascending esplanade of steps to the National Gallery stood six coffins, also draped in black. Five contained the exhumed remains of Nagy and four others executed with him. One stood eloquently empty. Officially, it was for unnamed freedom fighters who had also perished in the uprising. Unofficially, it was for communism itself.

Grosz had summoned his Politburo several days before. "We have nothing to be ashamed about," he told the assembled ministers and top party officials. Grosz was angry that Nemeth authorized the ceremony. He had strongly resisted Pozsgay's efforts to recast Nagy's death as anything but the deserved fate of a counterrevolutionary. Already, in November, he had warned of a "white terror" if reform went too far. He alluded to Nagy's perfidy, unknown to most of those present, and would later distribute to the Central Committee copies of secret papers from Soviet archives showing that Nagy had long served as a KGB spy, incriminating friends and allies, as well as personal enemies, within Hungarian military and political circles, who then disappeared into jail, or worse. This is your national hero, he would say—this traitor, justly accused. As for this democracy you say he represented? Why, it would be political suicide for the party, as events in Poland had just proved. This staged funeral, he told his men, was another step into a dangerous morass. He ordered them not to attend.

This was a turning point in a way the funeral itself was not. The schism dividing Hungary's top leadership became, at that moment, unbridgeable. A line was drawn, and each person in the room had to choose sides. Imre Pozsgay spoke first. "I'm going," he told Grosz, but he qualified that by saying he would go as a "private citizen." Nemeth did not attend the day's meeting; his relations with Grosz, he told me, had by that point reached "zero." But when Pozsgay informed the party boss that Nemeth would also attend the funeral—in his official capacity as prime minister—Grosz turned nearly apoplectic. Nemeth might have been prime minister, but Grosz was general secretary of the Hungarian Socialist Workers Party! He was the power!

There was a moment of tense standoff. No one spoke. Pozsgay momentarily thought Grosz had lost the ability to do so. Then, abruptly, the party chief all but spat, "Go, then, and be damned!" And with that, he stalked from the room.

So it was, on June 16, that Nemeth and Pozsgay stood beside the caskets, shoulder to shoulder with families of the victims and leaders of the political opposition that they helped create. Nemeth would later confide that he had been deeply worried for their safety. "I got quite interesting phone calls, some threatening my life," he subsequently told an interviewer. " 'If you go there, we will kill you.' " Neither man spoke; that was for the organizers, who one by one called for tolerance and democracy. The crowd applauded politely. Then the last speaker, a young man, just twenty-six years old, stepped forward. He was Viktor Orban, the charismatic, wild-haired and outspoken leader of Fidesz, the League of Young Democrats, the new political party of Hungary's youth. Enough of allusive symbolism. He said directly what everyone else was merely thinking. "In the sixth casket we bury communism!" he shouted. "If we have learned anything over the past four decades, it is that communism and democracy do not mix!" He went on to condemn the communists' betrayal of the nation and its people. In 1956, he said, they promised forgiveness. Within weeks, they were shooting unarmed civilians. Thousands disappeared into jail. "We are not satisfied with the promises of communist politicians," he thundered. "We must see to it that the ruling party can never use force against us again. We can force the party to submit itself to free elections! If we do not lose the ideals of 1956, we can elect a government that will demand the withdrawal of Soviet troops!"

At this, the multitudes cheered. The music swelled to a triumphant finale. The funeral of Imre Nagy had just been turned into a political rally, televised nationally. Lost in the hubbub was the fact that

Nemeth, Pozsgay and others were on the verge of delivering all that Orban promised, and more, albeit less noisily. They had set the stage for fully free elections, without any protections for themselves, unlike Poland's communists. Soon they would announce a date. They had already won Moscow's agreement to remove its troops from Hungary. Indeed, the first withdrawals had begun in April. Orban would go on to become prime minister in 1998. Here was the new generation of Hungarian leaders, making their mark by laying claim to the victories of others. The moment was emblematic in another respect, as well, for Orban was giving voice to a sentiment shared by many others: no communists were to be trusted, even those who were setting the pace for change and who would ultimately win Hungarians their freedom.

As for Grosz, the standoff in the Politburo was his Waterloo. "He will be gone within weeks," Pozsgay told me the day after the ceremony. In fact, it would be one week. For the past few months, the party chief's position had been eroding. As many as a hundred thousand people had turned in their membership cards, defecting from the communist camp. Nemeth and Pozsgay's nascent political groupings, begun late in the previous year, had gone mainstream and developed rapidly as bona fide parties, exerting real popular power. On June 24, the communist party Central Committee met in a fractious session that all but spelled the end. Concluding that the party had no future under its current leadership, it reorganized itself under four new "presidents." Grosz was formally demoted, inveighing against enemies within until the last. Two weeks later, almost parenthetically, Janos Kadar, the embodiment of Hungarian communism, would die in his sleep. That same day, the Hungarian Supreme Court would "rehabilitate" the rebels of 1956 and formally award Imre Pozsgay his victory over history.

If Erich Honecker was fazed by events along his borders, he did not show it.

I had flown into Berlin from Warsaw for an interview a few days after the Polish elections. The plane was late and I tried to speed through Checkpoint Charlie by invoking a meeting with "Comrade Honecker." The East German policeman who had by this time become familiar with my comings and goings, and who usually treated me politely, gave me a stony look. *"Dokumenten, bitte,"* he said tersely. "Papers, please."

He went through my shoulder bag, examining each notebook page by page. Also the book, Tom Clancy's *Red Storm Rising*, that I'd been reading on the flight, as well as my wallet. *"Was ist das?"* A receipt for coffee and some confection that I called a doughnut, I told him. *"Was ist doughnut, bitte?"*

The interview took place at communist party headquarters, a graystone building on the main square of old Berlin where the Royal Palace once stood before being dynamited to make way for a bronze-tinted glass monstrosity known as the Volkskammer, or People's Parliament. Above the entrance was chiseled the crossed hammer and sickle of East German socialism; inside, the inevitable heroic workers tableaux of socialist realism. On one side of a long polished wood table in the cabinet room, where the Politburo usually presided, sat the reporters from *Newsweek* and its sister publication, the *Washington Post*. On the other, Honecker and a phalanx of aides.

It was a curious choreography, a ritual that governed every meeting with high communist leaders since the end of World War II. We from the West asked questions that we knew those of the East would not answer. Honecker gave replies that he knew we did not want and would not believe. His views could best be summed up as no glasnost, no perestroika, no Polish- or Hungarian-style tinkering with the system. Socialism might have its flaws, but look at heartless and warmongering America, with its crime and great gaps between rich and poor. The remedy was to advance toward communism, not retreat as his brethren were doing elsewhere.

Why preserve the Wall, we asked, this anachronism of the Cold War? To protect the East German people from the depredations of bourgeois capitalism. Was the shoot-to-kill policy at the border still in effect? We don't do that—except if people are "deserting," which by definition includes anyone trying to leave. The massacres in Tiananmen Square? "The task of students is to study. The task of every government is to ensure law and order." Beijing had shown great restraint, Honecker declared, despite the activities of agent provocateurs seeking to create an international incident. On it went. Thrust, parry. Thrust, parry. A fan circled overhead in the stifling heat. Flies droned against the windows as if they, too, sought to escape.

Afterward, we went to the garden for a photo. Honecker hammed it up for the cameras, smelling the roses growing luxuriantly in a brilliant sun, his white hair fluffy in the breeze. He seemed so calmly in control. It was hard to imagine him as a killer. He had joined the communist party as a youth. He was one of the courageous few to openly resist Hitler. He was hounded by Nazi secret police, beaten, jailed from 1935 to 1945. By all odds he should have died in the concentration camps. Yet he came out after the war, rose to the top of the communist party—and did to his countrymen what the German fascists had done to him.

This man who seemed to have learned so little from history and from life, what would he do if the people turned against him, as in Poland or Hungary? Watching him, I did not doubt his capacity for a German Tiananmen. It wasn't the cliché of the banality of evil, though that also was clear. Nor was it the mercilessness of true belief. Honecker seemed to have passed from passion into rote. What struck me was his apparent blindness, an inability to see the world other than as he willed it. I wondered if Honecker actually smelled those roses. Was their fragrance lost to him, an abstract irrelevance? Or did he take pleasure in them, the way he did in his pet dogs, in things that were not human or prone toward unorderliness?

As it turned out, Honecker's calm was deceptive. He had said nothing more to his cabinet on May 3, after his explosion over Hungary's treachery. But during the following weeks he watched events with growing concern. West German television kept airing footage of the wire along Hungary's border being snipped. Scenes of bulldozers uprooting the concrete posts that secured the fence and knocking down watch-towers were broadcast deep into the GDR. This was exactly what the Hungarians had assured Honecker would not happen. Bits of the Iron Curtain were already being sold as souvenirs in Vienna and New York.

None of this, he knew, would be lost on East Germans as they prepared for the summer holidays. At the communist summit in Havana, in early June, Honecker reported that Soviet foreign minister Eduard Shevardnadze had told him that he found the Polish situation to be "disquieting." Honecker said he replied that, in his personal view, Hungary was almost "lost" to socialism. Something had to be done, he told Shevardnadze, and he was prepared to do it.

Just what that meant was unknown to anyone but Honecker. "It was clear to the entire leadership that we had a problem," Gunter Schabowski would later tell me. "But was it discussed? Not once." Instead, East Germany's leader made his own moves, typically looking to what had worked in the past. On November 26, 1980, as strikes organized by Solidarity threatened to paralyze Poland, Honecker had written an urgent letter to the personal attention of Leonid Brezhnev, calling for a formal meeting of the Warsaw Pact to consider "fraternal assistance" to the besieged Warsaw government. "Counter-revolutionary forces in the People's Republic of Poland are on the constant offensive," he told the Soviet leader. "Any delay in acting against them would mean death—the death of socialist Poland. Yesterday our collective efforts may perhaps have been premature; today they are essential; and tomorrow they would already be too late."

As Honecker saw it, Hungary now posed a similar threat. He could not imagine Moscow viewing it otherwise. Thus in late May, he sent Foreign Minister Oskar Fischer to Moscow with a personal letter addressed to "Dear Comrade Gorbachev," insisting that "the Hungary problem" be added to the agenda for discussion at the Warsaw Pact's July 7–8 annual summit in Bucharest. "Of course, he did not intend to just 'discuss' the Hungarians," said Schabowski, describing the gambit. "He wanted to stop them. As he saw it, it was time for the entire bloc to hold together."

Honecker obviously misjudged Gorbachev. He could not have missed the Soviet leader's repeated disavowals of the Brezhnev Doctrine, nor his insistence that Eastern Europe's communist regimes had to change with the times. But Honecker appears to simply not have accepted it. Perhaps he believed Gorbachev's rhetoric was ultimately mere propaganda, and that faced with a genuine threat to socialism's survival he would be quick to roll back change. If Miklos Nemeth could have harbored similar concerns, traveling previously to Moscow to judge for himself, it is not illogical to conclude that a man as cloistered and conventionally communist as Honecker would have thought so even more strongly.

The masters of the Eastern empire converged on Bucharest, citadel of perhaps the most repressive of all the bloc's regimes. They spoke of many things, but only one topic held their full attention. That, of course, was Nemeth and what his "reformist" policies portended for the rest of them. He was the quarry, the hunted. His host, the Romanian dictator Nicolae Ceausescu, made that plain, Nemeth would recall. "He would not address me as 'comrade,' I am proud to say."

As the meeting commenced, the leaders of the most reactionary states of the East bloc lined up against him: Romania, Czechoslovakia, Bulgaria and the German Democratic Republic. Like Honecker, they wanted to stop his "counterrevolution," just as the alliance had in Berlin in 1953, Budapest in 1956, Prague in 1968 and Warsaw in 1981. "Ceausescu led the attack," according to Nemeth. Seated next to Gorbachev, he rose to his feet, gesticulating and shouting his impassioned indictment. Hungary would "destroy socialism." If these "dangerous experiments" were allowed to proceed, they could bring down the entire Soviet Union. Honecker and Czechoslovakia's Milos Jakes soon joined in. General Jaruzelski of Poland sat silent, sphinx-like, betraying no emotion.

Nemeth had been in office only seven months. This was his first Warsaw Pact summit. He was nervous, but he knew his enemies could only act with Soviet support. The man who could give it, Mikhail Gorbachev, sat roughly opposite, about thirty feet away on the other side of the large rectangle of flag-draped conference tables. As Ceausescu ranted on, calling for armed intervention in Hungary, Nemeth glanced across at the Soviet leader. Their eyes met, and Gorbachev . . . winked.

"This happened at least four or five times," Nemeth told me. Strictly speaking, it wasn't a wink. It was more a look, a bemused twinkle. "Each time he smiled at me, with his eyes. I don't quite know how to describe it. But I clearly saw he was trying to tell me that he did not share these views."

For Nemeth, this was yet another important sign, as decisive in its way as the conversation the two men had had in March, when Gorbachev forswore any intervention in Hungary's affairs, and as telling as Moscow's silence in May when the Hungarians had cut their hole in the Iron Curtain. This was a signal, at a key moment, that it was safe to go on. It was as if Gorbachev were saying, "Don't worry. These people are idiots. Pay no attention," as Nemeth put it to me. So he didn't. As the dogs of the Warsaw Pact brayed for his head, he went outside to smoke a cigarette.

Honecker's defeat in Bucharest had a deeper consequence back home in Berlin. By failing to stop his enemies in Hungary, he called attention to his own weakness. Not only could he not influence Gorbachev, but he seemed not to grasp the implications. Schabowski explained, "Our dilemma was that of the East German state itself. We needed the support of Gorbachev and the Soviet Union to survive. Without it, our leadership always feared, we would fall like a ripe plum into the hands of the West Germans." Yet there was Honecker, talking about his close friendship with Ceausescu and Jakes and ridiculing Gorbachev, mocking his anti-alcohol campaign in Russia and the corruption of his so-called Soviet reformists. Meanwhile, Gorbachev himself was cutting a swath through Europe. From Bucharest, he had flown straight to France, where he called for a "Common European House." In Bonn, a few weeks before that, he had been mobbed by tens of thousands of Germans chanting, "Gorbi! Gorbi! Gorbi!" All this planted a seed of doubt within the East German Politburo, according to Schabowski. "To ally with Ceausescu and resist Gorbachev, and to boast of it? Some of us thought it odd. It made us think about a change in leadership. For the German Democratic Republic to continue to exist, we had to get in step with Gorbachev. If Honecker could not cooperate with him . . ." Schabowski completed the thought with a shrug.

From that moment on, Honecker was a marked man. Just as Karoly Grosz effectively met his end at the sharp point of a symbol, so Honecker's fate was sealed with Gorbachev's wink. Henceforth, the East German caesar would be surrounded by conspirators, awaiting with knives. *Et tu, Brute?*

Of course, neither Schabowski nor anyone else on the Politburo said anything that might reveal themselves. They did not discuss their unease with one another. Silence ruled, as it always did. "You must understand that Honecker's authority was absolute. What if you were denounced?" Treason, said Schabowski, begins first in the heart, then in the mind, a party of one. "You start by having your own ideas. A heresy, such as wondering whether Honecker should go. Then you watch the reactions of the people sitting around you, to sense if they are thinking as you are. You might make a remark to test them and judge whether to go further." In May, Schabowski saw little sign that others shared his doubts. After Bucharest, he was certain that they did.

Miklos Nemeth also flew home from Bucharest to a world markedly different from the one he had left. Suddenly, America woke up.

In early July, President Bush embarked on his first official trip through Eastern Europe. At a reception in Warsaw, he regaled guests with a list of Polish baseball "greats"—Stan Musial, Tony Kubek, Phil Niekro. He went on for half an hour about the American-Polish connection. The next day in Gdansk, the birthplace of Solidarity, he shot V-for-Victory signs and reveled in the crowds and banners reading DOWN WITH COMMUNISM and SOVIETS GO HOME. We like democracy, he told anyone who would listen. Try it. You'll like it, too.

Writing of the trip in his memoir, *A World Transformed*, Bush noted that "change was in the air" in Poland and Hungary, and that the West had an obligation to act as a "responsible catalyst" in shaping events in Eastern Europe. As they followed the president around Warsaw and Gdansk, many reporters wondered. Baseball greats? Change in the air? The horse was out of the barn. The train had left the station. Communism, by the time Bush visited, was all but officially dead in both Poland and Hungary. To speak of "catalyzing" events that were accelerating faster than any of us could comprehend seemed either arrogant or, worse, out of touch. Naturally, any administration would want to claim a role in such dramatic history. But the facts were otherwise.

At least, that is how I felt at the time. We now know that, during that trip, Bush experienced something of a transformation. Once on the ground, he was quick to grasp the full dimension of what was happening in the East. In Warsaw, he met General Jaruzelski for what was to be a ten-minute tea. It turned into a two-hour heart-to-heart talk. Solidarity's overwhelming victory meant the general might not have the votes to be elected president. He could not bear the humiliation of defeat and was thinking of resigning. That would leave Poland in potentially severe straits, because oddly enough Jaruzelski had emerged as the one man both Solidarity and the communists trusted enough to lead them through a perilous period. "I told him his refusal to run might inadvertently lead to serious instability and I urged him to reconsider," Bush wrote in his memoir, conscious of the irony: "Here was an American president trying to persuade a senior Communist leader to run for office." He also discussed the problem with Solidarity leader Lech Walesa the next day in Gdansk, where he drew a crowd of 250,000 people. His efforts helped. When Bush left for Hungary, James Baker would report, Jaruzelski was positively "beaming."

In Budapest, on July 13, the political situation was no less delicate. The anticipated flood of East German tourists was beginning. The campgrounds around Lake Balaton were filling up. Publicly, Bush came to Hungary offering a modest package of economic aid and trade concessions. Privately, he thanked Nemeth for all that he had done so far to dismantle the Iron Curtain and spark change at home and across the region. Then the president suggested that the time might not be far off to go even further. "We both knew what he was hinting at," Nemeth said in a later television interview. "It was very simple. We could feel it in the air. Our East German 'tourists' were not going to go home." As the men parted, Nemeth gave Bush a memento—a bit of barbed wire clipped from the Iron Curtain.

The oceanographer Jacques Cousteau, asked why he did what he did, used to reply, *"Il faut aller voir."* It's necessary to go see. From the moment George Bush set foot in Eastern Europe and saw for himself, U.S. policy perceptibly changed. From a cautious wariness of Gorbachev and his intentions, it morphed into a realization that events had gone well beyond his ability to stop them, even had he wished. The focus quickly became how to help, even how to keep up. Cold War diehards allied with Cheney and others were pushed to the fringe. From then on, "these guys were excluded from the inner circle," not entirely to be trusted, one White House adviser later told me. The trip also helped pry Scowcroft "out of his box," the set way of seeing that characterized the conservative general's worldview, according to this official. A policy of engagement, constant communication and partnership with America's European allies—and even, to a surprising degree, the Soviet Union—became the order of the day. U.S. policy went from out of touch and even obstructionist to a model of restrained, sober and knowing competence, helping to shape the international climate for change and culminating in the brilliant management of something that at this moment still remained almost unthinkable: the fall of the Wall and, in its aftermath, German unification.

CHAPTER EIGHT

Déjeuner sur l'Herbe, or Hieronymus Bosch's Hell

Otto von Habsburg, scion of the Austrian monarchy, was driving from Vienna to Budapest, and hence to Debrecen in eastern Hungary, where he would deliver a lecture at the university founded by his father before the First World War. At dinner that night, following his talk, he mentioned how beautiful the border region was. Conversation soon turned to the political changes under way. The Iron Curtain still divided East from West, everywhere but in Hungary. Why not celebrate this fact, a local activist named Ferenc Meszaros suggested.

He meant it as a joke, a sort of conversational lark. Those gathered convivially around the table, wineglasses in hand over a fine meal of game, vied with one another to come up with ever more inventive proposals. Among the more bizarre was to convene a picnic on the Austrian-Hungarian border. There would be a blazing bonfire, complete with a pig roasting on a spit. Hungarians could sit on one side of the border fence, while Austrians sat on the other. They would toss tasty morsels back and forth to one another over the Cold War barrier. What better way to call the world's attention to the unfairness of this ugly geopolitical divide?

Everyone had a good laugh. But ten days later, Meszaros again brought up the idea, this time more seriously, at a meeting of one of Hungary's new political parties, the Democratic Forum. As before, it was treated as a joke by most, but not by a young woman named Maria Filep, who was organizing a political retreat called the Common Fate Camp for students from around the Soviet bloc. Thinking a picnic would be a fine way to wrap up her program, she and Meszaros set about organizing it.

They settled on a name, place and date—the Pan-European Picnic, to be held in Sopron, Hungary, at 3 p.m. on August 19, 1989—and invited Habsburg and Imre Pozsgay to act as sponsors. For the passionate Pozsgay, the invitation was a godsend. Fresh from his triumph in revising the official history of 1956, he was looking for ways to publicize that Hungary was quietly opening its borders and bolting from the communist bloc. He immediately went to see Nemeth. Right then and there, the two men decided. "That's when we began to make the picnic into something else, something much bigger," Nemeth told me. "It was to be the solution to our East German problem."

As anticipated, East German tourists had begun their summer travels. Tens of thousands had already arrived, filling hostels in Budapest and descending on the campgrounds around Lake Balaton; many more thousands would soon follow. Nor had they missed the message in the very public dismantling of the border fence. Since May and early June, hundreds had ditched their cars in fields and woods along the border and hiked toward the frontier with Austria. When caught, they were politely turned back by Hungarian guards, often with a smile suggesting they were free to try again as soon as the patrol had passed. Many of them found their way to the West. But so far, those were an intrepid few. The vast majority of East Germans seemed too frightened to try to escape. For Nemeth and Pozsgay, the challenge was how to embolden them.

So these poor East Germans became pawns in an elaborate plot, one of the most creative geopolitical double games ever played. Under a 1969 treaty, East Germany and Hungary were obliged to honor one another's travel laws. Hungarians enjoyed remarkable freedom; they passed to and from Austria and other European countries largely without restraint. East Germans, by contrast, were confined to the East bloc. The Hungarians could not simply ignore the treaty, throw open their checkpoints and, like pharaoh, let their people go.

Besides, what they were doing was dangerous. Twice in the past year, communist hard-liners made moves to cast out the reformers, once even contemplating the use of force. Only a few months before, Russian troops had brutally put down pro-democracy movements in Georgia and Uzbekistan. Beijing's Tiananmen Square massacre was a more recent reminder. Immense subtlety was therefore required, and the Pan-European Picnic seemed the perfect instrument. "This invitation gave me a chance to do something quite different, not what the picnic organizers had in mind at all," Pozsgay said in an interview. "We decided to make the picnic a precedent. We would use it to show that East Germans could freely leave Hungarian territory."

Officially, the organizers went about planning their picnic. With backing from the sponsors, they put together a group of partners: students, activists from political parties in Sopron such as the Democratic Forum, local environmentalists and civic action societies. They settled on a logo—a white dove breaking through barbed wire (on some, a white rose)—and arranged for food, tents and buses to ferry guests to the site. T-shirts were made, maps were drawn up, invitations went out by fax to national and international media. Radio Free Europe would be there, broadcasting news of the event across the bloc. Western television networks arrived, including many from West Germany, which were viewed daily throughout the German Democratic Republic, as well as in Hungary. Of course, the organizers duly applied for permission from the local authorities, especially the commander of the Sopron border guard. They assumed that Hungarian police would keep a close watch. This was the frontier, after all. But they requested a special dispensation: to symbolically open a border gate that had been closed for the past forty years so that a small number of Austrians who wished to attend the festival could do so and be greeted as they arrived by an even smaller group of official Hungarian delegates.

Behind the scenes, Pozsgay moved to put his parallel plan in place. He telephoned an ally in the government, Interior Minister Istvan Horvath, and told him of the invitation. Then they sat down with Nemeth. Would Horvath please arrange for the border to be opened, as the organizers had requested? "Horvath's involvement was vital," Nemeth later told me. "He supervised the police and militia. Without his instructions, the whole affair could have ended in tragedy." They also contacted the head of the Hungarian border guard, Gyula

Kovacs, who relayed the instructions to the commander in Sopron: not only was the border to be opened, but guards were not to be stationed in the immediate vicinity. The only barrier separating Hungary from Austria would be a small mesh net designed to keep wild animals away. All this had to be done in strictest secrecy," Nemeth recalled. "I did not tell anyone else in the government."

Then came the master stroke. As the day of the picnic approached, flyers similar to those distributed by the official organizers—but coming from a different source—appeared in the camps where East German vacationers were staying. They were plastered on walls and in hotels, wherever East Germans would see them. Priests holding religious services in the camps helped spread the word; camp managers passed out leaflets. Come one, come all, to the Pan-European Picnic. Eat, drink and be merry. Snip a piece of the Iron Curtain as a souvenir. But be careful not to stray. The border is unguarded. Why, you might stumble into Austria and no one would notice! Handy maps were disseminated that provided directions on how to find one's way on the Austrian side of the border. So as not to "stray," of course!

Nemeth, Pozsgay and their allies had been attempting to lure East Germans to cross the Hungarian border for months, ever since May 2. They even staged a replay of that telegenic moment, on June 27, when the foreign ministers of Austria and Hungary, Alois Mock and Gyula Horn, met at the border and ceremoniously picked up outsize wire cutters and began snipping at the fence. Never mind that much of it had already been removed. With laughs and handshakes, they handed out bits and pieces as souvenirs for the journalists summoned to witness the occasion. Nemeth later told me he wanted to make sure the world got the message. "Something important is happening," he sought to say. "Pay attention."

The Hungarians thought the message was clear. But East Germans still didn't seem to get it. The Pan-European Picnic hence became what an American football quarterback might call a Hail Mary—an all-or-nothing throw downfield, aiming for a touchdown. For the Hungarian conspirators, this translated, essentially, into a plan to lure a bunch of East Germans out of the country, over the border to freedom, in hopes that thousands of others would follow. Nemeth called it "priming the pump."

Pozsgay organized the operation as secretly and discreetly as possible. Honecker had been increasingly insistent that any East Germans caught trying to cross the border illegally be returned for prosecution. East German secret police had been making themselves ostentatiously visible in the camps around Lake Balaton and the border regions, urging GDR citizens to return home and warning of the penalties of escape, not only for themselves but for their families left behind. Neither Pozsgay nor Nemeth knew whom to trust. Authorities reporting to allies such as Interior Minister Istvan Horvath could most likely be counted on. But in addition to the border police there were armed members of the so-called Workers' Guard, a paramilitary organ of the communist party controlled by conservatives under Karoly Grosz. In a subsequent BBC/Spiegel TV documentary, Pozsgay would describe the picnic as a "nerve-racking operation," all the more so because it was organized in cahoots with the West German government.

The day of the event, August 19, arrived. In effect, it was two events—the one very public, and the other private. Once combined, their effect was explosive. The official program began around 2 p.m. in Sopron, with a press conference in German, English and Hungarian. Buses then took the delegates and their foreign visitors, including a small army of reporters, to the picnic site. The organizers were aghast. They could barely get near the picnic area. They expected only several hundred people. Ten or twenty times that many showed up. People were everywhere. "A mass of Austrian guests, invited and not invited, had come across the border, rushing through the cornfields, making it impossible for anyone to move about," one of them recalled. "It was impossible to control such a crowd. No one was expecting anything like this. It was absolute chaos."

This was the private "party." When the buses arranged by Pozsgay's people arrived at Sopron's overflowing hotels and campsites outside town, East Germans clamored to get on. Hungarian and West German consular officers escorted them to the picnic site. Many of the East Germans had already been given Federal Republic passports, issued by the consulate in Budapest and stamped with the exit and entry visas required to leave Hungary and enter the Federal Republic via Austria. But many, freshly arrived, had nothing. Others drove themselves. On the other side of the border, the Austrians had set up Red Cross tents, clearly notified to expect a deluge. A fleet of buses stood idling nearby, organized by the mayor of the nearby Austrian town, St. Margarethen, at the behest of the West German government. It was arranged that any East Germans who crossed the border would be transported to Giessen, in central West Germany, that very day.

Imagine the scene. Four hundred miles from the Berlin Wall, the Pan-European Picnic began. A brass band played. Folk dancers in traditional Hungarian and Tyrolean garb cavorted in the meadows. There were banners and balloons and beer and good things to eat. Bewildered families of East Germans were set loose upon this surreal stage set, clutching their maps and turning nervously this way and that, trying to get their bearings. No frontier police were visible; Gyula Kovacs had ordered them to keep a distance of one kilometer. Instead, senior Hungarian and Austrian diplomats wandered among the crowd, nodding amiably as if this were merely what it appeared to be—a festive party in a field, where neither borders nor the Wall nor the Iron Curtain meant anything.

A bit before 3 p.m., this untenable facade cracked open, according to Laszlo Nagy, a local activist who helped put the event together. A group of some three hundred East Germans disembarked from their buses. Ignoring the festivities, they made straight for the border gate, opened wide for the first time in four decades. As one of the organizers moved to welcome them, they burst into a run. "They rushed through," Nagy recalled, "with the speed of a fast train." Not that there was anyone to stop them. The few Hungarian border officials stood with their backs turned ostentatiously to the East Germans, obsessively checking the passports of incoming and outgoing Austrians, who laughed aloud at the spectacle and moved to form a line on one side of the crossing so that the charging East Germans could exit on the other.

More were to follow. All afternoon they kept coming, in groups, singly or by family—"a constant stream," as Nagy described it. As if in willful neglect of the rules the organizers themselves had laid down, the Hungarian border officials seemed blind to the exodus, continuing to concern themselves only with Austrians despite occasionally being so jostled by the passing East Germans as to almost be knocked down.

Amid this maelstrom of calculated human confusion came moments of true absurdity. The family of one Silvia Lux, who braved the crossing with her husband and children, told of getting lost. Dozens of East Germans had "strayed" ahead of them, but they could not find the way. Suddenly, a man they identified as being from the West German consulate popped up from behind a bush. "Family Lux," he shouted, consulting a list of names in his hand. "Not that way. This way! Some nice border guards will open the gate for you!" And so, as she told Western TV reporters, they did. "It was all very well planned," she added, relating how West German officials had taken them via taxi from Budapest to Sopron, installed them in a hotel with instructions to "stay out of sight," then driven them the next day directly to the picnic site.

Back in Budapest, Nemeth and his men heaved a collective sigh of relief. They had spent all afternoon huddled in his office, equipped with special communications links for the occasion, monitoring the situation moment by moment. As for the real guests, they busied themselves with the beer and the wine, the food and the sheer entertainment of the show going on about them. It would have gone on all night, save for an evening thunderstorm. As Laszlo Nagy got into his car to head home, he was struck by the number of abandoned Trabants and Wartburgs, all with GDR license plates, lining the sides of the roads. "Their owners would not return for them."

That night, Hungarian state TV showed a brief clip of the festival but made no mention of the more than six hundred East Germans who had "escaped" across the border that day. Soon, however, members of the communist party brownshirts, the Workers' Guard, would begin directing cars with East German license plates away from the Austrian border. Shots could be heard at night; most were suspected of being fired by frontier guards, units loyal to the party, or by the Workers' Guard, intended to frighten away anyone trying to cross the border under cover of darkness. On August 21, a young East German named Kurt-Werner Schultz, trying to cross with his wife and six-year-old son, was shot and killed in a scuffle. It was unclear who was responsible, or who had ordered the border crackdown.

In any case, Erich Honecker, who witnessed coverage of the Pan-European Picnic on West German television, protested strenuously to the Hungarian ambassador in East Berlin and demanded that East German citizens be forcibly returned to the GDR.

In certain respects, the Pan-European Picnic was a disappointment. Nemeth had hoped that as many as ten thousand East Germans would leave that day, setting a mass exodus in motion. That so few East Germans seized the opportunity showed just how afraid they were. Some feared the Pan-European Picnic was a trap, as the Stasi secret police in the camps were claiming. Nemeth did not actually know how Moscow would react to a mass exodus. He had gone to great lengths to conceal Bonn's role in the planning. West German officials revealed themselves only at the last moment, and arrangements were negotiated in the greatest secrecy. Now everyone sat back to wait. "This was the Big Bang, the real test of Moscow's tolerance," Nemeth told me a decade later. "Will we get a bang on the door from the Russians? If something went wrong, or if Moscow protested, then we would have learned something. But nothing happened."

Several days passed, and Nemeth concluded it was safe to go further. On August 22, his top advisers met to consider their next move. The vacation season was ending. Soon, the weather would turn cold. Several hundred refugees were now leaving Hungary each day. But 150,000 East Germans remained. The situation had to be resolved. "We discussed several options," Nemeth recalled. "Someone suggested spreading rumors that the refugee camps would be dismantled in the night, and that anyone there would be sent home. Another was to tell people that unguarded trains were waiting at the border, ready to take them to Austria." The point was to frighten the East Germans into trying to "escape." In the end, Nemeth decided he did not like the pretense. "I thought it better to just open the border. Which is what we decided to do."

Three days later Nemeth and Gyula Horn flew secretly to Bonn to brief Kohl and Foreign Minister Hans-Dietrich Genscher. Genscher emerged from the hospital, where he was recovering from a heart attack, just for this meeting. "It was just the four of us in a room, without aides," Nemeth recalled. He began by telling them, tongue in cheek, that East Germans visiting Hungary in the future would soon find it far easier to leave. Hungary would go its own way, he informed them. It would break with the Warsaw Pact and allow citizens of the GDR to freely emigrate. It would officially and fully open its borders, as soon as the Federal Republic was prepared to receive the exodus. "Rarely had I been so filled with anticipation before a meeting," wrote Genscher in his memoir, *Rebuilding a House Divided.* Kohl was profuse in his gratitude. "He asked me two or three times, 'What would you like in return?' " said Nemeth, discussing reports that Hungary was given a 500-million-deutsche-mark federal loan (roughly \$250 million) in recognition of its services. "We really needed this money. Everything was ready to be signed. But I asked them to delay. We did not do this for the money, and I did not want to be accused of taking bribes."

Nemeth and his reformers would not make their announcement for another two weeks. Clearly, they did not fully realize just how decisive it would prove to be. Flying back from Bonn, Horn had speculated on the history of the moment. Who knows? he told Nemeth. Perhaps in three or four years, it could produce a real change in Hungary's relations with the West.

It would turn out to take just two months. Four hundred miles from the Berlin Wall, the Pan-European Picnic, with its folk dancers and brass band, had set in motion developments that would build with such incredible speed and force as to bring down Erich Honecker and topple his Berlin Wall.

Directly to the east of Hungary, now boiling with change, was Ceausescu's Romania. How to describe it? By metaphor, it would be Dante's Ninth Circle, the ring of frozen stillness closest to the Darkness. That was the first thing you noticed, the stillness. It wasn't an absence of sound but rather an almost existential mutedness, as if nothing were quite real.

Nicolae Ceausescu, Europe's Last Stalinist, bestrode his unfortunate country like some oddly frail colossus. He began as a shoemaker, rising in 1965 to become chief of Romania's communist party, famous as a maverick East European leader who dared to defy Moscow. His independence from Soviet influence was conspicuously demonstrated by his refusal to participate in the 1968 Warsaw Pact invasion of Czechoslovakia. Ceausescu maintained relations with Israel after the 1967 war, unlike the rest of the East bloc, and in reward received a succession of world leaders, from Richard Nixon to Queen Elizabeth to Jordan's King Hussein. Romanians enjoyed a measure of free speech unmatched elsewhere in the communist world. During the 1970s foreign newspapers and books were on sale. Radio broadcasts were not jammed. People could talk freely with foreigners. The secret police stayed in the shadows.

But that was then. By 1989, at seventy-one, Ceausescu had grown old. No longer celebrated as a maverick, he was instead reviled as a tyrant. When world leaders stopped alighting in Bucharest, the flattery to feed the dictator's ego had to be homegrown. Romania's once flourishing intelligentsia became courtiers. Poets penned verses to Ceausescu, or at least those who got published. Books and magazines and television carried ritual incantations of praise for the Enlightened One. His speeches, two to three hours in duration, were aired on loudspeakers throughout the country, live, from the beaches of the Black Sea to the parks of Bucharest and every small-town square. Foreign journals and books were banned. Contact with outsiders was forbidden. Typewriters had to be registered with the police, along with copies of their typeface. Movies were throwbacks to the fifties and sixties—Jimmy Stewart westerns and Italian farces with Sophia Loren. The emperor's secret police, the vicious Securitate, were everywhere. Criticism of Ceausescu or his regime was quickly and brutally punished. Torture or a beating could be expected by anyone unfortunate enough to be arrested. "There is no forward here," an American diplomat told me. "Only variations on backward."

Early in August, as Hungary's closet revolutionaries prepared their Pan-European Picnic, I paid a first visit to Romania. I wondered if I would find any sign of change, a hint of the revolution happening elsewhere in the bloc. Perhaps a dozen passengers arrived aboard the flight from Vienna. We shuffled through the empty terminal, footsteps echoing. No one was to be seen at Arrivals or Departures, save men with guns and walkie-talkies. A policeman stood at every door. They paced the tarmac near our plane. They walked the runways in the distance or sat in little huts like duck-shot blinds, their guns poking out. The massive parking lot outside was also empty but for a few taxis. The drivers, in broken shoes and soiled clothes, pushed their vehicles forward through the queue to save fuel.

Bucharest was a ghost town with people. They trudged to and from work, lived cowed and furtive lives. A bus would pass. You could sense everyone looking at you, but when you glanced up, they turned away. Passersby would look at your shoes, however, especially Western athletic shoes—a privilege of the top communist elite. It was a habit I would pick up. The plainclothes police who followed me liked to wear white sneakers.

Every day I tried to shake them. Usually I would find a crowded place to stroll, then jump in a taxi. If the driver spoke English, I'd pay him an extravagant sum—say $10, nearly a month's wage—to just drive around and talk. One told me a common joke: "If only we had a little more food, it would be just like wartime!" Things had gotten so bad, he said, that it was almost impossible to live. Every day after work, he rushed to the market to see if there was anything to buy. It wasn't uncommon to wait three, four, eight hours in line each day. Often, grandparents would go out at 1 a.m. or so and wait on little stools outside the shop doors, hoping they might open sometime that day. If a queue formed, people joined it immediately, buying whatever was sold: soap, meat, cooking oil, tampons, toilet paper, milk—anything and everything was in short supply. "All day I worry, and at night I lie awake," my driver went on. "How to find enough food. How to get medicine for my children. Or shoes. Will there be electricity tonight? Or heat?"

We drove by the huge palace Ceausescu was constructing at the center of Bucharest, larger than any other on earth, a thousand rooms made entirely of white marble and costing an entire year's worth of the country's exports. "We call it the Big Building," the driver said, as we skirted its several-mile circumference. "He is mad, Ceausescu. Every Romanian thinks as I do. But if I went into the street and said, 'This is bad,' the police would come for me like that." He snapped his fingers. "For my family, even, I would no longer exist. I would be lost in space." Half amused, half despairingly, he laughed and said, "There will never be a revolution in Romania."

He dropped me off at the edge of a park where there were no

other cars or people so I could see whether I'd been followed. I sat down on a bench and after a time was joined by a man who described himself as a welder. "You cannot conceive how we live, how poor we have become," he said after we began to speak, glancing about to see who might observe him chatting with a dangerous foreigner. It was a sunny day, and we watched children playing on a carousel that gave out every twenty minutes for lack of electricity. He complained that authorities not long ago canceled a two-hour radio program of music, jokes and entertainment as "inappropriate." "The joys of life are few," this man concluded resentfully. "We no longer even have the right to laugh. We get one hour of radio each evening, and two hours of television. There is no news; only pictures of Him."

I walked back to the hotel through a neighborhood near the foreign embassies, the wealthiest part of town. Houses were decaying, some overgrown with vines. Doves rustled in their broken eaves—a scene from Piranesi, life amid the ruins. Along another empty boulevard, the American ambassador's gleaming black limousine glided silently and majestically by, Stars and Stripes aflutter. Near the Square of National Unity, a woman neatly dressed in office clothes carefully scraped the contents of a broken egg off the sidewalk and put it into her purse. At the front desk of the Intercontinental, the manager greeted me with a knowing smile. "Did you enjoy your walk in the park, Mr. Meyer?"

The day before I was to fly back to Germany, word came that Ceausescu had consented to an interview. The next morning, *Newsweek*'s editor and I drove out to the summer residence at Snagov, an hour from the capital along empty country roads, beautiful and green in the bright sun. The house Ceausescu used was a modest Romanian wood cottage; the nearby villa where we were received was a monstrous extravaganza of gilt vanity and pomp.

With full ceremony, we were directed to a reception room—two thrones on a dais for Ceausescu and *Newsweek*'s editor, a small stool for me off to the side. I replaced it with a decent chair—on the dais. Then we waited, nearly an hour, for the Great Leader to finish his nap. A dozen or so royal retainers arranged themselves into a semicircle in front of the door through which he would come. It was as if tiny x's, chalked on the floor, marked our assigned spots. When all was ready, the official crier, in stentorian tones, cried out, "Comes Ceausescu!" The assembly stiffened. The deputy foreign minister, a swarthy man whose bristly, short-cropped hair made him look like a boar, sidled up to me with a sidelong conniving glance and whispered, "Mr. Meyer, are you trembling?" The Great Conductor, the Beloved Leader, the Genius of the Carpathians, the Danube of Thought—the Last Stalinist of Europe—entered the audience chamber.

President Nicolae Ceausescu was a short, bent little man with deranged eyes and bushy eyebrows who spittled as he talked. He shuffled in wearing woven plastic shoes and a baggy gray suit and offered a moist, weak palm. His people feared this man as Satan. They referred to him simply as He—He whose likeness weathered on billboards along every highway, He whose collected works yellowed in the windows of every bookstore. While Hungary and Poland experimented with democracy and free markets, while the Soviet Union opened to the world, Romania turned ever inward, wrapped in old-fashioned Marxist conviction and one-man rule. For nearly a quarter of a century, it had been driven by Ceausescu's singular vision of a Romania dependent upon nothing but itself and him. To free Romania of foreign debt, he launched an all-out export drive that stripped shops bare and caused near famine in the countryside. Commerce with the West was largely reduced to barter. State control of the economy was complete. Romania, in the summer of 1989, was one of the last temples of the dwindling communist faith, an international pariah as isolated as North Korea.

We were the first American journalists to interview Ceausescu in a decade, and the last to see him alive. For more than two hours he ranted about the glories of Romanian communism and the perfidy and corruption of the West. Occasionally he seized up, like a broken doll, and spluttered in an almost epileptic grimace, his lips twisting, spitting, his face and body contorting in tics and sudden spasms, before breaking out again into speech. Chaplin's parody of the Great Dictator could not rival this alarming reality.

How could we claim his people are starving? Ceausescu demanded. "We have a bumper harvest!"

Why are the stores bare, we asked, with next to nothing on the shelves? Because food is kept out of sight in "storage," he replied.

What of Poland's and Hungary's experiments with democracy? "Disasters. They should be stopped!"

Does it bother you that people talk of a Ceausescu cult of personality? "If this is a cult of personality, I would like all the poorly developed countries to enjoy such personalities." Does it bother you to be likened to Stalin? "He made mistakes, but he did everything a person should do in his job!"

I asked, perhaps too casually, if he thought Romanians might one day rise against him. Ceausescu looked at me with the contemplativeness of a man who could have me killed with a word, and would, if I were Romanian. His eyes were at once immensely intelligent and totally dead: fish eyes, if fish could think. That was the look I saw again six months later, when he lay dead on the ground, executed by firing squad.

For now, he merely paused, then resumed his monologue. He waved his fist in the air, banged the armrest on his throne. The translator, a sensitive and learned man, knelt at his feet, a footman struggling to keep pace with the broken, angry tirade. The interview had by now degenerated into the sort of speech Ceausescu might make at a communist party congress. All pretense of give-and-take disappeared. We were expected to listen and take notes. So I did, though probably not what he might imagine.

"Balls," I wrote, not as editorial commentary but as literal observation. Ceausescu's were huge. They sagged grotesquely in one trouser leg, squatting on his seat like misshapen tomatoes. Them so big, him so small.

A more serious notation: we spoke of his "cult of personality," but it was hard to discern any personality here. He gestured, talked, shouted, waved his arms. But who or what was he, beyond a hollow vessel for power? The man seemed utterly without presence, charisma, aura. If Erich Honecker was an impenetrability, Ceausescu seemed a cipher. I have never met a man more lacking in human qualities. He appeared to be utterly cut off from ordinary life, from ordinary sentiment and emotions, from reality, from empathy, from understanding. He lived in a weird world of will and fantasy that was at once his strength and, ultimately, his fatal flaw.

Afterward we went out to the garden for photographs, a time-honored ritual with such men. Peter Turnley, *Newsweek*'s photographer, posed him in front of his personal cornfield. The corn was as high as the dictator's eye. Was it planted there as proof of Romania's bounty? Along the road leading to his villa, the first four or five rows of corn towered impressively. Behind, they were scrawny and wasted. In Romania, there was no fertilizer for ordinary farmers, except those who fed the emperor's ego.

Aides followed us around, grinning and sweating furiously as Peter led Ceausescu to and fro across the lawn, gently touching his shoulder to position him in the sunlight . . . actually touching this man, the aides couldn't help but notice, who was so concerned about microbes and poisons that he never wore the same suit twice and required even close advisers to take saliva tests and be strip-searched before entering his presence. Peter nudged him onto a little wooden dock jutting out amidst reeds into the lake. Again, Peter touched his shoulder to position him in the light, and for an instant Ceausescu lost his balance. He tottered on one foot. His little arms spun little circles in the air. From the phalanx of aides behind us, from all those peeping out from the behind the curtains of the villa, you could almost hear the collective intake of a hundred breaths. Would the Danube of Thought topple into the drink?

CHAPTER NINE

The Great Escape

By the end of the first week in September, the conspirators' preparations were complete. West German authorities set up a sprawling immigration center in Passau, hard on the Austrian border, capable of accommodating tens of thousands of people. An agreement was quietly struck with Vienna to grant the East Germans visa-free passage, negotiated by German diplomats who shuttled secretly between Vienna and Budapest. Fleets of buses waited at the crossing points for travel through to the Federal Republic.

And so the Hungarians shed their camouflage. On August 31, Gyula Horn flew to East Berlin to confront his counterpart, foreign minister Oskar Fischer. More than 150,000 East Germans were encamped around Lake Balaton, Horn told him. They weren't going home. Hungary did not want to damage its relations with the German Democratic Republic. Yet neither could it stand idle in a situation that he described as "inhumane." Yes, there was the treaty with Berlin to consider. But Hungary was also a signatory to European human rights conventions—and those dictated a change of policy. Then Horn informed Fischer of what Budapest intended to do: open its border with Austria, without hindrance.

Fischer was outraged. "That is treason! Are you aware that you are leaving the GDR in the lurch and joining the other side? This will have grave consequences for you!" Nemeth shrugged off the threat, knowing it was empty. Days before, Mikhail Gorbachev had told Chancellor Helmut Kohl that under no circumstances would Moscow intervene. Even without that assurance, Nemeth had decided: the time was ripe to deliver the final blow against Erich Honecker and his Wall.

The decision was made in great secrecy and held close until the final moment. Nemeth's own interior minister, Istvan Horvath, charged with managing what would turn into a mass exodus, was informed only days before, according to Nemeth. "He asked, 'Miklos, do you realize that by doing this we are siding with the West Germans?' And I said, 'Yes.'"

All along, Nemeth saw the immigration crisis as a way of establishing Hungary's bona fides as a member of *Europe*. His strategy was to be the first East bloc nation to rejoin the West, and he hoped to reap the rewards. "Yes, I foresaw that opening the border could lead to the collapse of the German Democratic Republic, and of the Czech regime as well," he told me. "But I did not forecast it so soon." Flying home from that August 25 rendezvous in Bonn, he and his aides had discussed the likely consequences—over a presumed time frame of the next two to four years! That events moved so much faster was unfortunate, from his perspective. "I aimed to keep maximum advantage for Hungary," he would later confess. Had the bloc's implosion not come so quickly, Hungary would have been the leading reformer, the most progressive nation of Eastern Europe. It would have been the gateway for Western investment, tourism, cultural exchange. A grateful Germany would have lavished aid and attention upon it, partly to inspire imitation by Hungary's slower-moving neighbors. "I specifically asked Kohl for his help in rejoining Europe, and the chancellor agreed," said Nemeth. But because the other regimes collapsed so quickly, thanks in large measure to the events Hungary set in motion, "we lost our advantage. The other countries of the East could catch up. As they did."

Ordinary East Germans knew nothing of these grand strategies. They had only one concern: to escape. Over the preceding weeks, the pressures had built. The Stasi in their midst started rumors that they would be sent home. More recently came conflicting reports that they would soon be let go. The presence in the camps of so many West German and Hungarian officials lent credence to this hope. Yet nothing was sure. Tens of thousands of people—whole families and their children—lived anxiously from day to day in an increasingly tense and nerve-racking limbo.

Then, in the early evening of September 10, the sun still warm in the sky, the waiting abruptly ended. A West German diplomat named Michael Jansen climbed on top of a table set up in the middle of a playing field at a camp in the hills outside Budapest. One of Germany's most senior career diplomats, he had been sent to the Hungarian capital in mid-July at the personal behest of Hans-Dietrich Genscher. "My friend, go and do whatever is needed," Jansen was instructed. He had done so, setting up the camps that fed and sheltered so many thousands of East Germans. Now he had one last task. Picking up a megaphone, he paused for a moment to think about what to say, then addressed the expectant crowd of three to four thousand people who quickly gathered. You may have heard the reports, he told them, for at just that moment Prime Minister Nemeth had gone on national television to make his own dramatic announcement. Those reports were true. "You are free to go!"

The effect was electric—and immediate. The borders were to be opened at midnight, sharp, and the citizens of Erich Honecker's workers' paradise couldn't clear out fast enough. Jansen watched as people literally ran to their cars, threw in their belongings and raced away, at least insofar as the rattling lawn mower that was East Germany's national car could race. Others clambered aboard buses Jansen chartered to take them to the border and beyond, to Germany. "Why the rush?" he asked one. "You have until midnight." The memorable reply: "Under communism, when someone says yes, we know that *nyet* could soon follow."

To Jansen, the moment lives as if it were yesterday. "It was very emotional—the most emotional moment of my professional life," he told me twenty years later, after his retirement from the German foreign office. By the next morning, his camps were all but empty. Long lines quickly built at every checkpoint on the eastern side of the Austrian frontier, stretching for miles. The autobahn toward Vienna became a parking lot. Families with small children dozed in their cars, fitfully awaiting midnight; others simply partied, singing and dancing and popping off bottles of champagne.

At 12:01 a.m., September 11, the gates lifted and the mad rush to the West was on. Austrian and Hungarian police stood to the side as a steady stream of vehicles, bearing license plates of the GDR, swept past in an unbroken tide. More than eight thousand people left that first day. By the third day, the figure was close to forty thousand. Television crews and reporters from around the globe flocked to the scene, reporting this astonishing development that came, by all outward appearances, out of the blue. CNN ran live coverage throughout the following days. So did Sky News and the BBC. The event dominated the news in every country of the world, save China and the police states of Eastern Europe. *Newsweek*'s cover that week gave the exodus the name that would endure: "The Great Escape." And it was only the beginning.

The gravity of the situation was not missed in Berlin. At the September 5 meeting of the Politburo, following Horn's visit, the leadership inveighed against Hungary's perfidy. They did so again at the September 12 meeting. Gunter Schabowski, the Berlin communist party chief who would figure so prominently in the events to come, recalled the debate with mixed contempt and incredulity. As the entire edifice of the GDR shook with the blow the Hungarians had just delivered, the assembled grandees of communism dithered and pointed fingers.

On and on they went. "It was a general attack on socialism, and we are the first target," one top official groused. "The Hungarians are in cahoots with the West Germans," said another. "They were bribed by Bonn." Said yet a third, "It is the doing of that Western reactionary Otto von Habsburg." It was all sound and fury, impotent querulousness. Nor were there any "grave consequences" for Hungary, and not only because Moscow showed no signs of interfering. Erich Honecker himself was in no position even to govern, let alone retaliate. The reason: he had just gone into the hospital. Officially, it was for gallbladder surgery. But according to West German intelligence, Honecker had intestinal cancer. That left a vacuum of power, into which no one dared step.

Thus the internal crisis of surreal detachment enveloping the GDR became deeper as the external crisis grew. It was clear, even before the Pan-European Picnic and the September 11 border opening, that East Germany's survival was at stake. Yet within the leadership there was no discussion of what to do, how to react. "We were silent," Schabowski would tell me. "The situation of our people leaving was not even discussed." Or rather, it was discussed precisely once, and then only elliptically.

At the September 5 Politburo meeting, Heinz Kessler, a reactionary, suggested that the leadership should at least make a statement, if only to indicate that it understood why its citizens were leaving, according to Schabowski. "I asked, 'What should we say? Would you say people are leaving because they can't travel or can't get modern computers or decent goods?' Many were against this, others were for it." After a time, Kurt Hager, the party ideologist, chairing the meeting in Honecker's absence, cut off the discussion. "'It is better to table this matter until Erich returns,' he said. And we accepted this."

That was a mistake, Schabowski believed in retrospect. "We should have spoken up. We should have said, 'We must do this at once.' We should have removed Erich Honecker then and there. He would have learned of it at the hospital. Would anything have come of it? No, probably not. The GDR by this time was finished. Kismet. So long. It was only a question of sooner or later. But it would have been a fight. Maybe other leaders would have emerged, younger people who could have changed the system and been partners with Bonn. Perhaps a confederation would have resulted, with the GDR lasting another few years before reunification, leading to different conditions of unification and its results. But this was the Time of Silence, as we called it. We were like a rabbit, struck motionless before the snake."

Meanwhile, the exodus went on, watched each day via West German television throughout the GDR. The exception was Dresden, where reception was poor. East Germans watched as thousands of their countrymen poured across the frontier from Hungary, seeking new lives in the West. They cheered and cried as they arrived in the Federal Republic. They hugged relatives and families they thought they would never see again. I interviewed many and spoke also with ordinary West Germans as well as senior government officials. As the weeks went by, I was struck by the growing ambiguity of the public mood. Here was the German Democratic Republic, in certain trouble. The U.S. ambassador described it as a "silent crisis." By rights, West Germans ought to have welcomed these events as a herald of the Cold War's imminent end. And yet, they did not. Emotions were weirdly mixed, on both sides of the German divide.

Once the initial blush of euphoria began to fade, concerns of every-day practicality entered in. Many West Germans wondered how the Federal Republic could absorb all the people who wanted to come. Two years ago, some 100,000 *Aussiedler*—East Europeans of German descent constitutionally entitled to citizenship—immigrated to West Germany. This year, the figure was expected to be closer to half a million, even before the East German exodus began. "What we have seen so far from Hungary is only the tip of the iceberg," one senior official told me in early September, adding that by some estimates as many as 650,000 of East Germany's 17 million citizens had applied for official exit visas. At the United Nations in late September, Soviet foreign minister Eduard Shevardnadze was asked how many GDR citizens he thought would flee, if given the chance. His answer, given almost offhandedly: 1 to 2 million.

The government in Bonn was haunted by the specter of this human tide. Publicly, there was no choice but to profess jubilation over the escape of so many East Germans; privately, serious reservations existed at the highest levels.

"If the East Germans tore down the Wall today," said one of the Federal Republic's ranking diplomats to the GDR, "we would have to build another tomorrow."

"We don't want to depopulate East Germany; we want to see living conditions improve, so that they will stay home," a top immigration officer told me.

"We might say we want reunification and the Wall to come down," a former deputy mayor of Berlin confided bluntly, "but not really."

Ordinary West Germans took to grousing about banalities. Housing was scarce, especially in Berlin. Competition for jobs could be fierce. Those *Ossies* (the pejorative that colors intra-German relations to this day first cropped up that September) were already getting too many preferences: subsidized apartments, immediate unemployment benefits, help in finding work. A poll released in late September, at the height of the exodus, showed that a quarter of West Germans feared their countrymen would come and take their jobs. "Distrust was above all evident among young workers who saw the equally young and mostly well-educated East Germans as competitors," the study found. It also reported that, while most West Germans worked an average thirty-seven-hour week, East German émigrés were already putting in sixty to seventy hours, often at lower pay, just to get ahead. That old-fashioned immigrant zeal, the report concluded, was destined to become a "social irritant." This new sentiment was so unsettling that Helmut Schmidt felt compelled to protest in *Die Zeit*. "We took in millions of new citizens after the war," the former chancellor wrote. "I am ashamed of West Germans who are envious of the help we are giving these new members of our society. I am ashamed of politicians who say they should stay where they are."

Those staying behind were no less ambivalent. "Do you see these houses?" a young East German asked me one evening in East Berlin, pointing out three town houses. We were walking down a battered street; the plaster facades of the buildings were falling off in great clumps. Most still bore the scars of World War II—pockmarks from shrapnel, bullets and artillery. "They are empty. All the people left last week. They had everything—houses, cars, money, a dacha in the country. They left all this behind, just to get more." He said this angrily, indignant at the greed that he believed drove his countrymen to flee. For all the problems they faced—shortages of many basic goods, declining living standards, political repression—most East Germans had no desire to leave their country, contrary to the impression fostered in the West. Many if not most were perfectly comfortable with the socialist system that guaranteed them work, low-cost housing and free lifelong health care and schooling. Their main worry was that the mass exodus of their countrymen would worsen the lives of those who stayed behind.

One night, I visited a favorite haunt, the Café Papillon, where one had a fair chance of talking without being watched by police. A pair of stylishly dressed young women spoke of those they called "stayers" and "leavers." One ran a small boutique, the other was an assistant in an art gallery. Ensconced at a table in the corner, they looked as though they would be at home in any Western capital. "I am an East German, and I will not go," one woman told me fiercely. The other nodded. Shops, offices and even whole factories had been forced to close or cut back because their staffs were so depleted by emigration. "Patients have died in hospitals because their doctors disappeared. Buses and trains don't run because drivers have gone. They are not leaving for political reasons," she said. "They want only the money to buy 'things.' They don't realize that what they are giving up is worth much more—family, community, friends. They will regret their choice." I wondered if they would feel the same once they had tasted life along West Berlin's glamorous Kurfurstendamm, let alone New York. But what they said was a fact nonetheless: it was the youngest, the best-educated and the most ambitious East Germans who were leaving, not the deadwood of an older generation, and their loss was acutely felt.

Kurt Hager, the conservative ideologist standing in for Honecker on the Politburo, geared up the party's propaganda machine. Clumsily, the leadership tried to play on the people's mixed emotions. Newspapers accused the Hungarian and West German governments of plotting the escapes in order to "discredit forty years of socialist construction." Lurid tales of an illicit "trade in humans" were concocted. One "firsthand" account featured a railway worker who was given cigarettes that "tasted funny" by a woman in Budapest. He fell unconscious, awoke to find himself aboard a bus to Austria and only just managed to escape. "I consider myself the victim of kidnappers and criminals," the man told *Neues Deutschland*, the official voice of the communist party, which Schabowski used to run. East German television "disclosed" that West German "spies" were offering money to those who left, interlacing these absurdities with reports of refugees failing to find jobs, of homesickness, of feelings of insecurity and depression in West Germany's uncaring "elbow society."

With each passing day, the crisis grew deeper. How much better (and smarter) it would have been to acknowledge the problems honestly and accompany that with a pledge to address the people's grievances, said Schabowski, looking back. The regime would not have seemed so isolated. He and a few others had wanted to do just that. But, again, it was the Time of Silence. Despite all that was happening around them, instead of changing their approach to suit changing times, the leadership hesitated. Honecker's continued absence only accentuated their sense of paralysis. Unable to decide on a course of action, divided among themselves, unsure of everything that they had hitherto taken for granted, whether it was the system that governed their lives or the sense of their own power, they opted for the tried and true, a Stalinist stonewall. As much as anything, perhaps, this foretold the bankruptcy of the regime and sealed its demise.

Klaus Bölling, a retired diplomat who had once been head of West Germany's mission to East Berlin, was one of the few Germans I met who saw all this clearly. The regime's response to the crisis, he said over dinner one evening, showed the extraordinary divide between the GDR's rulers and its people: "The old strong Honecker is gone." Age had taken its toll; so had illness. "He and his regime are utterly cut off from everyday life. They still see themselves as the defenders of the true faith, battling the evils of uncaring capitalism. Yet they move through the streets in Volvo limousines, blinds drawn. They spend weekends at isolated dachas in the country. They live well on party perquisites and have no conception of the shortages that beset their countrymen. They shun all contact with the real." Bölling told me a story of one of his East German counterparts who took a trip with Honecker some years ago. At a factory in Mecklenburg, Honecker stepped out of his limo to greet what he thought was a crowd of workers. In fact, all the real workers had been shooed out to make way for the communist chief. The crowd that remained was composed almost completely of party officials and secret police. Honecker stepped forward and began waving and shaking hands, delighted with his popular reception, thoroughly unaware that the public, as such, was not even there.

That distance, that almost unhinged detachment from reality, was profoundly alienating. Ask East Germans why they left, and it was always the same. It was the "sticky air," the unremitting interference in people's daily lives. Their wish to travel freely, now become the lodestone of unrest, was an expression of this more profound malaise. The regime's imperviousness to any reality, to any point of view other than the socialist orthodoxy propounded by the country's founders, robbed East Germany's younger generation of hope. One refugee put it poignantly some weeks after he arrived in West Berlin, perhaps only a mile from his old house in the East—but a point he had traveled a thousand miles, and forty years, to reach. "It is as if you were a child," he had said, "and your father were mad. He cannot see the world, and you cannot make yourself understood."

Blindness among the many—clarity from a few—was the common thread woven through the events of 1989.

*　　*　　*

Did blindness cause Erich Honecker to misstep at the critical moment? Just as Poland's communists agreed to an election they thought they could win, just as Hungary's Karoly Grosz and his conservatives chose Miklos Nemeth to form a government, thinking they could control him, so now did Honecker trip himself up by self-delusion.

It was late September. He had just left the hospital. The exodus was at its peak. Several thousand East Germans were leaving the country daily. Though frail, Honecker thought himself in command. Clearly, he had to act. The tens of thousands of East Germans in Hungary were beyond his power. He did not dare to bar those who remained in the GDR from traveling. That would only inflame the situation and potentially spark active unrest. Honecker seized on what, to him, was an obvious solution. Acting on his own, without informing his cabinet, he called a friend and hard-line ally, Milos Jakes, the communist party boss of neighboring Czechoslovakia. He needed a favor, Honecker said. Could Jakes close the southern Czech border to Hungary, blocking East Germans from passing through to Hungary and on to the West. Without demurral—or apparent thought for the consequences—Jakes did so.

Honecker thought himself clever. But the move backfired badly. Thousands of East Germans en route to Hungary were suddenly trapped in Czechoslovakia. Some returned home. Many others descended on the West German embassy in Prague, the ornately baroque Lobkowitz Palace. Perhaps they had heard that, in July, the West German government had secretly flown 120 GDR citizens who had taken refuge in the embassy in Budapest to safety in the Federal Republic. Perhaps they expected the Czech government to buckle under international pressure as they imagined the Hungarians had just done, not knowing the underlying reality of the Great Escape. In any event, the trickle of East Germans arriving in Prague soon became a flood.

Czech police cordoned off the street in front of the embassy to keep East Germans away. Instead, they merely swept into the alleys around back and hopped over a shoulder-high, metal fence into the safety of the legation's gardens. Thousands were already encamped there: men, women, children, living in hastily erected tents without running water or sanitation. Dysentery and disease threatened. World TV networks descended. East Germany's problem became Czechoslovakia's. It was an international embarrassment and, worse, an inspiration to the country's own restive population. On September 25, thinking better of his precipitous decision, Jakes informed Honecker that he had to find a different solution. And he did.

He announced it, grotesquely enough, during a reception at the State Opera House for a delegation from Beijing, arriving to show its appreciation for Honecker's support for Tiananmen Square. He invited the entire Politburo to the fete and, there, gathered them in a private salon to relate what he described as "a little surprise."

"Dear comrades," Schabowski remembers him saying. "I have just spoken with Comrade Jakes and I have a solution to our problem in Prague." As before, there was no discussion. Honecker was announcing his decision. He had called the East German embassy in Czechoslovakia, he told them, and instructed them to arrange the details, in coordination with the West German foreign ministry.

The men of the Politburo listened, at first in disbelief and then with appalled dread. For Honecker's "solution" was to get rid of the refugees holed up in the Czech embassy by giving them precisely what they wanted—free passage to the Federal Republic. Special trains would be ordered, express from Prague to West Germany. Their doors and windows would be sealed to keep any malcontents from getting on or off the trains, he said. The particular genius of the idea was that those aboard this Freedom Train would be transported through the territory of the German Democratic Republic. That way, Honecker explained with satisfaction, they would have to . . . acknowledge East German sovereignty.

It is impossible not to wonder what sort of mind could dream up such a bizarre scheme. Forget the eerie historical echo: locked trains as in locked cattle cars, loaded with social undesirables shipped off to where they wouldn't be heard from again. The bigger question is what to make of the sheer illogic of his logic. Because the trains would pass through East German territory, this was somehow not a crushing defeat for the regime, a symbol of its impotence and a summons to resist? As Foreign Minister Hans-Dietrich Genscher said at the time, rushing to Prague from the annual opening of the UN General Assembly in New York to supervise the operation, "This was more than the opening of the gates of the West German embassy."

In this season of surreal spectacles, it is hard to decide which was the most surreal. Was it the almost farcical pantomime of the Pan-European Picnic? Was it the dark comedy of the Polish elections, with pens wielded as sabers, or the monumental botch that opened the Wall? Among all the lunacies, Honecker's on this occasion must be a contender. On September 30, as the first of his sealed trains hurtled their way west, thousands of East Germans pressed into railway stations along the route. In Dresden, they tried to fight their way into the station, to be beaten back by police. Others lined the tracks outside Leipzig and other cities, waving to their compatriots headed for a new life. This was the beginning of the end for Honecker, the start of something entirely different. Until then, the German Democratic Republic had largely been inert. Its people sought merely to escape. But "Erich's Big Idea," as Schabowski sardonically called it, changed all that. He closed the safety valve, the exit through Hungary that those who would resist could use to flee the country. Then he confronted them with police and pushed them against his Wall.

In Hungary, change came from within, led by a few reform-minded communists around Miklos Nemeth and Imre Pozsgay. In Poland, revolution came via the ballot box and democratic elections—a model of peaceful compromise and accommodation. In East Germany, for the first time, the people themselves rose up. Erich's Big Idea set the stage for a wave of ever-larger mass demonstrations that within weeks would sweep the country. The police violently turning East Germans away from the trains passing westward was the spark. On September 25, eight thousand people marched in Leipzig, singing the "Internationale." The next Monday, October 2, Leipzigers marched again—this time close to one hundred thousand, in what would become a weekly rite. Protests erupted in other major cities, including East Berlin. *"Wir bleiben hier,"* the demonstrators chanted, defying row on row of police. "We are staying."

For the East German regime, there could hardly have been a more chilling answer to Erich Honecker's final solution.

*　　*　　*

George H. W. Bush returned from Europe in July, deeply moved by what he had seen and heard. More, he saw how much was at stake for the East Europeans, how delicate the situation was and how fast events were moving. For an administration that took office expecting the big game to be Asia, the focus for the next two years would be almost entirely on Europe. Bush's interest had become personal. He followed events closely and telephoned the region's leaders almost daily. Quietly and with characteristic circumspection, he decided on a plan of action. It could be summed up as restraint. He decided that in a fast-moving, fluid environment such as this, more could be accomplished by doing less.

With the Great Escape, America awoke in earnest to the reality of what was happening in Eastern Europe. It dominated the news, became topic A around Washington's political dinner tables. Columnists, lawmakers and the public clamored for action, anything to help the poor but plucky Peoples of the East to throw off the yoke of communism. In his journal that fall, Bush wrote, "I keep hearing critics saying we're not doing enough on Eastern Europe. Here these changes are dramatically coming our way—Poland, Hungary, the German Democratic Republic—and you've got a bunch of critics jumping around saying we ought to do more." Congress, he went on, wanted to "just send money," no matter for what. Conservative and human rights groups alike called for louder rhetoric, more chest-thumping and more finger-pointing at the Soviets. The hubbub worried the cautious Bush. "If we mishandle it," he wrote, "if we get way out making this look like an American project," the whole thing could backfire, perhaps even "invite a crackdown that could result in bloodshed," if not from Moscow then from some other hard-line East European regime.

Less publicly, bigger issues were being debated. On September 11, one of Chancellor Kohl's coalition partners, the Christian Democratic Union Party, held a party conference in Bremen, where delegates called for the restoration of Germany within its 1937 borders. This in itself was nothing new. But in the current climate it raised questions, especially in Moscow, which complained that Kohl had done nothing to repudiate such talk. Eduard Shevardnadze raised the matter with James Baker at their retreat in Jackson Hole in the third week of September, then brought it up more pointedly a few days later in a speech at the opening of the UN General Assembly.

Shevardnadze did so for good reason. For the Bush administration, so late in recognizing what was happening in the East, had now moved far ahead of the Europeans in assessing the likely consequences. In May, François Mitterrand visited the president at his summer home in Maine. Bush asked flat out about the prospects of German unification. "Unthinkable," exclaimed the French leader in dismay—at least, he added, "not in our lifetimes." Margaret Thatcher would be no less dismissive. Bush himself, though, thought differently. And he knew that Helmut Kohl and his chief national security adviser, Horst Teltschik, thought differently, as well. As summer gave way to fall, and the magnitude of the crisis in the GDR became ever more apparent, Bush pushed his staff to think through U.S. policy. As for himself, when asked by reporters in late September where he stood on German unification, he replied simply, "I don't fear it."

By this point, Washington realized it had little to say about developments on the ground in Eastern Europe, and even less influence. As one national security aide somewhat ruefully put it, "Events proceeded with such bewildering speed that U.S. and other Western policies could not hope to keep pace. We in Washington often found ourselves in the role of thrilled, if not to say astonished, onlookers."

CHAPTER TEN

Vortex of Change

Each year, every year, the herds of East Africa's Serengeti Plain begin a vast migration. They gather by the millions: wildebeests, giraffes, zebras, antelope, lions and hyenas. It is impossible to predict precisely when it will begin, but there are unmistakable signs. The animals grow impatient. They mill about, clashing with one another, pawing the ground in rising uncertainty and irritation. The atmosphere, the very air, becomes heavy with their heat. This may go on for weeks. Then one day, seemingly for no particular reason, they bolt—abruptly, all at once, a pell-mell, headlong run in this or that direction. They move as one, an irresistible force. Nothing could stop it, nothing can guide it.

By autumn, this was the mood in Eastern Europe. The air was heavy with a brooding, unpredictable inevitability. From afar, the prospects were exciting. A Warsaw Pact without Poland or Hungary was easily imaginable. So was another Prague Spring, even the fall of the Wall. Privately, Helmut Kohl began to talk about an end of communism and hinted at a reunified Germany. Yet those living the events were fearful. Where there are herds, there are also predators. Where there is change, there is danger. Who knew what abrupt ugliness the times might bring? Hope was checked by caution, bred of the bitter experience of 1953, 1956, 1968 and 1980.

Traveling through the region in late September and early October was to run with the herds. By then, the sheer velocity of change had, in itself, become the most powerful force for change. Events in one country immediately spilled over to others. Overnight, Eastern Europe became less a geography than a volatile physics: plasma in motion, a blinding and bewildering kaleidoscopic whirl. Everyone seemed to be going at different speeds, in different directions, toward destinations unknown. In Poland, only months before, Solidarity had sought at most a restoration of its legal standing; now, it was grappling with the ambiguous spoils of victory. Hungary stood on the very threshold of success in its drive to bring down communism. By contrast, Czechoslovakia had scarcely begun to move. Tantalizing glimpses of what might be possible were obscured by dust, commotion, frenzy and fear.

My editors in New York suggested I take a sweep through the region, to look at it as one story rather than several, to watch it as a process and try to figure out where it might all lead. Stephen Smith, the executive editor of *Newsweek*, came along. We dubbed ourselves the Marx Brothers, lost in the unrecognizable terrain of Absurdistan. Down was up, and up was down. Sometimes it was hard to tell the heroes from the villains. No fantasy could match the bizarre realities and jarring contrasts that we encountered. Certainly, no fantasy could match its pregnant drama.

We began in Poland. Once again, Solidarity was fighting for its life, only this time as a government rather than a broken opposition. What a curious evolution! In early July, after its tumultuous election win, the once-banned union found itself to be the dominant political force in the country. When the new Polish parliament convened for the first time, a smiling and joking Lech Walesa found himself seated next to a dour Jaruzelski, the man who had imprisoned him eight years before. Indeed, the general's very presence was an eloquent symbol of the communist party's comeuppance. For the new parliament to elect him president—as both sides had planned—Solidarity's leaders found themselves in the bizarre position of voting with the communists to thrust their former nemesis into power. On July 19, they got him into office by a margin of one vote. At the swearing-in ceremony, his entire cabinet watched from the visitors' gallery. Not one had won a seat of his own.

After that, events took on a life of their own. When Jaruzelski and his communists proved unable to create a government, Solidarity negotiated a power-sharing arrangement: "Your president, our prime minister," one of its leaders, Adam Michnik, famously quipped. At the time, Michnik's compromise was laughed off. "Oh, come on, Adam," replied Tadeusz Mazowiecki, who had guided that winter's Round Table talks. "We have to go slow. It will be years before we enter the government." Yet just a few weeks later, on August 24, Mazowiecki became *the* government—Poland's new prime minister, the first noncommunist since the Soviet army swept across his country in 1944. On his first day of work, he skipped the official limo waiting outside his humble apartment and rode his bike to work. Exploring his new office, he pressed a hidden button. An armed guard leaped out from behind a partition. Mazowiecki was aghast.

The problems he faced. Inflation of 50 to 100 percent a month. Shortages of food and medical supplies. Panic buying that emptied stores. Endemic corruption. Economic incentives so skewed that barter threatened to displace currency. The specter of strikes if not social implosion. No wonder the communists had wanted to share power. How long would it be before they sighed with relief to be removed from responsibility altogether? Meeting for a late-evening interview, Mazowiecki inhaled hard on his cigarette. Fatigue was etched into his face. Perhaps, he joked, Solidarity should not have won the election, after all. For Solidarity's new ministers, it was the revenge of Oscar Wilde: "When the gods wish to punish us, they answer our prayers."

Like so many other journalists before us, we asked the obvious: Solidarity won the election. Now what? The neophyte prime minister, so accustomed to his role as an opposition leader and a champion of human rights, thus spoke to us of tax reforms, the elimination of subsidies and state planning, how to spark entrepreneurship and replace Poland's command economy with one based on demand. "The most important thing is to lift Poles out their sense of hopelessness," he said. "We need a reawakening. That's our first task, to release the energies of the people. Everything depends on it." To another typically American question—in the face of such difficulty, how long did he think his political "honeymoon" would last?—he smiled ruefully. "What honeymoon?"

At dinner that night in Warsaw's faded Hotel Victoria, three Solidarity leaders seemed at sea. They needed time, but there was no time. They needed money and kept asking for it from the West, but so far none was to be had. They needed knowledge, but they had none: monetary policy, fiscal policy, supply and demand? "We don't even know what a market is," said one. Innocent of the mysteries of Economics 101, they talked authoritatively of quack remedies. "What we need is a good dose of corrective inflation." By that they meant sudden price increases that would, in theory, put goods on store shelves and discourage panic buying. "Shock therapy," said the man who would soon be finance minister, Leszek Balcerowicz.

These were good and simple men, the sort you might find in the Vermont statehouse, thrust into the middle of world-shaking events. Yet they were so inexperienced. "I've never eaten in a restaurant like this," marveled a prominent member of parliament, as though the down-at-heel Victoria were the George V in Paris rather than a poor East European version of a Quality Inn. The man touted as a future defense minister spoke of commerce and history—that is to say, Germans. "Yes, we Poles have a thousand-year history with Germany. It is a thousand years of war." Bafflingly he solemnly advised, "Beware of the German Jewish conspiracy against the Polish army." It was an age-old shibboleth, too complicated to go into. Let's merely note that victims of history are not always ennobled by their victimhood, nor are devils forever damned.

Communists were quick to take advantage of Solidarity's troubles by recasting themselves as progressive "social democrats." Marek Krol, the newly appointed secretary of media relations for the party, was the epitome of the new New Man. Sleekly besuited and slick of hair, flaunting his uninflected English, he disdained the C-word. "Communism," he explained with distaste. "I don't like these religious attitudes, these socialist deities, holy leaders, the scriptural dogmas of belief. 'Class struggle.' 'The working class.' Paah. We have become the party of the lumpen proletariat. There is no future in that." Poles, lazy and demoralized, have to change their "mind-set." They must become more enterprising and self-reliant—in a word, more "Western." The path of his party, Krol assured us, was unfettered capitalism, not the messy "third way" likely to be favored by Solidarity. Why, look at how many former top communists, leaving public life, were going into business. "Already, they are making piles of money!"

The man they called the Fox would soon be counted among them. Prime minister a short season ago, now the new communist party chief, Mieczyslaw Rakowski likened himself to an Eastern "Reagan Republican." The effrontery of the assertion, the sheer audacity, at once shocked and made us laugh—all the more so because he so evidently believed it, that with a wave of his hand he could reinvent himself as a new-age free marketeer. With his short, silvery hair and craggy face, he more closely resembled Julius Caesar. Affecting an emperor's disdain for the masses he once led, Rakowski derided his countrymen for clinging to the comforts of the old system. "Society is not prepared to make sacrifices," he said. "We are too attached to our peaceful life. We Poles would rather live in capitalism and work in socialism."

George Bush, visiting Warsaw in July, liked what he heard. "He told me I was the first Pole who hadn't asked him for money," Rakowski told us proudly. Never mind that he, too, had once hounded Polish dissidents seeking change, or that he had helped create this nation of "slackards," as he called them. Ousted as prime minister when Solidarity came to power, an architect of Poland's era of martial law as well as its later reforms, he counted himself a realist. Clearly, he was skilled in both realpolitik and aphorism. "If the economy is clinically dead," he said, "we'd rather Solidarity were the undertaker." Why? Because it would be that much easier for his communists to retake power. "Democratically, of course," he added with a smile. He would have no way of knowing that, within three years, precisely that would happen.

Nor were the communists the only opportunists. Lech Walesa, Solidarity's leader, had been relegated to the sidelines under the new government. His problem was the perennial one for revolutionary politics. The elections were done. Solidarity was ascendant. What's in it for me? Walesa had wanted to know. I'm the hero of Gdansk! Truth be told, Solidarity's brass had turned against him, largely because of his high-handed arrogance. Behind his back, their tongues loosed by cognac, they called him "fatso" and "pontoon." They derided his pinkie ring and penchant for riding in sleek black limos and hinted he was in the pay of the Catholic Church. The one job to which Walesa might have been suited—president—was occupied by

Jaruzelski. So the man who had been the face of a movement, who perhaps did more than any other individual to bring Poland its independence, was out.

Beware the fury of a founding father scorned. Poland's first post-communist government was only six weeks old, but Lech Walesa went after it like the Doberman he was. The scornful rhetoric he once reserved for the communists was refocused on his former allies. "The government is not moving fast enough," he trumpeted in speeches. "It is making the wrong decisions. Society is furious and fed up. Poland is a powder keg that could erupt in civil war." Ever the canny politician, and perhaps taking a leaf from the communists, Walesa was also distancing himself from the government he'd helped create. Fail or succeed, its reforms would cause deep and politically unpopular pain to a majority of the electorate. He was quite sure he wanted no part of that.

Unlikable Lech showed his colors during an interview in Gdansk. I had flown in with a photographer, later in October. Violent winds and rain bounced the plane like a kite; visibility was zero. This being the national Polish airline (LOT, for lots of luck), we were not equipped for an instrument landing, nor was there enough fuel to return to Warsaw. We circled and circled before finally, through a break in the thunderclouds, diving onto the tarmac. It was lined with ambulances and fire trucks. Throughout the ordeal, Elvis Presley's "Blue Suede Shoes" played on the intercom. Music to die to, I thought ever after.

Walesa sat at a desk reading (or pretending to read) *Politika*, an intellectual political journal. "He can barely read," a former ally once boozily confided. True or not, Walesa had no time for the likes of me, now merely a lowly journalist. German businessmen, potential partners, awaited outside his door. "What do you think I am? An actor?" Walesa demanded when *Newsweek*'s photographer asked him to pose for a photo. "Hurry up. Hurry up. You are so slow. You would not earn much money from me!" I asked about his accusations against the new government: that its proposed economic reforms cut too deeply, that it risked igniting a "civil war," that Poland would be better served by a traditional nationalist strongman such as Marshal Pilsudski (or himself) than by democracy.

A shrug. "Walesa is an initiator," he said in fitting third person. "He initiated political change, now he will initiate economic change." It bothered him to hear talk of his being pushed aside; to the contrary, he insisted, it was his choice. "Such is life." I asked whether other communist regimes of Eastern Europe would find inspiration in Poland, hoping for some insight on events to come in Czechoslovakia or East Germany. "Walesa is many things," the Great Man replied. "But a fortune-teller he is not." Were we through yet? "I am a slave of time! I am sorry. I know you are important. I should treat you better. But Walesa is a slave of time!" With that, he abruptly got up and hustled off to his Germans, beaming.

The snub was weighted with unintended meaning. All those journalists pestering him about the past: Would the communists ever cede full control of the government? Could Solidarity govern? What was the future? Pisssh. It didn't matter anymore. As far as Walesa was concerned, the Polish revolution was over. Everything had changed. The future lay with commerce and the West, with his Germans, whose money would bring new prosperity, whose very presence, Walesa rightly saw, represented the Poland of the coming decades, firmly anchored in Europe. "It's the economy, stupid," he might have said, a phrase soon to be popularized in America by a rising young political candidate named Bill Clinton. Look West, not East. Look to the future, not to today. We journalists, with all our questions concerning the moment, didn't see the bigger picture. We did not see the new world. Walesa did.

If Poland was all motion and commotion, East Germany yet lay frozen, at least on the surface. Beneath, it was cracking up. Erich Honecker could not see it, or perhaps would not. But others in the regime surely did. They saw what was happening in Warsaw and Budapest. They saw the threat to the GDR. And they were appalled by Honecker's gross mishandling of the crisis.

Exhibit A was his latest folly—the decision to send East German refugees from Prague to the Federal Republic via rail through Dresden and Leipzig. Could he not foresee the popular reaction? An "idiocy," Gunter Schabowski called it, scarcely able to believe it. Yet he welcomed the move, if only because it gave him a weapon. "You see," he told me, "by this time Egon Krenz and I were in talks about how to end all this. Our solution was to push Honecker out."

A conspiracy was afoot. It had been slow in coming, for a variety of reasons: Honecker's illness, his absolute power, the mutual mistrust among members of the Politburo, the sheer blindness of some, the silence of others. Schabowski sensed an ally in the head of East German internal security, Egon Krenz, widely regarded as Honecker's eventual successor. The first sign came in early May, during the phony "elections" the communists periodically held to demonstrate their democratic bona fides. When the ballots were counted, it was announced that the party had garnered 98 percent of the votes. "It was rigged, of course," said Schabowski. "But 98 percent?" It was so transparently nonsense, given the temper of the time. "We looked like clowns. Ridiculous. I looked at Krenz, and he looked at me, and we saw we were thinking the same."

Neither man spoke. Schabowski struggled to explain why, to express how frustrating it felt to be so stymied. Here he was, this lively, intelligent man of immense energy and independence. Yet he felt utterly powerless, a ceremonial fixture in a government of one man—Honecker.

In the third week of September, another occasion arose a few days after Honecker emerged from the hospital. At a wreath-laying ceremony commemorating some alleged socialist triumph or another, Krenz had been relegated to the second row of party officialdom. Normally, he would be in the first, as befit his rank as Honecker's number two. But the head of the secret police, Erich Mielke, stood on one side of Honecker, and on the other was the party ideologist Kurt Hager. Schabowski found himself next to Krenz, so he tried a little experiment. "'Egon,' I said. 'Why are you in the second row? You should be in the first. Why is this asshole Hager in there?' Krenz laughed a little. He could tell, from the way I said it, that I was on his side."

A few days later, Krenz came by Schabowski's office. "We began to speak," he said, beginning with the recent lunacy of Honecker's handling of the problem in Prague and moving on to the mounting crisis at home. They had to do something, they agreed, and soon met again, first at Schabowski's house in Wandlitz, a leafy suburb of Berlin favored by senior communists, and again at his office near the Central

Committee building, which Krenz could reach unseen using a secret underground corridor. "We both agreed that with Honecker the GDR could not survive. So we began our little conspiracy. The murder of kings begins like this. But how to do it? In a palace revolution, you can only speculate who will sympathize and who will not."

The two began to quietly approach a select few members of the Politburo they felt could be trusted and settled on a propitious date to make their first move: October 7. This was to be Honecker's special day, his big Jubilee marking the fortieth anniversary of the German Democratic Republic. There would be parades, festivals, fireworks and many receptions where potential allies could innocently be approached. Mikhail Gorbachev would be there, along with the heads of the entire Warsaw Pact. The conspirators agreed that they would try to send the Soviet leader a signal, perhaps ask for his support for a change in leadership. "We could not try to contact him before then," said Schabowski. "We could have been found out. We had to protect ourselves. We did not think it would matter whether we waited another week or two."

In fact, it mattered immensely, for during those few weeks a popular German resistance movement arose and gathered strength. But neither that nor anything else fully engaged Schabowski's attention, neither the continuing refugee drama in Prague nor the growing protests in Leipzig and Dresden. "Getting rid of Honecker was the only thing that mattered—how to do it, and who would be with us." So intent were he and Krenz on killing the king that they missed the mortal peril to themselves.

Vaclav Havel sat calmly at lunch, smoking by the window of his favorite restaurant, a riverside barge on the banks of the Vltava. It was midafternoon, October 3. The sun sparkled on the water. Elvis Presley sang on the jukebox, "Blue Suede Shoes," yet again. We joked about whether Havel would win the Nobel Peace Prize, to be announced in Oslo the next morning. (It went to the Dalai Lama.) Wouldn't that make him popular with the secret police, waiting outside? We pretended not to notice them; they pretended not to be noticed.

Havel was the face of East European conscience, a legend in his own time, more famous, perhaps, than even Poland's Lech Walesa. He was Czechoslovakia's dissident of dissidents in a nation of dissidence, the philosopher-playwright banned from the theater after 1968 and embodiment of the Charter 77 human rights movement in a land where the penalties of outspokenness were painful and high. Signatories were denounced by the country's communist regime, variously, as "traitors," "renegades" and "misfits." They were barred from any but the most menial jobs, arrested frequently and interrogated harshly. The secret police were everywhere. Anyone involved in the liberalizations of 1968 was persona non grata. Former foreign ministers ran the elevators in downscale hotels. Future foreign ministers, once communism toppled, worked as boiler stokers, shoveling coal. Havel was jailed half a dozen times—once for four years, after which he wrote *Largo Desolato*, a play about a political writer who lives in fear of being sent back to prison. He was best known for his essays articulating the dilemmas of life under totalitarianism. His credo was to live "as if"—that is, as if he were free, and to deal with the consequences as humanly as possible. He was as close as you come, in our day, to a true hero—the very human face of all those who stood against an inhuman oppression.

I'd first met Havel in early June, not long after his latest stint in jail. It was about six in the evening. We were drinking coffee in his library, resentfully offered and grudgingly served by his wife, Olga. She wanted her husband to rest and stop talking and talking and talking. He was pale, tired. Western reporters had been traipsing through the apartment overlooking the Vltava since early morning. Havel had been patient with them all, but he didn't have the stomach for another long interview. Could we just have a conversation? I had come to ask Havel about the future—what would happen next, how events in Hungary, Poland and East Germany would affect Czechoslovakia, and what all that would in turn portend for him personally. But a conversation? "Of course," I replied. And so we began simply talking, a sort of surreally quiet and reflective interlude in an otherwise frenzied dash of history.

Leaning back on the pillows of his sofa, I mentioned that I had just seen two of his plays in Warsaw, *Audience* and *Temptation*. Havel himself had never seen them publicly performed, banned as they were in

Czechoslovakia and elsewhere in Eastern Europe, including Poland until recently. The audience's reaction, I told him, was "electric." It was as though they had been waiting, seemingly forever, for someone to speak out and say such things as they, too, were thinking, and wondering how those in power would react. Everyone knew, as well, that the leading character, Ferdinand Vanek, was Havel's alter ego. He, too, had recently been released from jail for antigovernment activities. He, too, was stuck in a dead-end job—a brewery rife in bureaucracy, pettiness and paranoia. Driven to drink, on the verge of insanity, Vanek nonetheless lived "as if." He refused to inform on his friends and colleagues, as most Czechs did in one way or another, despite the blandishments of better pay, perks and promotions within the communist hierarchy. The play evolves as a conversation: Vanek sitting in a chair across from his foreman, speaking his mind, and ending with him in the foreman's seat, roles reversed by dint of his hidden strength of character, Vanek as Everyman. It closes with the question on which it opened, how's life? But this time he responds as a leader, no longer the ordinary downtrodden Czech. No, things are not "okay." In fact, they're a "bloody mess."

It was a metaphor for life at that moment in communist Poland, Hungary and East Germany, as well as Havel's own Czechoslovakia. Things were not okay. They were a "bloody mess," and suddenly people weren't taking it anymore. Prime Minister Rakowski was in the audience, I told him, though no doubt unofficially, accompanying his actress wife. The couple applauded. Havel delighted in the irony. His plays were opening in New York and Los Angeles, to good reviews. "Vienna bombed," for reasons that eluded us both. But Hungary would stage a production soon. Everywhere but Czechoslovakia.

Havel seemed to gain energy at this thought, and we talked about the special responsibility writers in a totalitarian society had to speak the truth when few others did. "I never wanted to be a political figure," he told me. He was the country's foremost dissident almost by default, the intellectual voice of an almost nonexistent opposition. There was no Solidarity in Czechoslovakia, no reform communists seeking to join the West, no Gorbachev. The Czech communist party was as hidebound and repressive, in its ways, as Honecker's German Democratic Republic. "I live in such a strange and paradoxical world," Havel said, "that to be a writer, and to write the truth, makes you something more than a writer. It has political consequences, and you acquire political authority. This is all the more so because people know I do not want power. And so, perhaps, they trust me."

We stood at one point to look out the window, over the river and across Prague's rooftops, as picturesque as those of Paris. Did I know, Havel asked, that thousands of Czechs signed petitions demanding his release from prison? He received hundreds of letters every week from students, workers, people all over Czechoslovakia. This was significant, a sign of a coming thaw, as though the ice that had for so long bound the country might finally be breaking up. Writing to Havel, or petitioning for his freedom, was dangerous and deliberate. It was to choose sides, to stand up and be counted, declare yourself as one of those who resisted the regime and do so in the knowledge that those who watched Havel would now know you. "I read these letters, and I reread them, and each time I am again shocked at how things are changing." Havel paused, sipped his coffee, drew on his cigarette. "We lived so long in a state of helplessness," he went on reflectively, giving each word its weight. "There has been no progress, only stillness. So we wait, hoping for history to resume."

Havel delivered these lines almost diffidently, leaning forward in his easy chair, elbows on his knees, hands cupping his chin or stroking his mustache. Then he glanced directly into my eyes, a look almost more eloquent than his words. "We Czechs, we are finally finding our courage."

This was rather too good to be unrehearsed. Havel was a playwright, after all. But it excited me, even so. Czechoslovakia was an absurdity. The most talented people worked as bricklayers or night watchmen. The only good artists were those whose works could not be shown. The most honest people spent their days worrying whether the next would be spent in jail. The gentlemanly elevator attendant at the Hotel Esplanade, where I stayed, with his beautiful English and neat tweeds and bow tie, in such contrast to the brusque and unkempt manager, was a deputy foreign minister in 1968. Poles envied Czechoslovakia as a consumer paradise. Food was ample. Everyone seemed to have a weekend country house. Prague was a well-tended jewel. Czechs, on the other hand, envied Poles their freedom. For decades,

Prague's austere leadership enforced a tacit social contract: political subservience in exchange for a decent living standard. "We pretend to work, they pretend to pay us," the old joke went. It was a formula for stagnation. Czechoslovakia's communist leaders were determined to cling to power and preserve the party's "leading role" in society. They wanted nothing of Poland's chaotic economy and political turmoil. They saw Hungary "reforming" and recognized it for what it was—the destruction of socialism and the communist party. The question was whether they could resist those very changes, and how? They, too, felt the movement from within and without their borders.

Still, Havel was right. Something *was* changing. Dissidents such as himself were speaking out, and being jailed for it. But for the first time, new voices were joining them. In January, five thousand demonstrators rallied in Prague's central Wenceslas Square to commemorate the death, twenty years previously, of a young student named Jan Palach, who set himself on fire to protest the 1968 Soviet invasion of Czechoslovakia. Police dispersed them using truncheons, water cannon and tear gas. In February and March, half a million people signed a petition demanding greater religious freedom. A more recent manifesto called for an end to censorship and drew thirty thousand signatories. A bizarre group calling itself the Society for a Merrier Present had lately taken to marching around the streets of Prague outfitted in helmets carved from watermelons, spoofing fellow citizens into a sort of irreverent consciousness—always a threat to communism. A friend of mine, Tomas Ruller, went about setting himself on fire. He was a performance artist and had some technique for not getting burned. But it was weird to see this human torch stalking around like Frankenstein's monster, stiff-legged and arms out as flames enveloped him from head to toe. He did this in public spaces, abruptly appearing and lighting a match. He lurched around for a few moments, then fell facedown into a pool of mud. Crowds loved it. The authorities kept beating him up. "For some reason, they see it as a political statement," Ruller complained, an echo of young Jan Palach. For some reason.

To Havel, these were important signs. "We see what is happening next door to us, in Poland and in Hungary. We are frustrated and want change, too. People know it is necessary to do something. But they do not know what or how. So they seize on slogans. 'Freedom!'

'Reform!' Or my name, 'Havel!' But these are only feelings. All is embryonic. We have no Solidarity. We have no political 'reformers,' dismantling communism from above, as in Hungary. This is something new in history. I do not know what will happen in my country, but personally I think the trend is irreversible. It is Europe-wide and not an affair of this country or that. This puts the regime in a complicated situation. They are in a corner. One day they permit a rally, the next they do not. One day they jail me for eight to ten years, three months later they release me. They do not know what to do." One day, Havel predicted, the authorities would make a mistake. "The police would beat some student protesters and forty thousand people will turn out in Wenceslas Square." It would be up to him to channel that anger, when it finally broke.

Such was the situation in early October, when I met Havel once again during my romp through Eastern Europe with my *Newsweek* colleague. Prague is in the midst an "invisible crisis," he told us at lunch. Everyone was waiting, watching, seeking a sign, a spark, like the herds of the Serengeti. "The government knows it," said Havel. "We keep telling the people in power that they do not have to wait until the bitter end before starting a social dialogue, much like Poland's. A lot of suffering could be prevented." Yet that was precisely the problem: paralysis. "The leadership is tired and growing old. They are becoming petrified and cannot respond to these new things." Amid the waiting lurked dangers. "A dictatorship in crisis typically makes contradictory moves," said Havel. "I can imagine a situation that one day my play will open in Prague, and the next day I'll be in prison. This may seem implausible, but at the moment of crisis, when power is shaken, anything can happen."

Rumors were that party chief Milos Jakes would be ousted, Havel said. Others reported that the secret police were planning a coup. "It will happen. The only question is when and how. Even those plotting against him do not know." Havel suggested that we think of Prague's subterranean politics as a poker game. "Each player sits with many cards under the table and none on the table. They wait for each other to show his hand. Not until then will they make their calculation. It is also possible that no player will show his hand."

Looking back on this conversation, I am reminded of Gunter

Schabowski's description of Politburo intrigue. What would it take to move a player to action, to tip his hand? Would the impetus come from inside or outside? At the critical moment, who would side with whom? "Do not forget," said Havel, "in a totalitarian system we can observe an interesting phenomenon. People in power, like their citizens, speak out only when the time is ripe. Our leaders all wear a uniform mask and declare identical phrases. Perhaps at the moment of history, the masks will fall, and it is only at that moment that we know who is who. It is possible then that we may be surprised to find that the masks concealed an intelligent face."

This, also, was an echo. Around Poland's Round Table, enemies became partners, even friends in common cause. Hungary's reformers took power in late 1988 wearing one mask, then dropped it to reveal the visage of a wise humanity devoted to a better future. Meeting Gorbachev many years later, I asked why he had not cracked down when he saw how events were coursing. "In the name of what?" he asked indignantly. "In the name of . . . brutality? In the name of . . . coercion, or slavery?" He did not intend to destroy socialism, not by any means. But he acted with intelligence and out of essential humanity. Perhaps Havel, too, would soon recognize the faces of potential partners? I had heard from mutual friends that the opposition was in frequent and highly secret contact with disaffected members of the government, including the state security forces. "Perhaps," Havel replied, smiling.

After lunch, we walked to the West German embassy. Honecker's "solution" to the problem of the East Germans encamped inside had predictably proved illusory. It served only to highlight his regime's weakness. Within days, thousands more would-be refugees had descended on Prague, vaulted the fences around the German mission and were again encamped in the gardens inside. Havel wanted to see them but feared he would be arrested. "I have my own policeman," he joked at lunch, considering it perfectly conceivable that he would be arrested leaving the restaurant, as he often was when authorities suspected trouble. As we neared the embassy, Havel grew more nervous; he had already recognized five secret police, he told us, as we made our way along a twisting cobblestone street packed with scurrying East Germans and curious Czechs. Steve Smith and I linked our arms through Havel's, walking on either side, and shouldered through the crowds. "Don't worry," we assured Havel with cocksure bravado. "We're meeting Jakes tomorrow. He won't dare arrest you today!"

It was an extraordinary scene. The squares and street around St. Nikolaus Cathedral near the embassy were crowded with abandoned Trabants. They were parked everywhere: on streets, sidewalks, in parks. The keys were often left in the ignition. Some were even left running, as East Germans, loaded with belongings, jumped out to dash for the embassy, fearing that they would somehow be stopped. A crowd of a thousand or more stood before the ornate wrought-iron gates of the embassy itself, an ancient baroque palace in the heart of the old city. Hundreds more trooped up the street behind us, lugging their belongings in suitcases and rucksacks, holding young children aloft so they would not be hurt in the crush. Czech police tried to cope, pitifully. "Where are you going?" one Czech policeman demanded. "To West Germany," responded a young couple with their suitcases, defiantly pushing past.

Not all waited patiently to be let in the front door. Many worked their way around to the back of the embassy, where a shoulder-high fence surrounded the gardens. By now, roughly five thousand people were there, living in tents, their numbers growing by the hour as East Germans vaulted, climbed or were pulled up and over the barrier. *"Entschuldigen,"* said one young man, politely accosting me as I stood by the fence talking with a few of those inside. "Excuse me." I moved to the side so he could loft a heavy suitcase into the embassy compound. Then he clambered up, holding a hand to his wife to help her over. With a boost from me, she quickly joined him.

The first trains to the Federal Republic had left on September 30 and run steadily ever since. Every evening, with almost military precision, the West Germans marched refugees out of the embassy and into waiting buses for the trip to the station. As soon as one group left, the space they occupied filled with new arrivals. But soon the flow would stop. At 3 p.m. that afternoon, October 3, East Germany closed its borders. "I was on the last train from Dresden," one young man told me, speaking through the embassy fence as a light rain pattered on the plastic-sheet tents. "I knew we had to get out now or we never would. I fear a crackdown is coming. A catastrophe as in China. This regime would fire on its own people."

We escorted Havel away. He was elated, not only by the size of the crowds but by the reaction among Czechs. "This is solidarity," he enthused. "People are taking children into their houses and offering the East Germans food. This speaks not only of the social situation in the German Democratic Republic, but also of the situation in Czechoslovakia." Standing on a street corner, he politely thanked us, turning to give a diffident little wave as he departed. He would be fifty-three the next day. I remember wondering, could this shaggy-haired, amiable man with his well-worn army jacket and gentle manner have what it takes to channel an uprising, if and when it came?

The next morning, Czechoslovakia's communist party chief, Milos Jakes, laughed uproariously at the notion that he might be deposed. That Havel. "Do you know why he stopped writing plays?" Jakes asked in the accents of the plumber he once was. "Because they're no good."

We had asked Havel what question he would put to Jakes. It was, do you not realize the depth of social discontent, and your own impotence, that this is the last moment to solve the crisis without strikes, unrest or violence? The answer, Havel anticipated, would be to ask why Western journalists always visited Havel. This is a man who always complicates the situation, who wants only to destabilize society. We know the problems Czechoslovakia faces, and we will solve them.

Jakes answered precisely as predicted. Havel was a troublemaker, a cynic. Authorities could not be accused of persecuting him, however. "He is at large," Jakes said, as though this icon of humanity and Czech culture were a bank robber or murderer. As for the structure of Czech society, "we see no reason to change. . . . The communist party plays the recognized leading role in society. . . . We are not going to tread the path of private ownership." Yes, the situation at the West German embassy was "quite unpleasant." But now the border was closed. The problem was resolved, except for one detail, said Jakes. "What are we going to do with all these abandoned cars?"

October 6. As Prague stayed fretfully still, waiting, Hungary approached the culmination of its *refolution*, a term coined by Timothy Garton Ash to describe the country's unique admixture of reform and revolution.

"Communism is dead," Mark Palmer, the American ambassador, told us over dinner the evening we arrived. All that remained was to hammer a few final nails into the coffin. Only a month had passed since the Hungarians had opened the border, but the effect had been like pulling the plug in a bathtub. The foul waters of four decades of tyranny, repression and brute failure ran out, seemingly in an instant. In Palmer's analogy, it was all over but the death rattle.

Who would write the obit? Most likely Imre Pozsgay, rumored to be planning to officially abolish the party at a meeting of the Central Committee next week. Pozsgay hoped to be elected president in the country's first popular vote, a presidential plebiscite scheduled for late November, but Palmer thought he was deluding himself. Remember Poland? "People want revenge. They hate communism." It wouldn't matter that men like Pozsgay and Miklos Nemeth brought it down and ushered in democracy. "They, too, were communists," said Palmer. "They will go."

It seemed a terrible irony, an almost disgraceful ingratitude. After all, Pozsgay was one of Hungary's best. He had pushed for change when it was dangerous to do so. It was he who called 1956 what it was: a national uprising of the people against a system that was no good. "Communism does not work," he had said when we first met. "We must start again from zero." He was the hidden impresario behind the Pan-European Picnic, priming the pump for the Great Escape, one of the first men to deliver a hammer blow to the Wall itself. Yet he would not be elected president of Hungary in November. Palmer was right: revenge. A cabdriver spat when I asked to be taken to the head-quarters of the Central Committee, a marble hulk on the Danube that the citizens of Budapest derisively called "our White House." Across the city, workers were removing the socialist hammer and sickle from official buildings. The flowers planted in a red star at one city traffic circle had been dug up. Motorists kept driving through them.

Still, there was Pozsgay, the next morning, hammer ready and coffin nails in hand. Communism is "finished," he said again, as declaratively as ever, obviously relishing his role as coexecutioner. The Hungary of the future will be similar to West European social democracies, he explained. The party state will cease to exist. Dictatorial socialism will disappear. Hungary will be a constitutional state, with a government freely elected from among competing parties, much as Kalman Kulcsar and Miklos Nemeth had told me nine months before. "We have always been like a ferryboat, plying the river between East and West," said Pozsgay. "For too long we have been moored to the Eastern bank. Perhaps soon we will have a berth on the Western shore."

Almost parenthetically, as we prepared to leave, he added that he was preparing a four-day party congress, to begin the next day. Why didn't I come back when it was over, say on October 11 at 8:30 a.m.? He might have a little story for *Newsweek*.

And so, on the appointed day, I showed up early at his offices in the houses of parliament. "We don't know how all this will end," Pozsgay told me over coffee, making small talk about the changes taking place across the bloc. I was a little puzzled as to why I was there. Then, around nine o'clock, he smiled like the Cheshire Cat and got up, as if to go. He walked me to a door, different from the one I had entered by, and opened it, not for me but for himself. It was the entrance to the Assembly of the People. This morning, he explained, he would abolish the communist party. The Hungarian Socialist Workers Party would be no more. The old apparatchiks, the hoary edifice of dead-wood and social repression, the whole rank legacy, we could kiss it all good-bye. Pozsgay put his hand on the doorknob, smiled broadly and, with a hint of a chuckle, walked through the door.

CHAPTER ELEVEN

A Kiss of Death

History can be intimate, accidental, impersonal, ironic. It can seemingly just happen, implacably, or it can be cruel, as if by design, animated now and again by some cosmic sense of justice. How else to explain the bizarre fall of Erich Honecker, with all its uncanny symmetry?

The iconic May Day parade marked the zenith of Honecker's rule. No less important a date marked its nadir: October 7, the fortieth anniversary of the birth of the German Democratic Republic. It was to be the celebration of a communist lifetime. There would be a torchlight parade; one hundred thousand fresh-faced Freie Deutsche Jugend—Free German Youth—would march. Very Important People were arriving—the leaders of the East bloc, among them Mikhail Gorbachev. None knew, of course, that for most it would be their last hurrah. As for Honecker himself, it was as if fate were weaving three final strands into his destiny. The first bore the face of a titular ally, Gorbachev. The second was the secret conspiracy within. The third was the East German people, awakening from their long sleep and chanting, *"Wir sind das Volk*, We are the people,"* and who would no longer be ignored.

Thus the final drama commenced. Gorbachev starred as a sort of modern Cassandra, she of Greek legend whose prophecies, unheeded, came to pass. Honecker greeted him at the airport. They kissed in the style of communist leaders, on the mouth. It was an infamous photo: a pair of aging men, lip-locked. It quickly became an anticommunist opposition poster across Eastern Europe: THIS, it proclaimed, featuring a pair of young lovers; NOT THIS, with a red *X* over Gorbi and Erich. Honecker imagined it to be a seal of fraternal kinship. In fact, it was a kiss of death.

I had been told in Prague that Russian foreign minister Eduard Shevardnadze, two weeks earlier, delivered a stiff warning to his East German counterpart. Resolve the situation of the East German refugees in the West German embassy in Prague, or Gorbachev would cancel his trip. To what degree that element of added pressure figured in Honecker's mishandling of the crisis is not known, but it must have been considerable. In Budapest, a senior Hungarian official, also briefed by Shevardnadze, told me that Gorbachev's visit had only one purpose: to persuade Honecker to change. If he did not abandon policies of force and coercion, if he did not embrace some measure of glasnost and perestroika, Gorbachev would diss him at his own party.

Behind the scenes, meanwhile, the conspirators plotted. Between October 2 and October 6, the day Gorbachev and other East bloc leaders arrived, Egon Krenz and Gunter Schabowski secretly approached ten or so of their most trusted colleagues. Schabowski spoke with Werner Eberlein, the communist party chief of Magdeburg, and Harry Tisch, head of the workers' union, as well as several district secretaries. Krenz contacted Willi Stoph, the Politburo's elder statesman and head of the Council of Ministers, among others. They were surprised how little resistance they encountered. It was clear to all that Honecker had to go.

Ignorant of the net closing around him, Honecker welcomed his guests. But he wasn't always first to do so. Milos Jakes later told BBC–Spiegel Television how Egon Krenz had met him at the airport and driven with him to his hotel. "He told me that changes could be expected within the next few days," Jakes said. "The general secretary would no longer be Erich Honecker but Comrade Krenz himself." That evening's festivities brought a more visible sign of Honecker's troubles, in the shape of East Germany's communist youth marching in the torchlight parade. It was a stirring sight, all those young people with their uniforms in the firelight. But what did they cry out, according to Schabowski? " 'Gorbi! Gorbi! Gorbi!' They did not shout, 'Erich! Erich!' It was a clear repudiation."

Certainly Gorbachev saw it that way. The next afternoon, on October 7, he met with the East German Politburo. He had carefully thought about what he wanted to say. "I polished the text to the last letter," he told an aide over the phone. "You know they will scrutinize it under a microscope." He began by talking about glasnost and perestroika, how difficult it was to change. He mentioned the "mess" Poland had made of its economy, and how wise it would be to avoid such problems by acting sooner than later. "That's when he dropped that famous line, 'He who arrives late is punished by life,'" Schabowski told me, reconstructing the scene. "He was very tactful, very polite. Though he spoke about his own problems in the Soviet Union, it was clearly an invitation to speak frankly about ours."

But Honecker did not. Instead, he painted a bright picture of the country's future, congratulating himself that East Germany did not share in Russia's troubles, let alone Poland's. He boasted that East Germany had recently produced a four-megabyte computer chip. "It was surreal," Schabowski said. "There are demonstrations in the streets, and everything is beautiful?"

A long silence followed. "No one said anything," according to Schabowski. The conspirators, half a dozen of whom were in the room, knew they should agree with Gorbachev. "We should have gotten up, banged the table and said, 'Erich, enough of this foolishness.'" But knowing they would soon move against him, they stayed mum. Speaking out would only show their disloyalty and possibly jeopardize their plans. Gorbachev himself sat quietly for a moment, looking around the room as if astonished. No one met his eyes. "Then he snorted, a dismissive 'Tsk-tsk' of disbelief. He could not believe it. He shook his head, stood up and without any remark left the room. My impression was that this was the last straw. Gorbachev had concluded that nothing could be done with Erich Honecker."

At the state dinner that night, Honecker assigned the seat of honor on his right to Gorbachev. To his left sat old friend Jakes. Honecker rose to speak, flushed with high spirits and good feeling. As at the Politburo meeting that afternoon, he was unstinting in his praise of himself and his country and raised a toast to the GDR's fiftieth anniversary a decade hence. The political allies gathered in his honor were less sanguine. Gorbachev was positively rude. "During Erich's speech, he kept making sarcastic remarks," Jakes said in a subsequent television interview. "He made it plain that he stood apart from the East German leadership. It was quite out of keeping with the occasion."

As the celebrants dined in the splendor of the Palace of the Republic, protesters gathered in the square outside. Even within the salon where Gorbachev and Honecker sat, their voices could be heard: "*Gorbi, hilf uns!* Gorbi, help us!" Police barricaded the street, so the demonstrators marched along the river Spree behind the palace. Krenz and Schabowski left the hall to see. They also compared notes. Soviet foreign ministry spokesman Gennady Gerasimov was at Schabowski's table. "I told him things would change soon." Krenz spoke with one of Gorbachev's aides and made a similar allusion. Neither knew for sure whether the Soviet leader would know what they meant. Meanwhile, Schabowski noticed secret police chief Erich Mielke leaving the reception. The few hundred marchers outside the Palace of the Republic at the beginning of dinner had now been joined by thousands of others. Mielke had gone to tend to the messiness. How dare they, on this of all days? "He gave orders to beat them," Schabowski said.

I had arrived from Budapest that afternoon, too late for the official celebrations. The center of Berlin, near Honecker's ministries, was empty of life. But some blocks to the north, in the gritty working-class neighborhood of Prenzlauer Berg, young people were gathering in the thousands. At Gethsemane Church in Schonhauser Allee, known as the "rebel church" because of its support for the suddenly growing East German protest movement, so many people had come to debate the political situation that I could hardly wedge inside. In the surrounding streets, in windows and along tramlines, people held lit candles. "*Keine Gewalt,*" they called out. "No violence." They did not want to provoke the riot-clad security forces who in the darkness were erecting metal barriers and deploying around the neighborhood.

At one intersection, a crowd of several hundred protesters gathered to cheer themselves and jeer the regime. They waved to passing trams; the riders waved back or flashed victory signs. A double row of white-helmeted riot police, armed with clear-plastic shields and truncheons, faced off against them, closing the street. It was a close space and eerily intimate. Kids sat on the cobbled paving stones and sidewalks, candles cupped in their hands, flickering with a gentle yellow glow. A young man started up a conversation with one of the policemen:

"If you are for law, why are you beating us up?"

"We don't have to be having this conversation," the policeman replied.

"There's only one way to avoid violence. That's to talk."

"Why don't you talk through the newspapers? Or wait to see what happens in 1990," at the upcoming party congress.

The youth lit a cigarette for the cop, who lifted the Plexiglas visor shielding his face, saying, "We have to start now. That's why we are on the streets tonight."

At precisely that instant, the commander of the guard barked an order through his megaphone. "This is the People's Police! Disperse!" Abruptly, the visors went down and the police charged into the line of protesters. With surprised shouts, the crowd turned and fled. Some went down and were manhandled into police vans. Police dogs strained at their leashes. I'd taken off, too, an Olympic sprinter going for the gold. In all my travels through Eastern Europe's turmoil, this was my first brush with violence. I did not shine.

The demonstrations that erupted that night and the next were the first in Berlin and, so far, the largest in the country. Similar protests broke out in Dresden, Leipzig, Plauen, Chemnitz, Jena and Potsdam. Mielke dispatched sixteen thousand police into the streets of Berlin alone that night, wielding truncheons and spraying demonstrators with tear gas and water cannon. Many came from special antiterrorist units; others were thugs from the so-called People's Militia, uniformed in jeans, white sneakers and leather bomber jackets. They were particularly vicious, swaggering and cocksure, picking fights and randomly grabbing people and kicking them to the ground. More than a thousand people were arrested, many spending more than a week in jail, where they were beaten and packed into densely crowded cells. Hundreds were injured. Foreign journalists were expelled from East Berlin. Phone lines to the West were cut. "Happy birthday, police state!" one protester shouted as he fled. Another described the scene as a "Stasi Oktoberfest." Gorbachev was not impressed.

*   *   *

For years there was no opposition to speak of in East Germany. The ubiquitous Stasi, the largest and best-trained secret police in Eastern Europe, ruthlessly rooted out dissent in virtually every sphere of life. But the landscape had recently begun to change. A nascent opposition emerged and quickly gathered strength. As Havel put it of the Czechs, East Germans were finally "finding their courage." The question was how far Erich Honecker would go in putting them down. The fear in all quarters was a German Tiananmen.

At first, these groups were not overtly political. That spring, a tiny group of eco-activists, Umwelt Bibliothek, called on the government to take sterner measures to combat pollution. A group of several dozen rock musicians wrote an open letter to a West Berlin newspaper complaining that they were "sick of being criminalized" by the regime. An association of several hundred union and party officials calling themselves the United Left emerged over the summer promoting "free democratic socialism." Then, in mid-September, as East Germans began their sprint through the hole in the Iron Curtain cut by Hungary, four thousand people in Leipzig signed a petition supporting a new independent party known as Neues Forum, or New Forum. In a country where initialing a political manifesto could mean interrogation, loss of work and possibly jail, this was a dramatic development. Significantly, the signatories included a large number of young, reform-minded party officials, including a deputy chairman of Honecker's ruling State Council. Clearly, people were beginning to feel safety in numbers. The implications were not lost on East German authorities. When leaders of the New Forum applied to register their organization in twelve of the country's fifteen election districts, they were summarily rejected as "hostile to the state," an accusation nearly tantamount to treason.

Honecker himself gave this fledgling opposition both a louder voice and a broadly populist cause. The deal he conceived with the Czech government, allowing East German refugees free transit to the West by rail through the GDR, was the proverbial spark that ignited a firestorm. If so many other East Germans were winning their freedom, via Hungary or Prague, why couldn't others be free to travel, as well? On October 4 in Dresden, where the trains were still passing through to the Federal Republic, a mob of demonstrators gathered near the station, hurling paving stones and shouting epithets at police, who forcibly repelled them, beating many severely. The clashes became daily confrontations, featuring as many as thirty thousand citizens on October 7. The following day, with the security forces preparing more draconian measures, Dresden's mayor met with local churchmen and a citizens' committee to negotiate a "dialogue"—a sign of flexibility by the East German authorities that turned what otherwise promised to be a bloody riot into a delirious street party.

The events in Dresden were merely a curtain-raiser. A far more dramatic confrontation came the next day—October 9, a Monday—in Leipzig, the country's second-largest city. In a weekly rite beginning that spring, Leipzigers had been gathering at the Nikolaikirche in the center of the old city for a 5 p.m. prayer meeting. At the appointed hour, every Monday, they grouped together to inveigh against the regime's emigration policies and decry its inability to change. Only rarely were they more than several hundred people; with the September exodus from Hungary and the refugee crisis in Prague, however, their numbers swelled into the thousands. On September 25, they spilled out of the church, singing the American spiritual "We Shall Overcome," and onto Karl Marx Platz, where they were joined by some ten thousand others in a peaceful march around the city's central thoroughfare known as the Ring. The following Monday, October 2, the crowds were even larger. *"Wir bleiben hier,"* they shouted. We are staying!

Honecker saw the danger. Even before his embarrassment in Berlin, with protesters calling, "Gorbi, help us," he issued his orders: that Monday's demo would not be allowed. Three days before, on October 6, the party newspaper *Leipziger Volkszeitung* delivered a blunt warning. The state security police would no longer tolerate what the Leipzig Stasi chief Hans Geiffert described as "illegal and unauthorized" gatherings. *"Um diese konterrevolutionaren Aktionen endultig und wirksam zu unterbinden. Wenn es sein muss mit der* [sic] *Waffe in der Hand."* "We must be ready to suppress this counterrevolutionary action if need be with a weapon in our hand."

By early afternoon on that Monday, October 9, the Nikolaikirche was full. Those who could not get inside stood on the steps and surrounding streets. By 5 p.m., they numbered some seventy thousand. The stage was set for a bloodbath. The night before, Minister of State Security Erich Mielke ordered a full mobilization. Factory militias were reinforced with police reservists, called up on emergency footing. All through the preceding night, thousands of extra troops were trucked into the city. The Ring and the neighborhoods around the Nikolaikirche were thick with armed riot police. One commander told how he began distributing weapons and ammunition from the local armory. "I started with the lower ranks, giving out rubber truncheons, shields and helmets," Jens Illing told the BBC in a documentary reconstruction of the evening. "Then I gave the officers personal handguns—Makarova pistols, nine millimeter, with rounds. Each officer had at least two magazines. Then the company chief gave the order to ready a large number of Kalashnikov automatic rifles. These were loaded onto trucks and driven off."

The preparations worried many of the police, particularly local men such as Illing. He knew his mother and stepfather would be among the marchers and telephoned beforehand to warn them away. Another police commander, Silvio Rosler, told the BBC how officers tried to screen out "unreliables." "They interviewed us. You were unreliable if you weren't prepared to shoot at the demonstrators. It would be just like Tiananmen Square. 'It's them or us,' we were told. They were winding us up for a fight." Hospitals had been told to expect casualties. Doctors and nurses were on alert. Extra blood supplies had been stocked. Ambulances stood ready in streets along the Ring.

But if the hard-liners in the Politburo were prepared for violence, others were not. Egon Krenz would later claim that at the last moment he telephoned the commander of state security in Dresden and countermanded Honecker's orders. In truth, it was messier (and more typically communist) than that. Krenz clearly did not want blood on his hands. After all, he and others would soon move against Honecker, and authorizing violence against the people at this juncture would have doomed his own political future. But having been ordered by Honecker to personally "take charge in Dresden," what was he to do?

Krenz opted for a strategy of delay. In time-honored custom, he telephoned Soviet ambassador Vyacheslav Kochemasov late that afternoon, who according to some accounts disobeyed Gorbachev's orders to "listen but not advise" and argued forcefully against a "Chinese solution," especially one that might involve the use of the East German army. (Some suggest Krenz went out of his way to solicit Moscow's advice to proceed cautiously, should he later be called to account by Honecker.) He then told local commanders that it was best to avoid violence as they considered how to execute their orders from Mielke—and that they should act at their own discretion.

Krenz ducked, in other words. He knew that local communist leaders were divided, like the Politburo in Berlin. He apparently also calculated that, in the absence of direct orders from Berlin, they would avoid bloodshed. All that it took to tip the balance was the intervention of a modest outside force. It came in the form of art, as it seemed so often to do in Eastern Europe in 1989: a plea for "dialogue" from the director of the Leipzig orchestra, Kurt Masur, supported by local communist authorities and broadcast over the radio.

That was enough. Shortly after 6 p.m., the local party chief, Helmut Hackenberg, called Krenz—choosing, after careful deliberation, not to call Mielke or Honecker himself. The protest showed no sign of degenerating into violence, Hackenberg told Krenz. In his judgment, it was best to allow it to proceed. Krenz told him he would get back to him. He did so forty-five minutes later. "I have consulted with several ministers and members of the Politburo," said Krenz, "and we have concluded that your decision was correct."

And so the citizens of Leipzig marched. October 9 was to be the decisive victory of raw "people power" in all of 1989. Yet the danger was not over. At the weekly Tuesday morning Politburo meeting the next day, October 10, Honecker blamed the preceding night's unrest on NATO and Western provocateurs. As he stood up to leave, according to Schabowski, he once again asked, "What should we do about the demonstrators?" Perhaps, he suggested, it would be necessary to use force after all.

The conspirators were alarmed. The next march in Leipzig would take place the following Monday, October 16. They had chosen that following Tuesday meeting to stage their putsch. "This was a great crisis," Schabowski said. "What were we to do? It would utterly discredit our new government." Their solution was to do as they did the last week: ask Leipzig's leaders to restrain the demonstrators and nothing else. As the protesters filled the streets that night, Krenz waited until the last moment before issuing explicit instructions to the police not to interfere. "He waited until six p.m. to fax his orders," according to Schabowski. They feared Honecker would otherwise be alerted and personally direct the police to intervene.

That next day, on that fateful Tuesday, Honecker arrived at the Politburo at 10 a.m. He bid everyone good morning and shook hands with all. Then he opened the meeting. "I felt very bad, like Brutus," Schabowski recalled. Willi Stoph, the longest-serving party leader, was the first to plunge in the dagger. "Erich, I would like to propose a change in the agenda."

Honecker looked puzzled. He was not accustomed to interruptions. Stoph continued in bland apparatchikese: "I would like to propose the removal of the general secretary."

There followed a moment of "grotesque silence," Schabowski remembered. "Honecker's face went icy. Then he started again as if he hadn't heard, picking up where he left off."

"Erich," Stoph interjected, almost gently. "We must discuss this point."

Honecker appeared to recover his presence of mind. "All right. Let us have a discussion."

Incredibly, he then proceeded to lead it, as if it were the most normal thing in the world. He did not recognize even then how decisively events had turned. He asked who wanted to speak. As hands went up, he recognized those who would, he thought, support him. None did. Not even Erich Mielke, the hard-line head of the secret police.

Finally there came the vote, and with it Honecker's moment of truth. Gazing around the table at those who raised their hands against him, the dictator sat back in his chair and blinked. Then abruptly, he did what no one expected. Humbly, mutely, said Schabowski, "Erich raised his hand with the rest of them," a true communist to the end.

Poor Egon Krenz. The revolutions in Eastern Europe began as a subtle interplay of signs and symbols, but lately the message had become quite plain. Had he heeded the placards brandished by the crowds outside his offices, he could easily have foretold his future.

Among the more vivid was one composed of the word *Alt* (old) repeated dozens more times in small black print to create the letters of two larger words—*Neu?* (New?) *Nein*. Another featured a caricature of "Egon the Krenzman," with his toothy smile and bristly hair, nestled in bed and dressed in the bonnet and nightgown of Little Red Riding Hood. "Grandmother, what big teeth you have!"

To say that East Germans greeted their new leader with skepticism would be an understatement. "Grinning Egon"—another appellation—stepped into Erich Honecker's shoes only three weeks after visiting China, where he praised Beijing's bloody repression of the democratic protests in Tiananmen Square. After ousting Honecker, he immediately set about casting himself as a reformer, promising *Wende*—a dramatic change of direction, new openness and discussion, "dialogue." Welcome, glasnost and perestroika, GDR-style. He spoke of free elections, an end to censorship, a new constitution. Most important, he promised to rewrite the country's travel laws, offering East Germans what they wanted above all else.

No one believed him. He was, after all, a creature of the system—Honecker's protégé who rose through party ranks on his coattails. Like his mentor, he once headed the Free German Youth. As a member of the Politburo, he exercised ultimate authority over Mielke's hated Stasi. What he promised with one breath, he took back with the next. His first speech to the people whose hearts and minds he hoped to woo was a pastiche of contradictions and false starts. After proposing elections, he reaffirmed the "leading role" of his communist party. Though talking dialogue, he made no concessions to the country's newly emboldened opposition and instead spoke ominously of maintaining "law and order." As for material prosperity, he proposed to close the gap between East and West with something he called a "market-oriented socialist planned economy." Not even his own party bought that one. When it came time to approve him as head of state, twenty-six members of the normally rubber-stamp parliament voted against him and another twenty-six abstained. Such a display of independence had never before been seen.

Krenz could not comprehend that he was cursed, that his world had changed elementally. It mattered little that he came with good intentions. People sensed that he was an opportunist, that he was Honecker's man. His predecessor made sure of that, at least. As a last cruel gesture, in a brilliant act of sabotage, Honecker in resigning proposed a successor: not a "younger man," in keeping with the official fig leaf of his leaving for "reasons of health," but Krenz. Schabowski called it "the revenge of the pharaoh." Honecker knew who brought him down, just as he knew his blessing would do Krenz in. And so it was. Krenz was damaged goods, hamstrung from the get-go. His "reforms" would be seen as impotent holding actions, the cynical manipulations of one who wished only to hold power.

As the days passed, Krenz grew increasingly desperate. In an interview five months later, he would liken it to "riding a whirlwind." Everything was chaos, he told me. Nothing worked. In his book *Wenn Mauer Fallen*, he described how impossible it was to keep pace with events. "We decided something in the morning," he wrote, "and had to change it by evening." Meanwhile, the pressure mounted. On October 20, the day Krenz took office, fifty thousand people marched in Dresden demanding free elections. The next day, thirty-five thousand marched in Plauen and eighty thousand workers struck in Karl-Marx-Stadt. The weekly demonstration in Leipzig that Monday evening drew more than three hundred thousand. On November 4, half a million Berliners gathered on the Alexanderplatz in the city center to demand the right to travel freely.

If there was any moment when Krenz might have played the hero, salvaged some legitimacy for his rule, it was then. All he had to do was give people what they asked for: the right to come and go unhindered. But he could not break with the past. The very existence of the GDR was premised on social control, as was his own rule. So he moved by cautious shuffles and half steps, giving up as little as possible at every point, which turned out to be never quite enough.

He began in late October by promising "liberalizations" of the country's travel laws and assigned a "task force" to study the matter. Could there have been a more classically bureaucratic response than that? On November 1, as protests escalated, he reopened the border to Czechoslovakia and proposed to allow East Germans to visit the West from there. When that sparked even more unrest, he offered yet another timid compromise: travel abroad for up to a month a year, as approved by duly designated authorities. That very night—Monday, November 6—brought another huge demonstration in Leipzig, close to a million strong. This time the people demanded not only free travel but, for the first time, an end to communism itself.

Meanwhile, more East Germans than ever were fleeing the country. Krenz's decision to reopen the border to Czechoslovakia sparked a second massive exodus. Those who had not made a dash for freedom in September, and regretted it, now seized their moment. Once again, the West German embassy in Prague was overwhelmed with asylum seekers. This time, however, the Czech government played no games with trains. It quickly announced that East Germans would be free to cross its borders to the Federal Republic without condition. Over the weekend of November 4–5 alone, some twenty-five thousand East Germans did so. In a telephone call with President Bush on October 23, Helmut Kohl mentioned a conversation he had recently had with Gorbachev. The Russian leader told how he had pushed Honecker hard to reform during his recent visit. But neither man had much confidence in the leadership, including Egon Krenz. "The changes in the GDR are quite dramatic," Kohl told Bush. "Our estimates are that by Christmas we will have reached a total of 150,000 refugees, with an average age under thirty." (The actual number would exceed 250,000 by November 9.) It was the Great Escape all over again, only much, much bigger.

Late one afternoon on a wet and blustery day in early November—November 8, to be precise—I drove into the Bavarian mountains that range along the Czech frontier, just where East and West Germany and Czechoslovakia met. A long, narrow winding road ends near the town of Schirnding, hardly more than a few houses and a gas station clinging to the saddle of a piney ridge marking the border. On the way up, I passed caravans of Trabants trundling down in the opposite direction, their lights blinking feebly every time they hit a bump.

None of that prepared me for the scene at the border. Stretching into the distance, as far as I could see into the valley falling away below, was a double line of cars. Nearly every one was full. Beleaguered West German guards checked the East Germans' papers as Red Cross workers passed out tea and coffee. Volunteers from the West German automobile association worked around the clock to repair spluttering cars that were on the verge of giving out. The chief of the checkpoint looked as if he had not slept in days. "We are seeing more than ten thousand refugees every day," he said wearily. "They keep coming, all day and all night. We do not expect a letup." He figured one hundred thousand people had crossed over since the border opened roughly a week ago.

This was psychosis, a mass migration feeding on itself. "Twenty of my friends have gone to the West this year," said a twenty-three-year-old waiter from Jena. A young man, leaving with his girlfriend, told me how it had grown "lonely" back home. "We have as many friends in Frankfurt now as we do in Erfurt." A woman who hitchhiked through Czechoslovakia with her husband and young child said that the sight of so many people leaving made her pick up and go, too. "We didn't want to be the last ones to leave and turn out the lights."

At Schirnding, I realized with sudden and perfect clarity that this could not go on. The German Democratic Republic was hollowing out. In Leipzig, one refugee told me, half of the city's bus drivers had left. Retirees were coming back on the job; army soldiers were being assigned to fill in. A young East German from a village on the Baltic, sailboard strapped to the top of his car, told how his parents were having trouble finding the sugar, almonds and flour they needed to run their bakery. Food and other scarce goods were piling up in warehouses because so many truck drivers had disappeared. Buildings were without heat and water because the superintendents had left. Trains ran late because the brakeman or the switchboard operator or the engineer was gone. People would go home one day, as usual, never to be seen again. The manager of a factory sports team in Dresden crossed the border, a soccer ball in the backseat of his car. His team had recently gone on holiday in Czechoslovakia. Only half came back, he said with a rueful laugh. "How can you run a factory when you do not know how many of your employees will show up each morning?" Highly trained professionals were leaving in particularly large numbers. A third of the doctors at Magdeburg's prestigious medical academy failed to return from vacation over the summer; forty-one nurses and doctors had left East Berlin's Hedwig Hospital in recent months. Wittenberg's hospital for the disabled faced closure because of staff losses. So did its nursing home. "If you pull enough bricks out of a wall, it will fall down," a British diplomat had told me in East Berlin a few weeks earlier. He was right. The German Democratic Republic was close to collapse.

I had planned to spend the night in Nuremberg, the nearest large town to Schirndling and fly back to Bonn in the morning. My gut told me not to. *This cannot go on.* Sensing that I had to move, fast, I got in my rented BMW and made my way down the mountain, threading through the smoking Trabants. I accelerated to something exceeding 140 miles per hour, once I hit the autobahn, toward midnight, tendrils of fog coiled over the road in the cold dampness, interspersed far ahead in my headlights with faint, flickering red dots. What could they be? It was too cold for fireflies. . . . Almost too late, I realized they were the dim taillights of the little Trabbis, wandering down the center of the autobahn at about thirty miles an hour. They shook as I swerved and blew by.

Some I stopped to help. They parked by the side of the highway, sometimes in the highway. Which way is Hamburg? Cologne? Dortmund? It was so cold and windy that my map shattered, like glass. Did I have a phone book for Germany? They had relatives in the West and wanted to call. I asked in what city. They were not sure. "You mean, there are many phone books?" I arrived at my bureau in Bonn about six hours later, just before dawn, and wrote frantically through the morning about all that I had seen. It would become *Newsweek*'s next cover story. Then I caught a midafternoon flight for Berlin. A few minutes after I crossed into the eastern sector later that evening, GDR police closed the border. To this day, I still feel queasy at how close I came to missing all that would happen next.

CHAPTER TWELVE

The Fall

Thursday, November 9, 1989. Egon Krenz began his day early. He arrived at the office well before first light, having left it only hours earlier. By 9 a.m. he was presiding over an emergency summit of the Central Committee. His fledgling government was in meltdown. The communist rank and file were screaming. Like the ordinary citizens marching in a dozen cities, they too had lost faith—in their party, in the regime, in one another. The old policies obviously had to be scrapped. New policies were required. The generation of hard-line apparatchiks clearly had to go, for the times demanded new faces. But who, how, what, when?

Krenz had been in full crisis-management mode from the moment he took office. In a tumultuous session the day before, five holdovers from the old regime were brusquely tossed out. Among them, the titular prime minister, Willi Stoph, who had been the first to confront Honecker. Erich Mielke, the minister of state security, and a pungent bouquet of other retrogrades were also gone. In their place, Krenz appointed the popular, reform-minded mayor of Dresden, Hans Modrow, who had played a key role in preventing violence during the Leipzig marches, as well as an opposition writer named Christa Wolf. But even that was not enough. The communist party was consumed in a fury of self-criticism and mutual denunciation.

The historian Charles Maier captured the mood in his dramatic account of the GDR's final days, *Dissolution*. Delegates pointed fingers. You should resign! No, you should! The regime's handling of the demonstrations came under biting attack, with acrimonious calls for investigations. Specifics were deleted from the official minutes, for fear of pouring oil on the fire. "The working class is so angry that they are going to the barricades," one enraged delegate declared. "They're howling, 'Get the party out of the factories.' They want to cut the unions, get rid of the party secretaries."

The party faithful listened, aghast, as Gerhard Schurer, the country's economics czar, outlined the depths of East Germany's problems. No one knew, ever even dreamed, that the country was in such straits—near bankrupt, verging on collapse, dependent almost entirely for its survival on under-the-table handouts from the Federal Republic worth several billion dollars a year. To the rank and file, this was a revelation. In the popular mind, even among senior officials who might be expected to know better, the GDR was the industrial powerhouse of the East bloc.

Listening to Schurer relentlessly walk through the numbers, their confusion and dismay grew. Erich Honecker sought to make East Germany the model of successful socialism: a consumer society as well as a caring welfare state. But the dirty little secret was that a hidebound, centrally planned state-owned economy could not deliver. To assure the people's support, the government subsidized everything: housing, food and fuel costs, education, medical care, vacations and pensions. Investment in industrial productivity came a distant second. State revenue long ago began to fall short of needs. To fill the gap, East Berlin began borrowing—ever more heavily—from the West. As early as 1973, according to Maier, one courageous senior adviser tried to tell Honecker that his policies were a recipe for bankruptcy and showed him exact projections of how the country's debt would soon begin eating up larger and larger percentages of national income. Honecker brusquely ordered him to stop his work and destroy the data. It was not what he wanted to hear.

By the fall of 1989, the sky was dark with pigeons coming home to roost. According to Schurer, East Germany's foreign debt that October exceeded $26 billion. Interest payments alone cost $4.5 billion, nearly two-thirds of yearly national income and one and a half times export earnings. Putting the country's fiscal house in order would entail cuts in living standards of 30 percent, he estimated, if not far more. Everyone listening knew that such austerity was politically impossible. Labor strikes had already broken out in some cities where subsidies were cut.

There were runs on banks in Dresden and Schwerin. The more the assembled delegates heard, the more panicked they became. Clearly, the country could not go on this way. The GDR was doomed, as they saw it, not because of the inherent flaws of communism, but because of bad leadership. Erich, they brayed. You have betrayed us! You and your cronies! Fear, loathing, hatred, blame, recrimination took over. There was a frenzied biting, the rage of the mob devouring its ideals, one another, history, the future. As Schabowski mordantly put it, "Those who thought the party still mattered fought over who would lead it."

Amid this maelstrom, Krenz struggled with a second crisis: the continuing exodus and the right to travel. Above all else, East Germans wanted passports and the right to use them when and how they saw fit, without restriction. Krenz knew that to stay in power he must meet their demands. Yet everything he had tried so far was too little, too late, too communist. On November 7, even the once tame parliament shot down his latest plan—to allow citizens to travel up to one month a year, provided they applied for a visa and did not take their families along. Too timid, the lawmakers told him, and sent him back to the drawing board.

By the afternoon of November 9, Krenz was ready to try again. According to Schabowski, now the acknowledged number two on the Politburo, his hopes were high. The two men imagined the new measure as a beautiful "Christmas present." In their minds, they saw relatives in East and West Germany crossing the border, joyfully celebrating their reunion. As Schabowski put it, "We would be the patron saints of German unification!" Working through the preceding night and all that morning, officials of the Interior Ministry and the Ministry of State Security produced what they considered a revolutionary document. It declared that all East Germans who possessed a passport would be entitled to an exit visa allowing them to pass through any border crossing, anywhere and at any time, including Berlin. People lacking a passport could have their identity cards marked with a special *Stempel*, a stamp granting them an exit right. All the logistics were ready. Stamps. Visas. Pertinent rules and regulations. "This was our message to the people," said Schabowski. "'You are free to go, without restriction. We hear you, we are changing, here is what you seek. Send us your hosannas.'"

Of course, it was not to be. Anything involving the Wall was dangerous. It was a high-wire act, with no room for mistakes. Krenz proceeded carefully, despite his haste. In midafternoon, he took his resolution to the Central Committee. Stopping their acrimonious debate as to who would have power and who would not, he bade them pause to reflect. Here was a solution, he told them. Krenz read out his proposal. He read it sentence by sentence, he wrote in his biography, *Das Politburo*, and later told me. He read it slowly, emphatically, so that no one could claim not to understand. The policy would take effect "henceforth," meaning the next day. Tomorrow, November 10, he would open the border. At 4 p.m. or so, after desultory discussion, the Central Committee approved the plan—and went back to their intramural bickering.

And so it was. Around 5 p.m., Gunter Schabowski stopped by Krenz's offices. He was off to his daily press conference, a public hearing they had begun the week before as another sign of the regime's new openness. "Anything to announce," he asked so innocently. Krenz told him the good news. The new travel law had just been approved. Schabowski gave him a thumbs-up and turned to go. "Wait," Krenz said, as if deciding something on the spot, almost impulsively. Then he handed Schabowski that two-page document, the paper he had just read out so carefully to the Central Committee, along with the press release meant for tomorrow. "Take this. It will do us a power of good."

Krenz had placed all his hopes on that document. Everything hinged upon it. Krenz was a cool man under fire. He would not have gotten where he was otherwise. But at the decisive moment, he made a fatal misstep.

It was so small, a scarcely noticed misunderstanding of *ab sofort*— "henceforth," immediately. That was the word used in the document he handed Schabowski. As Krenz had so scrupulously explained to the Central Committee, "henceforth" meant tomorrow, November 10. Orders to that effect would soon be issued to all the relevant ministries and authorities—border guards, passport officials, all those administering the new regulations. But he explained none of this to Schabowski, who was even now scanning the memo in his limo on the drive to the press conference.

Did Krenz simply forget? Did he assume that Schabowski knew all this, forgetting that only he had sat through those endless discussions at the Central Committee, not Schabowski? Or was Krenz simply tired? The pressure of the last few months had been unrelenting. There had been no room for error, either in pushing Honecker out or in trying to hold the country together. Now he sensed a victory. He was doing something right, something that might work. Perhaps at that moment he let down his guard, relaxed just a bit, neglected that last crucial detail. Whatever the case, the mistake would change the world.

A few minutes after six o'clock, Gunter Schabowski stepped before the cameras. Among the various items to announce, he put the decree on travel close to last. "I read it out," he told me, reliving the decisive moment. "Then came that question: when does it take effect?"

No matter how many times you watch the video, the moment never ceases to amaze. There he was, confused. He propped his glasses on the end of his nose, shuffled through his papers. There was nothing about a release date, no mention of November 10. Only that cryptic *sofort*. So what did he say? *"Sofort,"* of course. Immediately, right now.

"What was I to do?" he would explain later, almost plaintively. "I couldn't exactly say, 'Oh, never mind.' "

Ab sofort. Those words, broadcast live, flashed across the country. I had crossed into East Berlin, through Checkpoint Charlie, scarcely half an hour before East German police closed the border. I was lucky. For Western correspondents, you were either already there or you watched what happened next on television.

It was too late to make Schabowski's briefing, so along with a *Newsweek* colleague, Karen Breslau, I headed for the Hotel Metropole on Friedrichstrasse. It was an *haut communiste* concrete wreck with only two telephone lines to the West. In the dirty-marbled lobby, plainclothes policemen, in their East European uniforms of leather jackets and cheap blue jeans, slumped smoking on shabby sofas and grease-stained chairs. Checking in, Karen overheard startling news. A young receptionist whispered incredulously to the hotel operator, "You mean we can just go?"

We dumped our bags and jumped in our rented car. It quickly became obvious something was happening. East Berlin's gritty streets, lit here and there by yellow arc lights, were usually dark and abandoned. Tonight, people were out, calling to one another. Some waved at our car, noticing the West Berlin license plates. Three young men in their early twenties frantically thumbed for a ride, an infringement of the rules that not so long ago could get you arrested. "Take us to West Berlin," one shouted out, telling us the news. "We're free to go. Schabowski said so."

Sven, Matthias and Sasha wanted to leave now, instantly. They clambered into the back of our Volkswagen. More people were on the streets now, flagging rides or walking in groups toward the Wall. We felt their excitement, even in the darkness. We stopped by Sasha's apartment so he could pick up some money and say good-bye to his parents; he feared it might be forever. Pools of water and mud collected on the broken pavement outside the sooty and decayed concrete edifice. Within five minutes, he was back. I remember being impressed less by his daring than by his nonchalance. For the new life that lay before him, he carried only a book bag and a change of clothes.

We drove to Checkpoint Charlie. A few dozen people stood about, keeping out of the floodlights and away from the guards and the dogs. "You must obtain an exit visa. You must have a *Stempel*," the police told people who approached them about the news, politely but firmly turning them away. But that in itself fanned the excitement. So, it was true, they thought to themselves. There had been an announcement.

We hopped in the car to see other checkpoints. People were gathering at all of them, confused but exhilarated, shouting to one another and, increasingly, to the guards whom only moments before they'd feared. "*Sofort,*" some of them began shouting, echoing Schabowski. "Open up!"

We went back to Checkpoint Charlie. The border police were obviously growing worried. There weren't just dozens or hundreds of people anymore, but thousands, milling and churning and threatening to get out of control. More kept arriving every minute, channeled toward the checkpoint along three streets that converged upon the gates to the West.

By 9 o'clock, people were becoming more brazen. "Open up! Open up!" Emboldened by their numbers, they pushed within a few meters of the barricades. Guards stood nervously with their weapons. If things got out of hand, I wondered, would they shoot? Inside his lighted, glass-walled command post, the beefy Doberman of a post commander stood dialing and redialing his telephone. Calls flew from checkpoints up and down the Wall to the Interior Ministry, to no avail. Top officials tried to reach the members of the Politburo, but the leaders of the regime seemed to have disappeared. Schabowski had gone home. He received the first alert from a fellow Politburo member around 9:30 p.m. What had he done? What to do now? No one had a clue, least of all Schabowski. Nor could Krenz be found. The minister of interior wasn't about to issue orders contrary to his instructions. The head of the state visa office, who'd drafted the new law and was responsible for enforcing it, was at the theater. When he returned around 10:30 p.m., the checkpoints were mobbed. He, too, telephoned futilely for instructions. "I couldn't find anyone to talk to," he later told TV reporters. "What a mess," he thought to himself.

Soon it was too late. On the Western side of Checkpoint Charlie, tens of thousands of West Berliners gathered. "Come over! Come over," they shouted. "We are trying," the East Berliners shouted back, shoving to within a few feet from the guards, their steaming breath commingling in the frosty air. Something, somebody, had to give.

The commander of the checkpoint surveyed the scene. Who knows what passed through his mind. Perhaps he heard that the larger Bornholmerstrasse checkpoint, to the north, had just opened its barriers. Perhaps he made his own choice, deciding: "Enough of this farce." Whatever the case, at 11:17 p.m., precisely, he shrugged his shoulders, just as Schabowski had done, as if to say, *Why not?*

"Alles auf!" he ordered, and the gates swung open. A great roar went up, the crowds surged forward. Among the first to cross to the West, to realize the dream of millions of her countrymen, and millions more East Europeans for more than four decades, was a woman in hair curlers, a coat thrown hastily over her baby blue bathrobe. I had watched her for hours, bobbing up and down on her toes, trying

to keep warm amid the throngs but also too excited to much notice the cold. There she was one moment, and the next, history literally swept her up. Like a flood suddenly unleashed, a wave of people arose and carried her away. Half riding the tide, she turned her head and shouted to a friend standing to the side, "I'll be back in ten minutes! I just want to see if it's real!"

With that, the Berlin Wall was no more. *"Die Mauer ist Weck,"* the people cried, punching their fists in the air as they danced atop it before the cameras at the Brandenburg Gate in the scene that played over and over and over around the world. "The Wall is gone!"

Egon Krenz called it "a botch." He blamed Schabowski, who blamed Krenz. He had not intended to just throw open the gates. He certainly did not intend to bring down the Wall, at least not in this way. The whole thing shouldn't have happened. Yet it did, with all the logic of human messiness.

Schabowski thought the Wall would have fallen regardless of the accident. But let's assume, for a moment, that Schabowski hadn't messed up and Krenz's travel laws had taken effect in an orderly, undramatic and efficiently German way. Strictly speaking, the Wall would not have "fallen." It would have been opened, not breached. The communists would have done it, not the people. Change might have come by evolution, not revolution. The bureaucrats would have gained time. Might they even have contained or channeled popular unrest, defused it, convinced people that reformed communism could work, possibly even kept themselves in power? Without the drama of the Fall, and all its inspiring visuals, would the Velvet Revolution in Prague have come one week later? Would Romanians have found the courage to rise against Ceausescu a month later? The dominoes of Eastern Europe might have toppled differently. A few might not have toppled at all.

Forty-eight hours after the first Germans clambered atop the Wall, I stood through a freezing night with several thousand West Berliners in the muddy no-man's-land that was Potsdamer Platz. An East German construction crew was knocking a new passageway through the Wall, and it was tough going. A giant crane strained to lift a twelve-foot-high slab, but it wouldn't budge. The crowd shouted encouragement: "Heave ho. Heave ho." A helmeted worker repeatedly hoisted himself up on the Wall and applied a blowtorch to the steel rods holding it in place. He became something of a favorite, and whenever he appeared the crowd burst into the German equivalent of "For he's a jolly good fellow." From time to time, he tipped his cap or waved. Sparks flew as the blowtorch did its work. The crane jerked the slab back and forth, twisting it like a broken tooth. Finally it gave way and hung suspended above the crowd, twisting slowly, as if from a gibbet. Television floodlights illuminated its broken surface, scrawled with grafitti. All the unresolved conflicts of Europe were on that chunk of painted concrete: a neo-Nazi swastika, surrealistic faces of . . . who, Europe's dead? Most notable was a word. *Freiheit*, it read. Freedom.

How odd that it should be that word, on this particular slab, the first to be torn from the Wall in the heart of old Berlin. That evening, as the sun settled in the west, a huge and perfect orange ball burning into the earth, the moon had risen to the east, as perfectly full and round as the sun, cool and bluish white. It was as though they were in balance, moving on an invisible axis, with Berlin poised between them equidistant, at once suspended and a fulcrum. *Freiheit*. It was almost enough to make one believe in destiny, here in this haunted land of ghosts. The word felt ambiguous then, more so now. Freedom to do . . . what?

Most immediately, it was the freedom to go shopping. East German noses pressed up against the storefronts of the West. My journals are full of images: traffic jams up to thirty miles long at border crossings. A new Berlin airlift—to get goods into stores, all the things Easterners could not for so long buy: stockings, decent electronics, sex magazines. An East Berliner riding around West Berlin on his battered old bike with big balloon tires, a map taped to his handlebars and a plump stalk of bananas on his back—all for him, who probably never had one. A farmer driving his smoke-belching pre–World War II tractor down the Ku'damm, Berlin's fanciest shopping drag, shouting, "Freedom for all" and shaking marimba gourds.

Intellectuals gazed loftily upon the scene. Freedom as travel and window-shopping? Yet what could be more human, after all these years? Of course, freedom meant freedom to think. East Germans had that. Lacking was the right to speak, which they began to do, cautiously at first and in small ways, but then all at once and as loud as possible, trumpeting, "Berlin is one again!"

Egon Krenz had been thinking, too. He had made his calculations to oust Honecker, to intervene in Leipzig, to free East Germans to travel. Go for it, his instincts told him now. The day after the Wall came down, he held a rally on the steps of the old State Museum on Unter den Linden. Ten thousand people came, chanting, "Keep going, Egon!" "We are the communists!" Half of them wore Stasi-style leather jackets and waved posters proclaiming such exhilarating sentiments as WE ARE FOR ACTION WITH A PROGRAM! Obviously, most of the people there were friendly plants. Krenz waded into their midst like a Boston pol, glad-handing everyone in sight and later talking for half an hour with reporters. He was convinced he could get out in front and lead the new changes. But other people were thinking. Toward the end of the rally, a man shouted out, "I wonder whether we really need a communist party in this country. I'm not even sure we need you." Party elders quickly beckoned the man with crooked fingers, among them Gunter Schabowski, as if to say, "You need a good talking-to."

Here was a face in the crowd. Everyone saw, everyone heard. Just as they would in Leipzig, the next week, at yet another of the city's huge rallies. Would the communists lose power after the Fall? Now that the Wall was gone, what would the people be marching for?

It was a freezing-cold night. Outside the Nikolaikirche, where the demonstrators gathered, a new mood was in the air. People were chanting the usual slogans: *Wir sind das Volk*, "We are the people." But they also sang a hymn to the German fatherland. Then, as if from nowhere, came the call, as immediately clear and commanding as a clarion. Not *Wir sind das Volk* but *Wir sind ein Volk*. "We are one people." Instantly it was taken up, and the rest was writ. Here, too, was a face in the crowd.

Jens Reich, the opposition leader who emerged from quiescence in the autumn of 1989 to help found the New Forum and went on to become a member of the German parliament, talked about the phenomenon of the individual within crowds. He told of addressing half a million people in Alexanderplatz on November 4, the largest protest in German history. "It was an almost mystical experience. You do not see just a black crowd. You see individual faces. It is impossible to say how such a crowd will react. That day, I feared it might march en masse to the Wall, where military force would have been applied to stop them. Why did they not? Why do some things happen one way, and not another?"

Within the crowd, within what he called the "exhilarating, uplifting mass of people moving and acting," said Reich, there is choice, oddly and persistently individualistic. The man who called out, "We are one people!" The one who asked Krenz whether he was needed—publicly posing the unwanted question, forcing the answer, desecrating the symbol. These were people making choices. This was not the crowd but the faces in the crowd, voices that moved it. Perhaps this is so obvious as to verge on banality. Yet so often we write and think of history as somehow inevitable, a culmination of great grinding forces and structures that can only lead to where they end up. Not so. The reality of 1989, said Reich, is that "it was possible at any point, at any time, for events to take a different course." Why this, not that? The answer seems to be those countless individual choices at key moments, the accidents of human messiness, such as Schabowski's "botch," so small and so understandable yet so earthshaking. Among them, too, were Reich's own choices: not to stay quiet anymore, to risk a beating and speak out, so as to not have to answer to the next generation, "We sat and waited."

It is immensely heartening, this view of history. So intimate, so uplifting, so human. Yes, the revolutions in Eastern Europe owed much to the power of the people. They also owed much to the power of some people, to what a few did or failed to do, to individuals fumbling about in the face of tottering totalitarianism, to courageous dissidents writing and smoking and plotting, to inspired reformers, to frightened conspirators, and later to powerful thugs manufacturing wars.

After the French revolution came the Glory. After the Glory came the Terror. So it was in Eastern Europe. Prague's Velvet Revolution was a party, a glorious exultation in almost effortlessly bringing down another communist regime. Romania was a troubling interlude, part people's uprising, part artfully concealed coup, with no happy denouement except for those who plotted Nicolae Ceausescu's overthrow. Then came the war, the slaughterhouse of Yugoslavia. As Robespierre followed upon Danton, Milosevic followed upon Nemeth and Havel. We celebrated the happier expressions of the power of the people, so wildly and enthusiastically, that we tended to forget the power of some people, for evil as well as good.

CHAPTER THIRTEEN

Aftermath

On the morning of November 10, Helmut Kohl flew from Warsaw to Berlin. That evening, returning to his residence in Bonn, he telephoned George Bush.

"I have just arrived from Berlin," he told the president. "It has the atmosphere of a carnival! The frontiers are absolutely open. At certain points they are literally tearing down the Wall. At Checkpoint Charlie, thousands of people are crossing both ways!"

Everything depended on the new government of Egon Krenz. "If the people see a light at the end of the tunnel," Kohl said, they will stay home. Otherwise East Germans will leave en masse—"a catastrophe for the GDR. They are doctors, lawyers, specialists, who cannot be replaced." The country would implode.

The situation required delicate handling, both men agreed. Above all there should be no triumphant geopolitical crowing, no premature talk of a brave new world. "I want to see our people continue to avoid hot rhetoric that might by mistake cause a problem," Bush said.

"Excellent," replied Kohl. "Give my best to Barbara."

Bush knew as well as Kohl that this was the endgame. From then on, they would work together for calm. The goal, as they would soon begin to discuss explicitly, was unification. Focused on Germany, they did not foresee how quickly the other dominoes of Eastern Europe would topple.

"Mike, I think you should be here."

My Czech translator, Zdenka Gabalova, was calling from Prague.

175

A "little gathering" would take place that evening in the old Vysehrad Cemetery, up in the hills overlooking the city. Fifty years ago, on November 17, 1939, nine Czech students were executed after demonstrations against the Nazi occupation. History, yes. But in the subtext of Czech dissidence, the commemoration would protest a more contemporary oppression. "It might be interesting for you," Zdenka ventured.

But I was in Berlin, I protested. The Wall had just come down. Who knew what might happen next? I couldn't leave now.

The "little gathering" grew into a demonstration of twenty thousand people, most of them students. They lit candles amid the terraced gardens and rising church spires of Vysehrad, the burial grounds of Smetana and Dvorak. They sang the national anthem, "Where Is My Homeland?" Poland, Hungary and now even East Germany had sloughed off bankrupt communist regimes. "We don't want to be last!" shouted the young people again and again.

Down from the hills they came, their candles glimmering in the darkness along the embankment of the river Vltava. "Down with communism!" "Jakes out!" At the National Theater, lit up in gilt Hohenzollern splendor, they turned into the street whose name would within hours become known to the world, Narodni. Riot police blocked their way, three rows deep, white-helmeted with plastic shields and truncheons. Another phalanx closed in behind, trapping the vanguard of marchers. The crowds halted a few feet from the wall of police. Those in the front tried to hand them flowers, placed candles of peace on the pavement before them, raised their hands in a gesture of youthful innocence. Then, from behind, the security forces advanced, using armored bulldozers to squeeze the people—perhaps three thousand in all—more tightly into their trap. Police with megaphones ordered, "Disperse!" Yet they would not let anyone escape the ring of steel.

Martin Mejstrik, a twenty-three-year-old theater student, worked for a year to organize the rally. Faced with a potential Tiananmen, he telephoned the police commander who had authorized the gathering and promised not to interfere. "You assured us there would be no violence," said Mejstrik.

"Don't be afraid," the man replied. "Nothing will happen."

Shortly after 9 p.m., Martin returned to Narodni Street, just in time to see the police hurl themselves upon the crowds.

Ten years later, we walked the street where it happened. "People were pressed so closely together that they could hardly breathe, let alone run," Martin recounted. "The police just beat them and beat them, swinging their clubs with all their force." Here, in front of the chic new Café Louvre, the police stopped the march. Down there, not far from a recently opened outlet for Just Jeans, they sprang their trap. Just here, down this narrow side street, no wider than an alley, was the only way out. It became a gauntlet. Special antiterrorist units in distinctive red berets lined either side, separated by about six feet. People were clubbed and pummeled as they ran between them—men, women and children. Those who fell were hit and kicked where they lay.

One young girl, a drama student, told me at the time how a policeman kicked out her candles, then slapped her. "Do you really need to do this?" she asked him. At that, he grabbed her by the hair and banged her head several times against a building, knocking her unconscious. A bland official announcement on state television later declared that order had been restored and that thirty-eight people had been treated for "light injuries."

Havel had predicted it. "Sooner or later," he had said in June, "they will make a mistake, perhaps by beating up some people. Then forty thousand people will fill Wenceslas Square." Black Friday, as the night of November 17 came to be known, was the spark that set Czechoslovakia alight. The challenge for Havel and his small band of dissident revolutionaries would be to fan that spark, stoke the fire and guide it.

How brilliantly they performed! Prague was Eastern Europe's happiest revolution, a delirium of good feeling. It was also the fastest, a revolution of passionate compression. Once it got going, the communists almost ran from power. This gentle revolution, this "Velvet Revolution" as Havel dubbed it, was sheer theater, a geopolitical spectacular as masterfully choreographed as the playwright's own absurdist comedies. It unfolded in vignettes, scenes and acts, with cameo appearances by famous faces from the past. Alexander Dubcek. Joan Baez. Dissidents just released from jail. Eminent émigrés suddenly returned home. The theme music was the Velvet Underground's "Waiting for the Man." The stage was the Magic Lantern, the underground theater that served as Havel's headquarters. The backdrop was Prague, impossibly romantic, the city of a hundred spires, tawny ocher houses and churches, sifting late-afternoon light, moonlight on the Vltava. The cast changed constantly, an immensely colorful cavalcade of friends and oddly assorted comrades-in-arms: philosophers, academics, journalists, students, boiler stokers, engineers, ditchdiggers, drunks, poets, hangers-on, hangers-out, pretty girls, all caught up in an intoxicating swirl of revolution, excitement, passion, sex and intrigue.

The audience, of course, was the world. We watched it happen on TV. We saw the people, standing in the hundreds of thousands in Wenceslas Square. It was revolution as a street party, the climax of the story that was the Year of the Fall, a turning point in history: cliché transmuted into Truth. We knew our heroes would win. Everyone swept up by it felt young again, as though the world had suddenly, mysteriously, euphorically been made new.

This revolution was counted in days. Day One was the "massacre," as everyone called it. Day Two was a call to arms. Martin Mejstrik and other student leaders at the theater academy of Charles University called for a general strike. By afternoon, the journalist faculty had joined them. Then the actors. Then the artists and musicians. Meeting at the Realistic Theater, not far from Charles Bridge in a neighborhood of twisting cobblestone streets and tilting medieval houses, these various groups combined forces and set a date: Monday, November 27, from noon to 2 p.m. Thus the Velvet Revolution began.

On Day Three, a Sunday, Vaclav Havel returned from his country house in northern Bohemia. He had chosen not to be in Prague the day of the Vysehrad march or the next, for fear of being arrested. In the early afternoon, a small group of dissidents met at his apartment overlooking the Vltava; the presidential palace, or Hrad, loomed in the distance. This was the time. They all knew it. They needed to create an organization, a Czech Solidarity. What to call it? A young dissident named Jan Urban—*Rambo* to his friends, in honor of his penchant for goading the police and leading them on chases across Prague's rooftops—proposed *Forum*, after the New Forum in East Germany. Havel suggested *Civic*, for the democratic civil society they wished to create. "That was that," Urban recalled. "Civic Forum was born." Havel would lead it. Jan and his best friend, Ivan Gabal, my translator's husband and a founder of a group called the Circle of Independent Intelligentsia, would be among the chief organizers.

They wasted little time. They demanded the resignation of communist leaders responsible for the Soviet invasion of 1968, most prominently President Gustav Husak and the boss of the communist party, Milos Jakes. They called for an investigation into the authorities' handling of the Friday-night massacre and the resignation of the men in charge. They appealed to all Czechs to support the students' strike. Then they disappeared into the night, hiding out in friends' apartments and other secret places, waiting to see how the regime would react.

On Day Four, I arrived. Driving in from the airport late that Monday afternoon, my taxi took a circuitous route to avoid the main bridges into town. "Closed by tanks," the driver explained. Shades of '68. But at the central Wenceslas Square, a surprise awaited. It was teeming with people, bubbling with fun and good spirits—and not a policeman in sight. Over the weekend, thousands of students had begun gathering in the Square to protest Friday night's beatings. Authorities did not intervene, and so the crowds grew. By Monday afternoon, they numbered in the tens of thousands, a mass of people already far too big for the police to easily disperse were they tempted to try. "I've never seen anything this big," said a twenty-three-year-old art student named Renata. "We are ready to fight. We have had enough. We want to be free to speak our minds." A well-dressed man with a briefcase told me that he had been a teenager in 1968. "I believe this is the end of the regime," he predicted. "There will be no more violence. The police are afraid. Soon, they will start thinking about how to save themselves." Besides, how could they resist this, he added, gesturing toward the people milling about us. There, a father with a child on his shoulders. Here, an elderly couple, he with a cane, she in a fur hat. A young woman said incredulously, "My mother is taking part. She used to say, 'Don't get involved. Stay away from all this.' And tonight, here she is!"

This was revolution as a family outing. Exuberant crowds invented a new Czech national anthem. Anyone could play it. You just took your house keys out of your pocket and jingled them above your head. Tens of thousands were doing it, and the noise drowned out everything, like the ring of a thousand alarm clocks. Time to wake up. Your time is up. The din was deafening. "Jakes! Jakes! Jakes!" "Freedom!" "Democracy!" "Down with the government!" A spade was planted in a trampled municipal rose garden. Attached to it was a sign: WHO'S THIS FOR? The answer was already obvious.

The evening news was a revelation. The state-run media had changed sides. After years of shading events, anchors truthfully reported that students were on strike. Martin Mejstrik was given airtime. "Things have gone too far," he declared on national TV. "There is no longer any room for talk, no other choice but to strike!" The chancellor of Charles University, a pillar of the communist elite, announced that he supported the movement. Students at universities across the country abandoned their classrooms, professors threw out their lecture notes. Theaters went dark as musicians, actors, sound technicians declared their support for the strike, as well. And all this on TV.

"They are finished," said Zdenka, shaking her head when Jakes issued a gray communist statement: "We agree with measures taken to maintain public order." Stupidly, he sided with the thugs of Friday night, for all to see. That night, I went to bed with my windows open, despite the cold, and fell asleep to the myriad jingling of keys from the streets below.

The Grand Hotel Europa, in the heart of Wenceslas Square, was built at the height of central Europe's infatuation with art nouveau. A down-at-heel gem of old-world style, from the serpentine ironwork of its balconies to the smoky ambience of its renowned café, the Europa became my home away from home. Each morning I would stake out a table by the windows looking out on the square, order coffee and read the newspapers, meet with friends, conduct interviews and write up my notes on the previous day's events. Each afternoon, a dapper man in threadbare tweeds and a bow tie would sit down at the grand piano and play lilting melodies from a Europe long gone. Everyone would take a break from overthrowing communism, come in for coffee or maybe a nice Becherova, a bitter Czech liquor, before heading back into the cold to deliver a next blow for freedom.

The morning of Day Five, all was confusion. Clutches of people stood outside, excitedly talking. The regime must go, all agreed. But who and what would follow? At the table, people debated what kind of society they wanted to live in. "Is capitalism good?" someone asked. In midafternoon, one of the leaders of the strike telephoned, frantic. "We have information from several sources that the army will crack down at three p.m.," she reported. "Martial law will be declared."

Outside in the square, there was no sign of trouble. A row of police vans was parked on a side street, but the men inside casually played cards. One passed a note through a window, drawing a puff on his cigarette: *Are you trying to provoke us?* it read. The cop laughed easily. Soon thereafter, the communist party's most outspoken moderate, Prime Minister Ladislav Adamec, went on television to announce there would be no violence. But it was a dangerous moment. The police were no longer prepared to act against the people, but elements of People's Militia, a private army employed by factories and the party, had boarded buses and driven into Prague. Adamec issued direct orders barring them from the city center.

By late afternoon, some two hundred thousand had gathered in the square, shouting, "Down with communism" and "Out with this regime." Every passing car honked in sympathy—a steady, unremitting blare. They carried on like this for two hours. Just before six, I made my way through the throngs to the third-floor offices of *Svobodne Slovo*, Prague's main newspaper, where I was told I could find Havel and his crew. He gave a little nod of greeting, conferring with a dozen aides seated smoking in a circle of chairs before a pair of tall French doors. Then he stood up, wearing a turtleneck sweater and the same shabby army jacket he'd had on when we met in October, and went out onto the balcony overlooking Wenceslas Square. It was the first of what would become daily appearances, climactic moments in the drama he himself was writing.

A great roar went up, ceaseless and so loud that those of us behind Havel could hardly hear ourselves speak. "The prime minister has guaranteed there would be no use of force," he told the people. He spoke forcefully, but briefly—how this was the moment, how solidarity coupled with restraint was key. "Thank you all for coming," he concluded ever so politely. "And see you again tomorrow at four p.m." A folksinger who had been banned from performing since 1968, Marta Kubisova, then sang. Another thunderous ovation, and everyone headed for home or a pub. "A very well-mannered revolution," I wrote in my notebook.

Havel told me on the fly that he deliberately muted his speech, for fear of arousing the crowd. It's a balancing act, he explained: to keep up the pressure without letting it get out of hand. He feared anything extreme, such as the possibility that inflamed radicals would do something stupid such as storm party headquarters, forcing the police or the military into what everyone called a "Chinese solution." He also worried that party or police extremists could stage a provocation, a pretext for cracking down. So it was "gently, gently," as Havel put it. I marveled at this man, who so shyly asked a colleague and me to escort him to the German embassy a few weeks ago. I wondered then whether he would have what it takes to lead a revolution, if and when it came. Watching him so confidently making decisions and uttering the words that would shape the future of his country, I no longer had any doubt.

So it went. Each day at 4 p.m. the people assembled. Students went about their general strike. The dissidents around Havel plotted and back-channeled with government officials, all but invisibly and always "gently, gently." I filled my hours, and notebooks, going around town recording scenes of the revolution. One morning, I dropped by the Academy of Dramatic Art, a headquarters of the student opposition, press center, publishing house and hub for national resistance all rolled into one—and run entirely by kids. They dashed this way and that, shirttails out, hair unwashed after days of no sleep or bathing. Xerox machines burned with overuse. One room was the Department of Proclamations. Writers dashed them off with panache, not always getting it exactly right: "We call on all Czechs to join a one-hour general strike from 2:00 to 4:00 p.m. on Monday, November 27." I pointed out the obvious error. "Oh, well. Thousands have already gone out," I was told, distributed by armies of volunteers. They covered every window, streetcar, lamppost and flat surface of Prague. For a time, police went around at night tearing them down. By now, they had given up.

I ran across Martin Mejstrik, who had just led a delegation to meet with Adamec. What a transformation. One day, this young man with his Yasir Arafat scarf, army boots and ponytail was organizing a rally at which he expected a few hundred people. A few days later, he was running a nationwide strike and meeting with the prime minister to negotiate the overthrow of a government.

Another day, I dropped by the Museum of the National Security Police in Ke Karlovu Street. An unsmiling apparatchikita handed me fuzzy bootees to put over my shoes, so as not to scuff the pristine marble floor of this monument to warped humanity. What a trove it was. There was a wall of guns, pointing menacingly outward, allegedly confiscated from 1948 counterrevolutionaries backed by foreign powers. Glass cases displayed hidden cameras, listening devices, secret poison pens and scuba gear taken from a Western spy caught trying to "penetrate" the country by swimming the Danube in 1951. There were "illegal" printing presses and their illicit fare—literature of the Jehovah's Witnesses, a hymnal—and pictures of secret police learning to shoot, snoop and body search. Most bizarre was the stuffed dog Brek, a "dog legend" who served along the border for twelve years. "His extraordinary abilities contributed to more than sixty arrests," read the plaque on the plinth upon which he stood, teeth bared in an eternal snarl. A medal was impaled in his chest—a modest little postmortem wound, in contrast, say, to that which would be inflicted by the bronzed heroic worker, portrayed in a trashy tableau, poised to spring at his oppressive capitalist boss with a pickax.

By now, Prague had become America's favorite revolution. Dan Rather, Peter Jennings and Tom Brokaw, the anchors of the big three U.S. networks, found themselves sitting together in first class on the same flight from New York. Meanwhile, hidden diplomacy took its course. One day Adamec flew to Moscow to consult with Gorbachev, as Jakes spoke threateningly of "restoring order." Not a chance, Havel's young foreign policy adviser told me. "The regime knows the Russians will not intervene. They also know that the people know. They've crossed a line." Sure enough, the next day the Soviet ambassador, Viktor Lomakin, called on Jakes for a wholesale "review" of their relationship. Then he ceremoniously welcomed a delegation from Civic Forum to his embassy.

At the foot of Wenceslas Square, where it meets Narodni Street, stood the theater known as the Magic Lantern. Enter the heavy brass-and-glass doors. Descend a twisting marble stair. Pass through the Theater Club, a salon crowded with people rushing about, smoking, talking self-importantly. Go down another set of stairs and into the theater itself. There, onstage, was the set for Dürrenmatt's *Minotaurus*, a great wall of papier-mâché rock with a cave for the Minotaur, a hole leading into the underworld. Duck your head, brave the darkness—and emerge into the inner sanctum.

There, in the backstage dressing rooms and lounges, Havel and an entourage of friends and advisers drafted and redrafted their ever-changing, always improvised script for the Velvet Revolution. In the early days, Havel would write little "tickets" for admission: a smiley face, or some other code for the day, signed by himself. One night, late, I stopped by for a little party in a narrow, dark room whose distinguishing feature was a series of wall-length mirrors reading SMOKING LOUNGE in different languages, with far too many people squeezed inside in a malodorous haze of cigarette smoke, sweat and beer. A grayish-haired man with a clipped mustache pressed me against a wall and introduced himself, in perfect English, as a great fan of *Newsweek*. This was Vaclav Klaus, an economist. Who do I think is the greatest living American? Milton Friedman, he answered for me. "I am our Milton Friedman." For the better part of an hour he told me how Czechoslovakia would dismantle its communist-planned economy. Within months, he would become finance minister (and later prime minister) of the new Czech Republic.

As we spoke, a delegation from Civic Forum, not yet including Havel, was meeting with Adamec. Members of the Politburo were initiating contacts with the opposition. Leaders of the Central Committee had called an emergency session to demand the resignation of the party's top leaders. "This puts all the pressure on them," said my friend Jan Urban. "We can afford to wait." All the while the numbers of people in Wenceslas Square kept growing, to half a million daily by the end of the revolution's first week—Day Seven, if you were still counting. Havel was astounded. "Half of Prague is out there!" said someone in the little speaker's room at *Svobodne Slovo* as Havel prepared for his nightly talk to the crowd. Their shouts made the windows vibrate: "Havel! Havel! Havel!"

It was intoxicating. Speaker after speaker stepped out upon the balcony and into a sea of . . . sheer energy. It was a palpable, physical, enveloping thing that you could literally feel and touch. A famous actor, Rudolf Hrusinsky, quoted a scrap of Neruda. The crowd went berserk. Jan Skoda, the publisher of *Svobodne Slovo* and head of the Socialist Party, spoke out for a democracy. The crowds screamed back, "Free elections! Free elections!" A renowned musician sang a protest song, and the people joined in. I remember looking out over the square, black with people chanting, dancing, waving, cheering. Who could possibly withstand this, who could not join in? Well, I thought, why not? So out on the balcony stepped I. It was only for a moment; just a big wave to the world. But what a moment. Half a million people cheered deliriously, as if I had pushed a button. "Holy shit!" I scuttled back inside.

That night was the tipping point. Over the past few days, Civic Forum had won promises of support from more than five hundred factories and workplaces. The roll call was read out each evening from the balcony: the Tatra engineering and defense group, the Skoda autoworks, the big CKD steelworks in Prague. To foreigners, these names meant little. To Czechs, they carried totemic power. CKD, especially, was not just any company. It was the General Motors and IBM of Czechoslovakia, the country's largest employer and the absolute core of the communist party. It was significant enough that CKD had gone over to the opposition. But what happened when its name was read out? Precisely on cue, ten thousand of the plant's workers came marching into Wenceslas Square. A place of honor had been cordoned off for them, right beneath the windows of *Svobodne Slovo*.

What exquisite choreography. Havel stood on the balcony to welcome them, his voice croaking with weariness. "We are at the crossroads of history—again. We are ready to talk but there is no way to return to the previous system of totalitarian government. Our leaders have brought our country to the point of moral, social and economic collapse. We want a democracy and a free Czechoslovakia. We want to rejoin Europe. Today!"

He closed with his answer to the regime's threats: an appeal to the soldiers, police and People's Militia to heed their own conscience, to think for themselves as individuals, to see what was happening around them and act independently of their officers, "first and foremost as human beings and citizens of Czechoslovakia." It was uniquely Havelian, a call to choice, for personal responsibility, a plea to people as people to give voice to their conscience and act within their own power. This was the velvet in the Velvet Revolution, and it had brought Czechoslovakia to the brink of freedom. With that, he slipped out a back entrance and into a waiting car for the four-hour drive to Bratislava, the capital of Slovakia. There he would make another speech and prepare for the next day's performance. It would be the climax of the entire drama.

On Day Eight—Friday, November 24—silence fell over Wenceslas Square as an aging figure emerged from Czechoslovak history. No one needed to ask who he was or what he represented. He looked much as he did in 1968: a bit older, a bit frail, his face more lined but wearing the same smile, at once ironic, tentative and touching. Alexander Dubcek stood on the balcony of *Svobodne Slovo*, bathed in television lights, and addressed his countrymen in their capital for the first time in twenty-one years. Quietly, he greeted them. Quietly, he called for democracy and freedom. Quietly, he urged them to throw off the Stalinist regime that had ruled since 1948. Perhaps six hundred thousand people stood for this man in his shapeless dark blue functionary's coat and rumpled hat. His voice fell into the reverent silence like the snow filtering down from the sky. The silence lasted a few eloquent beats after he finished, then exploded into the most extraordinary single-throated roar I have ever heard. "Dubcek! Dubcek for president! Dubcek to the Hrad!"

Once again, I was lucky enough to watch all this from a few feet away, in the speakers' room where Havel, smiling, and others awaited their turn. Dubcek waved, retreated, returned to the balcony to wave again. Surely, he could scarcely believe this was real. He had tried to give socialism a human face, was removed from office by Soviet troops, exiled to become a woodcutter and forester in his native Slovakia, probably thankful that he had not been jailed or worse. Did I see a tear in his eye, as he turned once again to acknowledge the crowd? The rally ended with the singing of the national anthem and that eerily spine-tingling music of half a million people jingling their keys.

An hour or so later, at the Magic Lantern, Havel and Dubcek emerged from the Minotaur's hole for a press conference with an assembly of five hundred world journalists. Gone were the fanciful, little handwritten admission tickets. Lately, Havel was guarded, as if he were the diminutive quarterback on a football team of giants, by a phalanx of sturdy Czechs weighing several hundred pounds apiece. They charged in, deposited Dubcek and Havel in chairs onstage, then glowered as the pack of reporters loosed a barrage of shouted questions from every corner. Dubcek had just begun a disquisition on the future of socialism—"I have always stood for a renewal of social-ism," he said, already getting himself into trouble—when Jan Urban jumped up with startling news: Jakes has resigned! The Central Committee has tossed out the entire ruling Politburo!

Hubbub. Consternation. My notebooks record Czechs falling in the aisles, screaming, whooping, crying. "One question, sir," a jour-nalist shouted to Dubcek. "What now?" "It's difficult to speak," the great man replied uncertainly, then stood and fell into Havel's arms. Urban magically produced a bottle of bubbly. "I think," said Havel, "that it is time for champagne."

When, precisely, was the Velvet Revolution won? Those swept up by the events often gave different answers. Martin Mejstrik thought it was the weekend it began, on Black Friday, when twenty thousand people turned up for his rally, rather than the expected few hundred. "I knew then that we had won," he told me as we walked Narodni Street so many years later.

For Jan Urban, the moment of victory came at the press confer-ence with the Politburo's resignation. "That was it," he would tell me afterward. At the Intercontinental Hotel, later that night, the nation's new communist leaders held a press conference of their own. The new top commie was one Karel Urbanek, who sat flanked by his peers of the refurbished Politburo. I still remember his looks: gray suit, scared beady eyes, nervous demeanor, a safe provincial func-tionary from the Central Committee. Someone asked about their plans for resolving the political crisis. "We did not discuss future developments." Have you read the declarations of Civic Forum? "I will as soon as possible." Do you believe in democracy and free elections? "We will continue our cooperation with the parties of the National Front," that is to say the tame parties that don't challenge communist hegemony. In other words, no.

At this point, the international media abruptly dropped its pretense of neutrality. "You jerks," shouted one Western reporter. Another called them "assholes" as someone else cried, "Get lost!" There are sides, and there are sides. Even journalists must sometimes choose. Urbanek and his minions began to twitch, then beat a hasty exit.

The resignation of the Politburo set in motion a kaleidoscopic chain of events, bewildering in their speed and complexity. Power changed hands, careers were made or lost, in what seemed like the blink of an eye. Already the bunch that had a few days before fled from the Intercontinental were gone. The moderate face of the communist party, Ladislav Adamec, yearned to take their place. Now he, too, was being set up for the fall, but so gently and so deftly.

On Day Eleven, Havel and his ascendant revolutionaries held a massive rally at the soccer stadium in Letna Park, in the hills above the city where a giant statue of Stalin once stood. Perhaps half a million people braved the cold and congealing winds, snapping flags and banners like whips. It might have looked like the usual gathering: people cheering, Havel and others exhorting. But it was not. Behind the scenes, the revolution entered a new phase. What began as a spontaneous outpouring of support had by then evolved into calculated political theater of the highest order.

That was evident in the meticulous stage management of the event. As thousands of people converged in streams upon Letna, student marshals directed them to their proper places. Sixty rock musicians had been working since early morning to set up an elaborate sound system. There were nursing stations and public-assistance booths. "A child is lost," an announcer declared over the loudspeakers, and the multitudes stopped what they were doing until the kid was found.

Havel stepped forward, speaking from the spot at the stadium where Jakes and other communist party bosses usually stood to watch their annual May Day parades. "If anyone had told me a year ago that I would see this, I would have laughed," he said, to guffaws from the crowds. Of course, a year ago he was in prison. With that, he turned the microphone over to none other than Ladislav Adamec.

What was Havel doing, giving this forum to a member of the ruling communists, one of *them*? Behind the scenes, Adamec had asked for Civic Forum's support. He calculated that with the opposition behind him, he could persuade the Central Committee to appoint him general secretary, a man acceptable to both camps who could unify the country and take Czechoslovakia down the path to reform. Havel was pretending to go along, an aide whispered as we watched this final act in the drama unfold only a few meters away. He at best considered Adamec to be a man of the minute, rather than the hour. By giving him his chance, Havel calculated that he could destroy the communists' last best hope.

And he was right. Adamec blew it, spectacularly. At Havel's behest, the crowds welcomed him. "Adamec! Adamec!" But then he opened his mouth. The first word out, incredibly, was "Comrades!" He called for discipline, an end to the strikes, economic rather than political change. Pausing for what he expected would be cheers, he realized he was undone. "No," the crowds shouted back, amid a mounting chorus of jeers and boos. Adamec struggled manfully to continue, all but drowned out by angry shouts: "Resign! Resign!" It was like watching a man being drawn and quartered. Weirdly, a spade materialized from somewhere in the crowd and was passed forward, shaken aloft by every passing hand.

So came the end, "gently, gently." Havel called for a moment of silence for those "fallen in the fight for freedom." Snow began to filter down, lightly at first and then more thickly. A horse-drawn cart left the park, decked out with banners and the wings of angels, and the people began to follow. One by one, the half million at Letna joined hands and in single file began to walk toward Wenceslas Square, more than a mile and a half away, scarcely saying a word in the gently falling snow.

For me, this was the moment. To this day, I can hardly remember it without tears. The rickety old cart with its angel wings, the bells on the horses. The people following, always hand in hand. It was so gentle, so strong and irresistible. Of course I followed, too. The procession slowly wound its way through the paths and woodlands of the park, now covered in white. It snaked down the medieval streets behind the castle and then into the square in front of the darkened presidential palace. There were no chants, no cheers, no hints of confrontation. Just the unbroken line of people passing silently in the white darkness, the line looping back and forth upon itself outside the forbidding gates. The snow muffled their footfalls. There was no sound but their soft shuffling, broken only now and again by a gentle shaking of keys.

For hours the procession passed. Half of Prague joined the human chain. From the castle it wound down the steep hills into Mala Strana, past the great baroque cathedral, its ornate spires lit in the snowy night, across the shimmering Vltava at Charles Bridge with its four-hundred-year-old statues of Czech kings and religious saviors, through the narrow streets of Old Town and finally into Narodni Street, where lit candles marked the savagery of November 17.

I watched three uniformed policemen join the procession, their caps set at jaunty angles, dancing along in tall black leather boots. What was it that Havel had said, back in October? At the moment of truth, our masks would fall, perhaps revealing intelligent and very human faces. And still the procession came, everyone swinging their arms, skipping, happy, joyous. The first of the marchers had reached Wenceslas Square, a pandemonium of honking horns, trolleys jingling their bells and the cheers of multitudes, while the last still waited patiently at Letna, high in the snowy hills. Hand in hand, they bisected the city. Hand in hand, they drew a line. Here, on one side, stood the people, on the other their oppressors. This was the moment. Everyone had to choose.

From above the city, I looked out at Prague, lighted and luminous in the snow, its people dancing. O silent night. O holy night. Never in my life have I seen anything so beautiful. I doubt I ever will again.

If only Eastern Europe's subsequent revolutions were so light of spirit, or so painless.

A few hours after the Berlin Wall fell, so did Bulgaria's communist leader of thirty-five years, Todor Zhivkov—notorious for so many nefarious geopolitical plots, from the poisoned-umbrella slaying of a Bulgarian dissident in London to the attempted assassination of Pope

John Paul II. This was no uplifting revolution by would-be democrats. It was a coup d'état that kept the old regime in place.

Darker still was the final act in the epic year. On the night of December 16, news broke of an uprising in the Romanian city of Timisoara, across the border from Hungary. Security forces fired on demonstrators, according to reports that were impossible to confirm. In the supercharged climate of revolutionary expectation, the wildest fictions were quickly accepted as fact: ten thousand dead in Timisoara, sixty thousand in other cities. Global TV networks aired lurid tales of Romanian secret police machine-gunning people from helicopters, executing soldiers who refused to shoot civilians, burying thousands of dead in mass graves or burning their corpses to destroy evidence of their massacres.

Christmas Day found me glued to the television, trying to figure out what was happening and how to get into Romania. A colleague from the Associated Press was shot in the arm attempting to drive through one crossing post. Another from the *New York Times* reached Timisoara, only to be shot through the back as his car inched along a darkened street. He would have died then and there had he not been directly outside the city hospital. That evening a friend from the German foreign ministry called to say that a military relief plane would leave from Cologne the next morning. Would I like to be on it?

Dusk was falling at Otopeni airport. Army troops lay prone on the concourse, snapping off rifle shots through shattered windows at enemies, real or imagined. Tanks were dug in along the runways.

I flew in with two German journalists aboard the Luftwaffe military transport. Officially, it carried supplies for the Romanian Red Cross; unofficially, it was delivering weaponry and commandos to reinforce the West German embassy, under fire downtown. A man from the local Red Cross greeted us as the plane lurched to a stop outside the terminal. "You're journalists? Fourteen of you were killed today!" The West German military attaché said four hundred people had been massacred in a subway little more than an hour ago. Neither report turned out to be true, but it was an unnerving welcome.

The center of Bucharest was afire. Tanks and armored cars blocked the boulevards near the university and the presidential palace. The

National Library was a smoking hulk. The front doors of the Intercontinental Hotel had been shot out. A bullet had gouged itself into the ceiling of my room. At the reception desk, phones rang unanswered. The staff gathered around a television in the dark and unheated lobby. Nicolae Ceausescu, the Great Dictator, had reportedly been caught and executed on the afternoon of Christmas Day, along with his wife, Elena, the equally fearsome Dictatoresse. Was it true? No one dared hope, for that would mean three decades of terror were over.

The TV screen flickered, blinked to life. The cavernous lobby filled with hisses: there he was, Ceausescu, dressed in the rumpled dark overcoat and scarf he wore as he fled four days ago. Those he'd tyrannized saw him, now, in a different light. Instead of standing loftily before them, surrounded by flags and aides and the ceremony of state, he sat at a bare table in a squalid little room facing an unseen panel of judges. "You are in front of the People's Tribunal, the new legal body of the country," an invisible voice intoned. The People's justice was about to be delivered.

The farce that followed was dark as Mamet. The hidden inquisitors barked questions, lashed Ceausescu with disdainful accusations that the dictator, equally contemptuously, refused to answer.

"Do you understand the charges against you," asked the prosecutor peremptorily.

"I am the commander in chief!" Ceausescu replied. "I do not answer to you!"

"You starved Romania!"

"Nonsense," the dictator heatedly replied. "Never in Romania's history has there been such progress."

Elena spat vitriol against the "worms" who presumed to challenge them, dismissing their claims as "lies" and "provocations." Ceausescu denounced the "plot" against them as an ill-disguised "coup" instigated "by traitors right here in this room." Occasionally the old couple patted each other on the arm, as if reassuring themselves. Within an hour, the court entered its verdict: guilty. The couple's "defense" lawyer was shown on camera, smiling as the sentence of death was read out.

Thereupon the film broke, to recommence, startlingly, in a rubble-strewn outdoor courtyard. Two bundles of what appeared to be rags lay on the paving stones. The camera closed in: Ceausescu, lying on his back, head tilted up toward a wall behind him, eyes open and staring. For nearly a minute, it seemed, we gazed upon him, the crowd in the lobby stunned. "The Antichrist is dead," whispered someone, as if this were the Wicked Witch in *The Wizard of Oz*. Then the screen went black, with the words FREE ROMANIA TELEVISION.

When Ceausescu was alive, he liked to hunt bear. With his retinue, he would retreat to a lodge in the mountains of Transylvania, then sally forth, guns locked and loaded. He was accustomed to good fortune, for his huntsmen took precautions. They would chain some poor beast to a tree, drug it to keep it still and conceal themselves around the blind from which the Great Man would shoot. One day they did their job haphazardly. Ceausescu took aim, then fell backward in fright when the bear, inadequately sedated, reared on its hind legs as if to attack. His shot flew into the tree-tops, even as three bullets entered the bear's heart from the snipers whose job it was to guaranty his marksmanship. This day, I was told by a forester who claimed to have witnessed the incident, Ceausescu did not acknowledge the applause of his retainers.

That could be the story of the Romanian revolution. The bear is the people. They rise up from slumber. The emperor, alarmed, fires wildly and misses his mark. The sharpshooters hidden in the forest take aim and shoot, only this time their target is not the bear but Ceausescu himself.

Romania's revolution was unlike any other. Elsewhere, it seemed as if communist regimes were racing to dismantle themselves. New leaders arose overnight. Old regimes collapsed and disappeared, scarcely leaving a ripple. People danced and celebrated largely pain-less victories. Not so in Romania. There, the struggle was written in blood. Communist masters ordered the police to fire on their citi-zens. They obeyed. A civil war was fought, albeit briefly. Revolution transmuted into a crypto-coup.

That it should have begun in Timisoara, a depressing industrial city of about three hundred thousand, begrimed with soot and human misery, was a matter of happenstance, a local issue of negligible importance to Ceausescu. A young but popular pastor named Laszlo

Tokes was told by his bishop that he would be transferred to another parish. His outspoken sermons criticizing the regime, coupled with his support for the large Hungarian nationality living in Romania, were causing trouble. When Tokes resisted, parishioners stood vigil outside his door. The crowd of a few hundred grew to several thousand, many of them high school and university students not altogether happy with life in the Epoch of Light.

At first, they sought only to protect Tokes, who was regularly beaten and harassed by the police. But the gathering soon turned into a more general protest. There were shouts for freedom, for bread, for an end to the regime. Singing the outlawed national anthem— "Awake Ye, Romanian!"—a group numbering more than a thousand marched into the center of town, tearing down posters of the Leader and stoning the headquarters of the communist party. Police responded with water cannon and tear gas.

This took place on December 16. The next day, a Sunday, Romania's revolution began in earnest. Early that morning, around 3 a.m., Securitate and local police burst into Tokes's house and, after a beating, forced him to sign a blank paper resigning his post. Meanwhile, army and Securitate reinforcements poured in. Stupidly, they made a show of it, parading through the city with banners flying and bugles blowing. Ten thousand demonstrators came roiling out of nowhere to pelt them with rocks, bottles and jeers.

If communist leaders elsewhere seemed paralyzed amid crisis, Ceausescu was not among them. How could they allow a simple protest outside a pastor's church to escalate into a riot? he asked his defense minister, General Vasile Milea, according to the minutes of an emergency meeting held that afternoon: "I gave orders for a show of force, with tanks, and you organize a parade!" Where were his troops last night? "Why didn't they fire? You don't put an enemy down with sermons. You have to burn him!"

Then Ceausescu turned on General Iulian Vlad, commander of the Securitate. "Don't you know what a state of emergency means?" Ceausescu complained that he had stayed up all night, talking to the two men every ten minutes. "Why were not my orders carried out?" At this point, bloody Elena chimed in. "You should have fired on them. They would have fled like partridges. And had they fallen, you should have taken them and shoved them into a cellar. Weren't you told that? Not one of them should have gotten out!"

Wrathfully, Ceausescu threatened to dismiss both men and take command of the army and security forces himself. He accused them of treason, suggesting they should go before a firing squad. Abjectly, they pledged their fealty and promised to justify his faith in them. "Good," said Ceausescu. "Shall we try once more, comrades?" Sometime after 5 p.m., back in Timisoara, Generals Vlad and Milea executed their orders. Troops and Securitate fired into the crowds of demonstrators, many of them women and children. One hundred people were killed. Between three hundred and four hundred were wounded.

If Ceausescu had no illusions about the threat in Timisoara, he did have a blind spot: himself. He treated his people as slaves—"worms," in Elena's phrase. He lied to them, stole from them, robbed them of life and liberty and happiness. Yet in the end he genuinely seems to have believed they loved him. In this delusion, he made a fatal decision. He would deal with the challenge to his rule by going to the People, live on TV and in the flesh. Of course, there would be the usual props. A crowd of loyal supporters was rounded up from Bucharest's factories and party bureaucracies. Banners and placards bore his likeness. "Long live Ceausescu," his subjects would shout. He would wave, deliver a fiery speech and all would be well in the kingdom.

And so, on the morning of December 21, Nicolae Ceausescu stepped before the microphones and cameras set up on the balcony of the Central Committee on Palace Square. In his dark blue overcoat and fur hat, he shouted out to the one hundred thousand subjects in the square below. He told them that the reports of uprisings and killings in Timisoara were false, that they were efforts by foreign powers to corrupt and disinform the people. He counted on the mass of tame functionaries, beholden to him and his rule, to applaud and cheer on cue. Instead, from the fringe of the square, some students not part of the select assembly started shouting, "Ti-mi-soara! Ti-mi-soara!"

Never had he heard anything like it. Never had he been so brazenly challenged. Then other cries, faint but loud enough to be heard on camera: "Killer! Murderer! Down with Ceausescu!" There were loud popping sounds. Guns? It was later determined to be the sound of exploding tear-gas canisters fired by police, but it was enough to unsettle Ceausescu.

Flustered, he stopped speaking. His face lost its confidence, sagged in sudden timid bewilderment, abruptly looking old and weak. He waved his hands to calm the crowd. Yet they were the flailing motions of a man in trouble, not unlike the moment Ceausescu tottered on his dock in Snagov, flapping his arms in danger of toppling into the depths. This moment of truth lasted only seconds, but it was enough. Everyone watching in the square and on national television saw his weakness. The emperor had no clothes.

The rest is well-known history. Security guards bustled Ceausescu off the balcony. Crowds stormed the Central Committee building. Ceausescu and his wife boarded a white helicopter and escaped from the roof. Fighting erupted throughout the city between the army, siding with the people, and the Securitate, loyal to Ceausescu. The Securitate sniped from rooftops or mingled with crowds of demonstrators, pulling weapons from beneath their coats and mowing down those around them. Tanks fired away in squares and boulevards; the city center blazed with flames and smoke. After a three-day chase, on Christmas Day, the dictator and his wife were captured, tried and summarily convicted by a kangaroo people's court.

Revolutions are probably never as they seem. They are admixtures of myth, idealism, opportunism, politics, intrigue, exploitation. Good and bad, the noble and the ignoble, the pure and the impure become so entangled as to be almost indistinguishable. Nowhere was this more true than in Bucharest. For at the moment of Ceausescu's speech, the revolution in Romania became two revolutions. One was public: the people rising up to throw off the hated dictator, seen on TV. The other was far more private: a behind-the-scenes struggle for power among elites amounting to a coup.

I would understand this better in later years, after further research. But even at the time I sensed something suspect about this revolution—happenings that simply did not fit the public picture.

Shortly after I arrived on December 26, a stocky man with a mustache approached me in the lobby of the Intercontinental. "Hello, remember me?" Actually, no, I don't think I've ever seen him before. "Good, I did my job well," he said, introducing himself as Andrei. He was one of my invisible "tenders" last August. Whom he worked for now wasn't exactly clear, either to him or to me. If anyone was in charge, it was a revolutionary council calling itself the National Salvation Front, headquartered at the Bucharest television station. He offered to take me over.

Out on the streets, I instinctively ducked at the crack of sudden gunfire. Andrei, however, seemed unfazed. At the television station, surrounded by trucks and army troops nervously guarding against an attack, he had no trouble passing through their lines. Inside, desks and chairs were piled into makeshift barricades, guarded by more troops and armed volunteers. As recently as last night, he told me, one floor of the building had been occupied by Securitate, shooting at soldiers occupying other floors. Oddly, there was no sign of blood, or bullet holes, aside from a few broken windows.

A few other reporters had gotten to the TV station as well, and we had an impromptu press conference with a man identified as Romania's new vice president, Dumitru Mazilu, a human rights activist who had only just been freed from years of house arrest. "The situation is extremely grave, extremely fluid," he said, confirming reports that Ceausescu had been executed. Mazilu added that, by now, the army had allied itself firmly with the people and the new government. The shooting outside came not from the main ranks of Securitate, numbering perhaps forty thousand, but from a specially trained Fifth Directorate of presidential guards, whose assignment was to sow terror and wage war on those revolting against Ceausescu for as long as he was alive. Mazilu put the strength of these "terrorists" at no more than two thousand, if that, working in teams of three and four men.

Wandering down a hallway, I ran into the foreign ministry official who'd arranged my trip in August. "Hello, Mr. Meyer," he said buoyantly. "What lies I told you!" The man was never at a loss for words. "That's okay," I replied. "I didn't believe anything you said anyway." It was a strange camaraderie, all the more so for the question he answered only with a smile: "What are you doing here?" He filled me in on the National Salvation Front, an odd mélange of poets, writers, students, dissidents and allegedly disaffected former government officials that was meeting in a crowded conference room nearby. I could understand why Laszlo Tokes, the priest from Timisoara, would be there, as well as dissident writers such as Doina Cornea and Mircea Dinescu. But General Stefan Guse, the army chief of staff who commanded the troops in Timisoara? Ion Iliescu, the self-appointed new president? Not too many years ago, he had been Ceausescu's chief propagandist.

Perhaps the most incongruous presence was that of General Victor Stanculescu, appointed acting defense minister only a few hours before Ceausescu fled from the roof of Central Committee headquarters. He had been a favorite of Elena's, the man she would have sent to quell the unrest in Timisoara, if she'd had her druthers. Stanculescu had organized the Ceausescus' evacuation from the Central Committee building, I would subsequently learn, and Elena had cried out to him as she boarded the helicopter, "Victor, protect the children!" By that, she meant the hundreds and hundreds of orphans recruited into the Securitate as a special guard, the "terrorists" who were now indiscriminately firing on the people in defense of their adoptive "mother" and "father," Elena and Nicolae. It would later emerge that Stanculescu had also arranged the Ceausescus' trial, according to Richard Hall in "Rewriting the Revolution," among others, and had personally chosen their prosecutors, helped select their place of execution and organized the firing squad—even before the legal proceedings began.

One evening, I again ran into Andrei at my hotel. Once again, he offered to show me something interesting. We drove to a walled compound in the diplomatic quarter. As before, a heavily guarded security gate slide magically open for him. A light snow lay on the gardens and pathways of the palace where Elena and Nicolae Ceausescu had lived and last slept.

For the dictator and his lady, home was a pink stucco neo-Italianate mansion in northwest Bucharest. Scrawled on one of the arched windows flanking the grand entryway, in bloodred paint, or perhaps lipstick, was the word *Victorie!* Wine bottles rolled on the floor of the gold-filigreed vestibule, beneath a sparkling crystal chandelier, amid scatterings of cigarette butts. A gas mask lay incongruously on a brocade chair. According to Andrei, "the people" stormed the palace in the late afternoon of December 22, after Ceausescu fled. But it didn't feel right. Here and there, expensive vases lay on their sides, as though carefully placed so as not to be broken. Small objects of art, mostly cheap china figures, had been trampled underfoot, along with family photos of the Ceausescus and their children. But there were no muddied rugs, no footprints in the snow outside, no broken doors or windows or smudgy handprints on the walls and white sofas. In fact, there was no evidence of damage of any kind, let alone the looting you would expect from an angry and unruly mob. Instead, it looked as if a bunch of teenagers had the run of the house while their parents were away and found the key to the liquor cabinet. The palace had been secured, it seemed to me, not liberated.

As Andrei promised, however, it was interesting. "Mike, you knew Ceausescu," he called to me as I sat at the dictator's damask-covered dining room table writing up my notes. "Have you ever seen anything like this?" To him, as to most Romanians, the luxury was inconceivable. The Ceausescus lived like princes of the French empire, or at least the more egregious of Hollywood moguls. Rich tapestries covered the walls. Silver and bronze statues and candelabra stood next to ornate Louis XVI clocks on extravagantly scrolled tables. Everything was gilt, mirrors and brocaded wallpaper—glitter without style, coherence or taste. There were no books. The paintings were of reclining nudes and cherubs, milkmaids frisking with lambs and little children.

Upstairs, empty boxes of perfume and cosmetics littered the floor of Elena's boudoir: Arpège, Nina Ricci, Mystère de Rochas. A can of Woolite rolled in a corner. Boxes of Palmolive hemorrhoidal balm crunched underfoot. Despite the closets full of haute-couture gowns, Elena Ceausescu seems to have preferred heavy woolen suits and metallic, stub-nosed shoes with square, no-nonsense heels. There were hundreds of pairs. Gauntly thin, she appears to have obsessed about her weight. Her pink-and-gold bath had four scales. A man in white athletic shoes and a leather jacket rummaged in the drawers of her nightstand. Finding a photo of the Ceausescus with their children, he balled it up and threw it into her rose-tinted bidet. Another gestured toward a pile of mink and sable coats laid out on a bed, his cigarette dripping ash on the coverlet.

An adjoining suite was His. Perhaps a hundred identical gray suits hung in his closet, all new and shrouded in hygenic plastic. Under each: a black pair of leather shoes, none ever worn, custom-made for a slightly clubfooted man. I sorted through Ceausescu's ties: a massive assembly of swirling, weird colors, specially made by the world's better haberdashers, all seven inches wide and never worn. Oh, ho, what's this? A pair of Swiss-made Jockey shorts, which I held up to my waist. They were hopelessly large even on me, over six feet tall. How must they have hung on such a small dictator. Did he hike them almost to his shoulders? On the floor, a photo of Elena in her forties, wearing a yellow raincoat and picking a flower, lay amid broken fragments of glass. It was the only faintly personal thing I saw.

A final bizarre touch awaited in the royal couple's bedroom. Papers and documents were strewn across the marital bed, presumably Ceausescu's reading the last night he was here. Among them was a study prepared for "Comrade Elena Ceausescu," dated November 26 and typed in the extralarge characters that her husband preferred for his reading. It was an analysis of the events leading up to the assassination of Egyptian president Anwar Sadat and the popular political climate of the time. To this day, I don't know whether it was genuine, suggesting that the Ceausescus were far more aware of the mood of the country than often supposed, or whether it was planted there for journalists like me. Its purpose? Perhaps a red herring, meant to suggest that Romania's revolution was indeed spontaneous and unplanned, rather than a plot by insiders. After all, the "people" stormed this palace, did they not?

The days and weeks following Ceausescu's death brought more intimations of conspiracy. From Timisoara came reports that, in the initial days of the unrest, a gang of Securitate went around deliberately smashing store windows and trying to provoke townspeople into fighting. Corpses laid out for photographers, alleged victims of the regime's massacres, turned out to have been dug out of paupers' cemeteries or borrowed from the local morgue. There were the extravagantly inflated casualty figures. "What genocide?" Elena Ceausescu had not unreasonably replied at the trial. The Ceausescus were charged with killing tens of thousands of people. But the official toll turned out to be closer to one thousand, with most in Bucharest and other cities after the dictator had fled. Why were the Ceausescus killed off so quickly, people began to ask. As for the new government, why all those familiar faces?

Not surprisingly, this led to subsequent speculation about the true nature of the revolution. Some suggested it was a plot from start to finish, masterminded by leaders of the army and Securitate to depose Ceausescu and replace him with one of their own. But the truth is more prosaic. The revolution began in Timisoara, just as it appeared, with a popular explosion of anger and frustration and the widespread sense, shared elsewhere in Eastern Europe, of having had enough. Amid the muddle of events, people made choices, quickly and irrevocably, sometimes out of courage, other times out of cowardice or expedience. Laszlo Tokes wouldn't leave his house. The people rose up and did not back down. Seeing the handwriting on the wall, the conspirators against Ceausescu seized their chance.

It was a near thing. After Ceausescu lifted off in that helicopter, he tried to make his way to a friendly army base, where he could mobilize his forces to retake control. He was caught, partly because Hungarian intelligence helped his captors to find him using electronic surveillance. Ceausescu's hasty execution was intended to stop the fighting. As long as he lived, the revolution was not won, a former president of Romania, Emil Constantinescu, told me a long time later. "They murdered him."

Scarcely seven minutes elapsed, approximately, between the time the sentence was read out and the firing squad did its work. The judge, also a member of the conspiracy, who would later become deputy prime minister, barely had time to gather up his papers before soldiers tied their victims' hands and hustled them down a hallway and out to the courtyard. During the rush, the electric cord powering the video camera was yanked from the wall. By the time the cameraman caught up, soldiers were already shooting. Some did not even wait for the official order to fire. Elena Ceausescu fainted and was shot where she lay.

CHAPTER FOURTEEN

Denouement

On a bleak afternoon on the next to the last night of the year, I felt an abrupt and overwhelming need to be out of Romania, out of Eastern Europe, before the New Year rolled in. Perhaps it was a visit to Bucharest's main cemetery. A light snow covered mounds of earth from hundreds of fresh graves, open and gaping in long straight rows. "Here are the fallen," a solemn priest intoned across the field of dead as four men placed a wooden coffin before him on a wobbly trestle. Jacob Stetincu, shot by a sniper while crossing the street, lay wrapped in a thin white cotton sheet, wearing a worn blue beret, snowflakes catching in his mustache. After a hurried sacrament the men nailed shut the lid, carried him to the nearest grave, his widow struggling to keep up, and shoveled in the heavy earth. A few feet away, others hacked at the frozen ground. The priest, working in shifts with a dozen of his brethren, was already shaking holy water on the next victim of Ceausescu's reign.

"Revolution overload," one friend called it. Too much, too fast, too intimately. The faded Orient Express left late that night. When it stopped the next afternoon in the switching yards of Budapest's Keleti station, for a three-hour layover, I climbed out a window, schlepped my gear a mile down the tracks and hailed a taxi for Vienna, several hours away. A flight to Frankfurt. Another two-hour taxi to Bonn. A few minutes after midnight, twenty-seven hours after leaving Bucharest, I walked into my house with a party of friends and neighbors singing "Auld Lang Syne," just as they were in Berlin, Prague, Warsaw and Budapest.

For the people living in these newly free cities, it was a time of joy.

In Berlin, so-called *Mauer*-peckers whittled the Wall away with hammers and chisels. On Christmas Day, Leonard Bernstein conducted the philharmonic at the newly opened Brandenburg Gate, playing Beethoven's Ninth ("Ode to Joy") with the word *joy* changed to *freedom*. Less than a year later, on October 3, 1990, Germany reunited.

The Wall began a long slow fade into historical imagination. Much of it was quickly knocked down. A 260-foot stretch stands today, as a tourist destination, near the old Gestapo headquarters in central Berlin, midway between Potsdamer Platz and Checkpoint Charlie. Another stretch runs along the river Spree near the Oberbaumbrücke, dubbed the East Side Gallery for its graffiti-covered face (all painted post-Fall). Still more chunks have been exported around the world—mainly to the capitals of the perceived victors in the Cold War: London, New York, Washington. They stand here and there, vaguely incongruous, providing shade for lunching bankers or secretaries, oblivious to their once ominous portent.

Mikhail Gorbachev deserves enormous credit. He was the geopolitical demiurge, the prime mover that set all else in motion. Without him, the history of Eastern Europe and the end of communism would have been vastly different. His reward for services to humanity was to be unceremoniously ousted, after an attempted coup, when the Soviet Union itself collapsed in 1991. He was awarded the Nobel Peace Prize in 1990.

Egon Krenz tried to claim credit. In an interview the summer after the Wall came down, he told me that he had "instructed border officials to open the frontiers," sometime around 9:15 p.m. But that simply doesn't jibe with the facts. He was thrown out as the GDR's last communist head of state on December 7, 1989, by a party desperate to change its image. In 1997, he was sentenced to six and a half years in jail for crimes against humanity, specifically manslaughter of Germans attempting to escape over the Berlin Wall.

Erich Honecker fled to Moscow after the collapse of the GDR, to be extradited in 1992, tried for treason and jailed in the Federal Republic. He died in exile in Chile on May 29, 1994, of cancer, unrepentant.

Gunter Schabowski would be one of the few top leaders to repudiate communism. I met him in early 1999, just after his seventieth birthday. He was helping a local newspaper in little Rotenberg am Fulda with their graphic design. Photoshop! Quark! "Are you a computer freak?" he asked disarmingly when I arrived to spend half a day with him. He chatted about his Macintosh and lamented its lack of processing power. Only 160 RAM! And it took so long to download digital photos. Even then the resolution was poor, he said, muttering about pixel counts. At the close of our interview, he took a picture of the two of us and processed it through his computer. "Just so you'll remember meeting this old toad," he said.

In Warsaw, Lech Walesa went on to become Poland's president, replacing General Wojciech Jaruzelski in December 1990. Jaruzelski subsequently faced charges for murder during the period of martial law and was defended by former leaders of Solidarity. In 2005, he apologized for his role in the 1968 Warsaw Pact invasion of Czechoslovakia, calling it a great "political and moral mistake."

On Sunday, December 10, 1989, International Human Rights Day, President Gustav Husak swore in Czechoslovakia's first noncommunist government since World War II. Then he himself resigned. Who would replace him? Jan Urban, tired but jubilant, wore the answer on his lapel, a little campaign button reading HAVEL FOR PRESIDENT. He was sworn in on December 29, 1989. The celebrations on Wenceslas Square went on all night.

We had one last conversation. Outwardly, Havel looked the same as ever, down to his faded green army jacket. But he seemed distracted, even evasive. The revolution was over and we both had the odd feeling that, for the moment at least, everything had been said. We spoke a bit about the whimsy of fortune, from jail to the presidency in six months. "Yes, a lot has happened," Havel said. "I learned in prison that everything is possible, so I should not be amazed. But I am amazed."

Then he told a story I've often heard repeated: "For a long time, I thought that all this might just have been a colorful dream, and that I would wake up in my cell and tell my fellow inmates about this dream. 'Oh, Havel,' they would tell me, 'you are becoming bigheaded about being an important dissident.' So from time to time during these days—we must still decide what to call these events—I would ask my friends if we were dreaming. They would say, 'No,' but it was not until yesterday that I really felt that it was so. I took a stroll through Pruhonice Park, outside Prague. It was the first time in a month that I could spend some time in the open air and feel the heavens above me, and for the first time I felt that from now on I could live in a different way, less dependent on messages of encouragement from, say, the Dalai Lama!"

Havel, like his country, was beginning a new life, not merely as president but as a person. But instead of asking more about this, continuing the conversation as a conversation, I lapsed into journalist mode. How did he feel about a writer as president? "Well, I could at least write my own speeches." He laughed, but he was torn. He wanted to return to being a playwright, and he wanted to be president. If asked, he said, "I would accept this post on the condition that I hold it only until another president is elected to a full five-year term." After that, he would prefer to complete the play he was writing when events interrupted. What would it be called? He didn't know, just yet. But his last one was aptly titled, didn't I think? *Slum Clearance*. It was about to open in New York, he added, and close in Prague.

As if in keeping with the quiet way in which it began, the year ended in Budapest with only the faintest echo of the celebrations elsewhere. A new national parliament adopted Kalman Kulcsar's cherished Constitution, modeled on that of the United States and enshrining free speech and private property (not to mention the pursuit of happiness) as inalienable rights of man.

Imre Pozsgay abolished the communist party and expected to lead a revived Socialist Party to the presidency. But voters would not elect a former communist to high office, however heroic a patriot he might have been, and he returned to teaching at the University of Debrecen, just as when he was on the outs with the ruling regime of yore.

In contrast to Poland, whose communists enjoyed a protected place in parliament, Hungary had scheduled completely free elections for March 1990. That fully democratic free-for-all would unseat all those most responsible for Hungary's freedom. Unlike Pozsgay, Miklos Nemeth anticipated that his term as prime minister would end with that historic ballot. "I saw it coming long before," he told me. "I belonged to the party. A member of the former regime could never last, no matter how good his works." His reward for changing the world would, when I first saw him again ten years later, be a job as a mid- to upper-level vice president of the European Bank for Reconstruction and Development in London, in charge of human resources.

Yet Nemeth had one last victory in those final days, a secret one that few ever knew about. Toward year's end, he received a letter hand-delivered from the Soviet ambassador in Budapest, accompanied by armed guards. The ambassador did not know what the letter contained, nor was he allowed to stay while Nemeth read it.

Privately he opened it. The Soviet Union is pleased to inform you, it read, that all nuclear weapons have been removed from Hungarian soil—weapons that Moscow had always denied deploying in Hungary or other Warsaw Pact nations.

This was the grim secret that Nemeth had become privy to in December 1988, after being named prime minister. He had raised the matter with Gorbachev in March, insisting that the weapons be withdrawn despite his only being in office four months. "I'll get back to you," the Russian leader had said. To this day, Nemeth does not know how the Soviets got them out without anyone in his government knowing, just as he does not know how they got them into Hungary in the first place. He went to inspect the bunkers, not far from his mother's village near Lake Balaton: empty, stripped to their twenty-foot-thick concrete walls. He liked to think of it as an independence gift.

Epilogue

"It's a poor sort of memory that only works backwards," the Queen remarked.

—Lewis Carroll, *Through the Looking-Glass*

Some memories fade, others remain vivid despite the passing years. Why? Perhaps they carry some bit of unrealized experience, a message not fully decoded that can help us decipher the future.

For whatever reason, I've never forgotten an image from nearly twenty years ago, scribbled in a reporter's notebook dated November 2, 1990. It was a beautiful autumn day in Berlin. The first anniversary of the fall of the Wall was coming up. A few weeks earlier, East and West Germany had been reunited. Almost overnight, it seemed, the once-divided city had become the world's top tourist destination. We journalists joked about it as a Cold War theme park, a sort of Disney East. Everyone wanted to come—to see what communism was really like, to savor victory—before it all disappeared.

Among the dinosaurs in this park, besides the remnants of the Wall and the oddly dressed *Volk* who lived to the east of it, was the Soviet Red Army. Within a few short months of diplomatic negotiations, Moscow had agreed to call its soldiers home—380,000 in twenty-one battle-ready divisions across a geography stretching a thousand miles from the Baltic Sea in the north to the Black Sea in the south. Meanwhile, there they were, smack in the heart of what was now democratic Europe.

This made for some surreal experiences. Driving in the newly open countryside of East Germany, or hiking in dense woods, you might hear a low heavy rumble. Suddenly, a long line of troop carriers and tanks would come into view, emblazoned with the Red Star. Hello, you were in the middle of a Warsaw Pact military exercise. Not so long ago, you got shot for less. On one such excursion, I drove south to Wuensdorf, headquarters of the Soviet high command. I had heard rumors that Russian forces were selling off weapons on a new black market and thought I would investigate. For reasons that seemed to make sense at the time, this adventure culminated in my climbing a pine tree to see over the concrete wall of a Russian base deep in a forest accessible only by a rutted logging road. I fell, broke my arm and had to be transported, whimpering, back to a hospital in Berlin. The doctor laughed at this tale. "You don't have to fall out of trees to see Russians," he told me. "Just go to the city dump."

Which brings me to that image from long ago, a mental snapshot of a day trip to a Berlin suburb called Dallgow, home to a municipal garbage dump and a Soviet garrison. Picking through mountains of stinking debris were a dozen uniformed Russian soldiers. These were not conscripts, notoriously underfed and seldom paid. They were officers: lieutenants, captains, colonels—field commanders in the vaunted Red Army that had vanquished Hitler and held half of Europe in thrall. One carried a plastic bag into which he stuffed recovered treasures: a broken toaster, an abandoned toy. Another stood amid the garbage casually smoking a cigarette, a scrap of frayed carpet rolled under his arm, along with a soiled corduroy pillow. He looked me in the eye and spat.

For decades Americans lived in fear of these men. Braced for war, we stationed hundreds of thousands of troops in Germany. We spent trillions of dollars on weapons, waged a nuclear arms race, battled the communist menace in Vietnam and Korea and underwrote proxy wars in a dozen countries from Somalia and Nicaragua to Afghanistan. All to fight off . . . these poor scavengers? Here was the true Russian army, a shell of a once mighty force, capable of spitting at a victorious America but scarcely able to clothe and equip itself let alone charge through the Fulda Gap into West Germany and on to the English Channel.

I wrote a colorful post–Cold War feature article to this effect, full of moody atmospherics. Recalling it twenty years later, I am a bit embarrassed, most of all by its triumphalist tone. Humbled though it may have been, the Red Army remained formidable. Russia was still a great power and remains so today, as its sway in Europe's energy markets amply demonstrates. As a matter of historical record, I knew the Russians were the chief victors in World War II. They bore the brunt of Nazi Germany's aggression; they battled back from the gates of Moscow and across the map of Europe to Berlin. They paid for that victory with 23 million lives. (U.S. losses were less than half a million.) And yet there I was, in that dump at Dallgow, spinning out my yarn that put us at the center of everything, from defeating Hitler to facing down the "Red menace" and, finally, emerging triumphant at the end of the Cold War.

Of the various interpretations one could give to this scene, more or less accurately, I chose what I wanted to see. Lewis Carroll's metaphor is apt. The world is always partly a mirror of ourselves. We see all things, enemies especially, through the lens of our own hopes and fears and desires, inevitably distorted. Memory works not only backward but forward, shaping the present and prefiguring the future. We live as much by what we believe happened to us as by what actually did.

I found myself thinking about all this, not long ago, at the George Bush Library and Museum in College Station, Texas. It is an odd place, so starkly in contrast to, say, the Jimmy Carter Library in Atlanta. Carter's memorial is a quiet refuge in a leafy park, a sober and respected center for scholarly research and substantive conversation on weighty global issues—climate change, child health care in Africa, the war against world poverty. The Bush library, by comparison, felt like a huckster's carnival. The former president's baseball glove from his college days is lovingly displayed, along with bats, balls, uniforms and photos of the star Yale athlete running, diving, catching and lounging—just a few of the two million photos, ten thousand videos, innumerable souvenirs and mementos documenting his life. The 1947 Studebaker in which he drove to Texas is there, not to mention the plane he flew as a pilot during the war and the cigarette boat in which he liked to race around Kennebunkport, Maine. Then, amid all this boy-racer bric-a-brac, one comes across something much more serious: a slab of the Berlin Wall, encased in Plexiglas. An accompanying video explains what it represented and how it came to fall, with America and the Bush administration very much at the center of the narrative. Lest one miss the point, a massive bronze sculpture of a herd of wild horses, unbridled and free, stands outside the library doors. The symbolism is far from subtle, and it takes only a moment to grasp the meaning of this Ceausescu-scale statuary: beneath the flashing hoofs of these mighty mustangs is the rubble of the wall that once separated the West from those oppressed under communism.

As I surveyed this epic and extravagant tableau, I couldn't help but wonder what it had to do with George H. W. Bush. This was a man, after all, who in the middle of the most dramatic events of the past half century worked so skillfully to keep the drama of Eastern Europe's revolutions from cascading into a broader East-West crisis. He shunned inflammatory rhetoric. He avoided rubbing Moscow's face in the reality of its collapsing empire and, indeed, went out of his way to engage America's erstwhile enemy in the responsible management of the Cold War's end, most masterfully in negotiating German reunification and the withdrawal of Soviet troops from central Europe. In other words, he disdained the crass triumphalism that today pervades his own library. What happened? Who hijacked George H. W. Bush's legacy? We might as well ask who hijacked American foreign policy.

The easy answer, embraced by many, is George W. Bush and the swaggering band of neocons who took us into Iraq. The truth, of course, is more complicated. Bush junior came to power at the dawn of the new millennium—January 20, 2001. Savoring the calendrical symmetry, he sought to portray himself and his administration as a breed apart from his last-century predecessors. He took office speaking of a "humble" America, one that played well with others. Yet he made clear that he hoped to break the mold of past presidencies, defined as he saw it by inertia and an unwillingness to make tough decisions. Most particularly, he shunned the restraint and caution of his father. His administration, he promised, would be defined by boldness and big thinking. It would, he liked to say, leave a "big footprint."

It's tempting to find in this the early signs of hubris, a classically Greek presentiment of decline and fall. Yet for all his rhetoric, it would be a mistake to see George W. Bush as representing a sharp break with the past. He was, rather, the extreme end of a continuum, the culminating expression of a deeper and more general and ultimately very American way of seeing the world.

It is eerie, and unsettling, the contrast between father and son. In the aftermath of 1989, and the subsequent collapse of the Soviet empire, the administration of George H. W. Bush was distinguished by its collective cool. Partly because of who he was, and partly because his worldview was so shaped by the Cold War, the elder Bush recognized—and accepted—the limits of American power. The United States may have emerged as the world's preeminent military and economic power, but that did not mean it could cut loose from its traditional moorings in the larger world. His New World Order had America at its center, but only as first among equals.

This sense of proportion—of geopolitical "place"—found expression first in his administration's deft handling of the potentially explosive issue of German unification. British prime minister Margaret Thatcher viscerally opposed it. So did the French under President François Mitterrand. Other European countries were similarly wary, not least the Soviet Union. Washington was the future Germany's only champion. Without Bush, it would not have come to pass as smoothly and harmoniously as it did.

Then came the horror of Yugoslavia. If you were on the ground, as I was in the early 1990s, you saw the war in the Balkans for what it was: a manufactured conflict, orchestrated by nationalist politicians in Zagreb and Belgrade. But from afar, and especially in the United States, it looked quite different. Reporters confused by the country's ethnic complexity reduced it to a stick-figure analogy. The civil war in Yugoslavia, most wrote, was the product of "ancient ethnic hatreds," unleashed with the collapse of communism and thousands of years in the making, as inexplicable and irresolvable as our own legendary feud between the Hatfields and the McCoys.

In fact, the Balkan holocaust might have been prevented. Early on, the thugs plotting war could have been confronted. But Europe would have had to do it, acting in concert with the United States and NATO, and that was not yet in the cards. Rightly or wrongly, the Bush administration read the situation and stood back. "We don't have a dog in that fight," said James Baker. In any case, the first Iraq war shifted the world's focus. When Saddam Hussein invaded Kuwait in August 1990, Bush declared, "This shall not stand." But he did not go on to Baghdad, fearing to embroil U.S. troops in a Middle East civil war from which there might be no exit. Hard-line conservatives never forgave him. Bush, as they saw it, was "pusillanimous" and "weak." At the time, the decision to stop the war echoed what *Newsweek*'s editors once memorably dubbed "The Wimp Factor." With two decades' hindsight, however, Bush's restraint might go by another name—judgment, perhaps, or wisdom.

This sense of moderation, of national place in the world, did not last long. As early as 1990, Charles Krauthammer made a mark with an essay on the United States in a post–Cold War world. The end of communism, he argued, did away with the old order of checks and balances of power among allies and enemies. In this new "unipolar world," as he called it, America could act with unfettered sway. Krauthammer might have been a neoconservative commentator, but his ideas reflected the temper of the time. Flush with Cold War victory, Americans of every political stripe embraced this robust new vision of the United States and its role in the world. If Bill Clinton won the White House on a domestic rather than a foreign policy agenda, he soon changed hats. Secretary of State Madeleine Albright spoke of America as the "indispensable nation," without which no good could happen. It was a nation with a mission, a manifest destiny stretching back over centuries, under Democratic presidents and Republican, from Woodrow Wilson's and Franklin Roosevelt's denunciations of colonialism and empire to Jimmy Carter's campaigns for global human rights. "We stand tall," Albright said. "We see further into the future." It was our duty, as Americans, to carry freedom and democracy forward into the world. "Humanitarian intervention" gained new currency, as international law and as U.S. policy, in Haiti, Bosnia and Kosovo.

During these years, the rest of the world began to view American power with misgiving. Europeans accused Washington of throwing its weight around. French foreign minister Hubert Védrine dubbed

America the "hyperpower," riding roughshod over the sensibilities and interests of others. Samuel P. Huntington, author of a 1996 bestseller, *The Clash of Civilizations*, decried Clinton administration officials who "boast[ed] of American power and American virtue" and "lectur[ed] other countries on the universal validity of American principles, practices and institutions." Public intellectuals from Ronald Steel (*Temptations of a Superpower*) to Robert W. Tucker (*The Imperial Temptation*) warned against the perils of U.S. triumphalism. Chronicling this history in *World Affairs*, Robert Kagan pointedly noted that the epithets *hegemonic* and *unilateral* were first thrown at the United States during the Clinton era, not that of George W. Bush.

All this became magnified under the second Bush administration, particularly after September 11. Just as the new president took office modeling himself on Ronald Reagan, so did many senior officials around him, few more happily than those who had been marginalized during Reagan's later years, or marginalized once more under the first Bush administration. Born-again, they resurrected the in-your-face rhetoric of early Reagan and amped it up. They made his myth—"Mr. Gorbachev, tear down this wall!"—into operational dictum. Traditional American idealism—the United States as a lamp unto nations, enjoying a special providence—morphed into a crude Manichaean dialectic: good versus evil, us versus them. Confrontation clothed as strength through power became the order of the day. Diplomatic "engagement" was for wimps, a form of modern "appeasement." Impatient with the perceived irresolution and half measures of the previous Bush and Clinton administrations, they wanted action— real solutions, not Band-Aids—and they derided those who thought differently.

Years ago, I remember reading an exchange between a writer for the *New York Times Magazine*, Ron Suskind, and a senior Bush administration official. You guys, meaning reporters like me, you live in the "reality-based" world, the adviser famously told him with sheer condescension. By contrast, the aide went on, the Bush team moved in the faith-based world, a sphere where American might was transformative. "We are an empire now," the man said. "We create our own reality." In this brave new world, the United States was free of the constraints and limitations that bound normal nations. Again Ronald

Reagan was the exemplar. He confronted the Evil Empire and the Berlin Wall fell. He ran an arms race that the Soviets could not afford, and communism crumbled. He confronted dictators, and they backed off. Their people, emboldened, rose up and democracy bloomed. It would take more than a decade for this vision of history to find its fullest expression in the faith-based foreign policy of George W. Bush, and it could be summed up simply: If you are America, you have only to will something for it to be. Stand up and confront the enemy, whoever he may be, and he will back down or collapse, by definition hollow at the core. This was the new American era.

Among the many problems with this worldview, none was more serious than the simple fact that it was a self-defeating fantasy. As we have seen, the myth that Americans spun around 1989—confront and they will fall—bore little resemblance to how the Cold War actually ended. The regimes of Eastern Europe were indeed rotten at the core. But the push to collapse came less from the outside than from within. Once the containing pressure of the Soviet system was lifted by Mikhail Gorbachev, they essentially imploded. This is not to diminish Ronald Reagan's contribution to ending the Cold War. To the contrary, it is important to recognize how he did so: not by uncompromising Manichaean confrontation, as many in the Bush administration believed, but by engagement. He embraced Gorbachev as a reformer, a potential partner in peace, and that made all the difference.

Mistaking cause and effect was the single most critical misreading of the lessons of 1989, and tragically costly. For it was a straight line from the fantasy of Cold War victory to the invasion of Iraq. Convinced that freedom could be won there as easily as it was in Eastern Europe, and that it need only confront the tyrant, the Bush administration scarcely bothered to plan for the aftermath of the war. There was no blueprint for building democracy. Little forethought was given to ruling the country during a transition to self-governance, nor to the hard work of creating institutions of civil society and the rule of law or even a functioning economy. The result was a loss of lives and fortune that will heavily weigh for decades to come.

Worse, it blinded Americans to the realities of a dramatically changing world. In recent years, the United States behaved less as an unchallengeable superpower than some oddly enfeebled giant, besieged by enemies. It increased defense spending by a quarter of a trillion dollars since 2001—more than the combined military budgets of China, India, Britain, and Russia. It waged a global war on terror despite the lack of subsequent attacks in the United States, and despite clear evidence that well-coordinated international police action is more effective in combating terrorism than aircraft carriers or bunker-buster bombs. It confronted North Korea and Iran—the remaining members of the once-vaunted "Axis of Evil"—as though these geopolitical bit players were existential threats to the nation. It frittered away billions upon billions of dollars, largely without accounting or responsible management, as though military might somehow meant that money grew on trees and that, as vice president Cheney memorably put it, "deficits don't matter."

Along the way, it all but missed the great transformation going on around it—one made possible by the end of the Cold War. In a recent book, *The Post-American World*, my *Newsweek* colleague Fareed Zakaria artfully dubbed this the "rise of the rest," the story of how global economic growth has changed the world. Japan was the first non-Western nation to awaken, then China, India and the rest of Southeast Asia, not to mention the emerging economies of the Americas. Today these newcomers wield substantial power of their own, and their rise makes the world a very different place from what it was even half a decade ago, let alone in 1989. Since the turn of the millennium, the U.S. share of world GDP has declined from 36 percent to 28 percent; that of China, India, Russia and Brazil has more than doubled to 16 percent. Meanwhile, America's low-cost industrial base and back-office services shifted to factories in Guangzhou and call centers in Hyderabad. China's foreign exchange reserves rose from $200 billion in 2001 to $1.8 trillion in 2008; India's have gone from $50 billion to $300 billion. Thanks to low savings at home, the U.S. government relies more and more on overseas borrowing to finance everything from Social Security and Medicaid to the ongoing war in Iraq. Europe has become a bigger market than the United States. The world's biggest banks are increasingly Arab and Chinese. You have only to look for the world's tallest buildings to appreciate, symbolically, how much has changed. Forget New York. Think Shanghai.

The crash of 2008 will not change this fundamental dynamic. As the United States and Europe slide into recession, virtually all global economic growth will come from Asia, possibly for years to come. Though hurt by the crisis, the economic and financial power of China, India and other formerly "emerging" nations will grow relative to that of the United States. All this will accelerate the trend away from the America-centric world that began with the fall of the Berlin Wall, and it will unfold in ways that are difficult to predict. Even amid the worst days of the Iraq war, when the world's anger at U.S. foreign policy was at fever pitch, people everywhere retained their faith in one thing quintessentially American: its economy. Nothing could rival it as an engine for growth, prosperity and innovation. Its capital markets ruled the world; its entrepreneurial and technological prowess was unchallenged. For nations rich and poor, there was but one path for economic and social advancement. That was the American model.

By early 2009, that model was widely seen as a sham. As the United States bailed out banks and automakers, the contagion of financial collapse threatened to spread around the world. Like Monarch butterflies fluttering north from Mexico, business and political leaders descended on the little village of Davos, Switzerland, for the annual World Economic Forum. Billed as a gathering of the Earth's most powerful men and women, it has traditionally served as a celebration of the capitalist way, leavened with talk of corporate responsibility and the greater global good. This year, by contrast, the crisp alpine air was filled with angry shouts and murmurs about the perils of America's "faith based" economic policies and its destructive "casino capitalism." For so long, Americans lived under the almost religious illusion that markets were inherently self-correcting and self-regulating, that good governance was unnecessary if not an outright nuisance. Yet suddenly it all came crashing down. This, too, was a legacy of 1989. Self-proclaimed victory in the Cold War not only made the United States the sole superpower. It psychologically freed the country to do as it saw fit, in whatever realm it chose. Not only was America unbound from the rules of the old world; it was unbound from its own. It awoke, abruptly and unhappily, to a new world, unfamiliar but very much of its own making.

Against this backdrop, America's enduring obsession with military supremacy—the default position of Cold War confrontation, with its eternal quest for new adversaries—seems dangerously dated, if not wholly out of touch with the new reality. The rise of the rest has created new rivals but few enemies. Most would be better viewed as partners, for the challenges of this new world are primarily those of collaboration. How to revive the economy and keep the great global boom rolling into the coming decades? How to handle the politics of global prosperity? Growing populations and rising wealth place unprecedented stress on the earth's resources. We see it in the volatile prices of oil, food and commodities. Malthus is back in vogue. Everything we have long taken for granted seems suddenly in short supply: energy, clean air and freshwater, all that nourishes us and supports our modern way of life. Climate change and environmental degradation threaten the very future of the planet. The Secretary-General of the United Nations, Ban Ki-moon, rightly calls this the defining issue of our age. Yes, Al Qaeda remains a challenge. But it is not remotely on the same scale as the threat of global warming or worldwide economic meltdown.

This world, too, requires American leadership. Yet increasingly, the converse is also true: in a changed world, the United States can accomplish little without the partnership or cooperation of the rest. Americans sense this. Polls show that less than 40 percent believe the United Nations, for example, is a particularly effective organization. Nonetheless, a whopping 79 percent believe that U.S. foreign policy should be conducted in concert with it. This is not idealism. It is pragmatism: some problems are simply too big, too complicated, to be dealt with alone. Leslie Gelb summed it up in his recent book *Power Rules*: "The reality is this: succeed together or fail apart."

America remains the indispensable nation so long as it sees the world as it is and operates in the realm of reality, rather than self-delusion. One of the smartest commentators I know, the historian Tony Judt, not long ago wrote an essay entitled "What Have We Learned, If Anything?" In it, he warned of the dangers of "mismemory" or, worse, the deliberate rewriting of memory (not unlike the onetime overlords of the Soviet empire) to shape the future. "In the wake of 1989," he said, "with boundless confidence and insufficient reflection, we put the twentieth century behind us and strode boldly into its successor swaddled in self-serving half-truths: the triumph of the West, the end of History, the unipolar American moment." If there is a real enemy, he concluded, it is less the rogues' gallery of Washington's "bad guys" than America's ignorance of itself and the past—a prescription, according to Judt, for self-defeat.

America will sort out its troubles. The country does that well, better than most others. But it begins with stock-taking—going back to where things went wrong and facing problems squarely. Nations, like individuals, occasionally need a reality check. Mine grew partly from that encounter with a Russian soldier smoking a cigarette on a garbage heap in Berlin, spitting at the feet of my arrogance. For me, it was the beginning of understanding. As a nation, on the twentieth anniversary of the end of Cold War, Americans should look hard at 1989. It was, truly, the pivotal moment, the end of something momentous but also, and more important, a beginning—a year that changed the world, the United States included. It's time to fully understand just how, and why, and move on.

NOTES ON SOURCES

I wrote this book to tell a story, largely unknown, and to do so simply and straightforwardly, in plain language for ordinary people. I would not presume to call it definitive history; this book might better be thought of merely as a firsthand account of the revolutions in Eastern Europe and the fall of the Berlin Wall.

Unusually among foreign correspondents, I was on scene for most of the events described, with few exceptions. My beat for *Newsweek* ran from Germany through every country of the East. Most other news organizations, by contrast, divided assignments among a few (and in some cases many) correspondents.

That is at once a strength and a weakness. If I can say with a certain authority how things happened on the ground, or at least how I saw them happen, I cannot claim the same about events elsewhere. I was not in Washington, reporting from inside the White House or the State Department. Nor do I have much sense, firsthand, of how Americans at home perceived them. I didn't watch U.S. television. I read contemporary news accounts only when I could get them—not easy in an Eastern Europe cut off from the West, before the days of the Internet. I have since done considerable research to fill the gaps. But this book's strength, in the end, derives from its eyewitness experience.

Last, it goes without saying that the views expressed here are my own and do not reflect those of my employers, past, present or future.

CHAPTER 1

It is no revelation that George W. Bush modeled his presidency on Ronald Reagan's. Lou Cannon and Carl M. Cannon make perhaps the best case in their biography, *Reagan's Disciple*, 2008, in which they describe the Reagan legacy as the "gold standard" for Bush's own. I also recommend Steven

Hayward's *Lion at the Gate*, 2005, as well as a *New York Times Magazine* article, "Reagan's Son," by Bill Keller, dated January 26, 2003, seven weeks before the invasion of Iraq—at which point, the Cannons argue, Bush broke with the Reagan model.

Quotes attributed to the president are drawn from transcripts of his speeches and remarks. Among others: Remarks Announcing the End of Major Combat Operations in Iraq Aboard the USS *Abraham Lincoln*, May 1, 2003; Remarks at the Twentieth Anniversary of the National Endowment for Democracy, U.S. Chamber of Commerce, November 6, 2003; Eulogy at the National Funeral Service for Ronald Wilson Reagan at the National Cathedral in Washington, June 11, 2004; Speech to the National Endowment for Democracy, Ronald Reagan Building and International Trade Center in Washington, October 6, 2005; Commencement Address at the U.S. Military Academy at West Point, May 27, 2006; Remarks at the Dedication of the Victims of Communism Memorial, June 12, 2007; Remarks to Conservative Union at the Omni Shoreham Hotel in Washington, February 8, 2008.

I drew additional background from contemporary news accounts, including "Raze Berlin Wall, Reagan Urges Soviet" by Gerald M. Boyd, the *New York Times*, June 13, 1987, as well as retrospectives on the twentieth anniversary of the speech: *Bild*, "The Great Speech That Changed the World"; Associated Press, "Reagan's 'Tear Down This Wall' Speech Turns 20"; *Time*, "20 Years After 'Tear Down This Wall'"; *American Conservative*, review of *Rise of the Vulcans*, by Georgie Anne Geyer, June 7, 2004.

For George H. W. Bush's reaction to the fall of the Wall, see Michael R. Beschloss and Strobe Talbott, *At the Highest Levels: The Inside Story of the End of the Cold War*, 1993. Peter Robinson's fascinating book, *How Ronald Reagan Changed My Life*, 2003, was a key source for the background on Reagan's immortal speech. Additional references: *Hoover Digest*, "Tearing Down That Wall," by Peter M. Robinson, reprinted from the *Weekly Standard*, June 23, 1997. Also by Robinson, "Why Reagan Matters," Speech to the Commonwealth Club, January 7, 2004. Ronald Reagan: Remarks at the Brandenburg Gate, West Berlin, June 12, 1987; Address to the Students of Moscow University, May 31, 1988.

I cite James Mann's masterly history of the George W. Bush administration's foreign policy and its ideological antecedents, *Rise of the Vulcans: The History of Bush's War Cabinet*, 2004, further elaborated in "Tear Down That Myth," a *New York Times* op-ed, June 10, 2007. An excellent analysis of Ronald Reagan's transition from intransigent Cold War warrior to flexible partner in peace can be found in Bradley Lightbody's *The Cold War*, 1999.

For the ultimate indictment of communism, I refer to *Perestroika: New Thinking for Our Country and the World*, Mikhail Gorbachev, 1987. "Chernobyl turned me into a different person," Gorbachev writes in his book *Man-*

ifesto for the Earth, 2006. The higher the future Soviet leader rose in the party hierarchy, the more clearly he saw the gravity of the social and economic crisis gripping the country: how heavy industry devoted mainly to military production was not only fueling an arms race and beggaring the civilian population but was, quite literally, poisoning the nation in its environmental effects. Chernobyl, as he saw it, was only the tip of the iceberg of a much deeper problem, propelling him to think differently about everything, from state policies on secrecy and information to Soviet foreign policy.

As for the account of the evening of November 9, 1989, at Checkpoint Charlie, I was there, on the Eastern side, watching events unfold. For further details on Gunter Schabowski's press conference, from 6:53 p.m. to 7:01 p.m., see the transcript filed as Document No. 8 at the Cold War History Project. The exchanges between Egon Krenz and Gunter Schabowski are based on interviews with both men, Krenz in 1990 and most particularly Schabowski in March 1999. The reporter who asked the fatal question was a friend, the British journalist and eminent literary critic Daniel Johnson. He, too, deserves a measure of credit for bringing down the Wall.

CHAPTER 2

My travels along the Wall and to East Berlin, at least as they relate to this chapter, took place in the fall of 1988 and early 1989 and culminated in a February cover story for *Newsweek International*. I spoke to diplomats, government officials on both sides of the Wall, analysts, polling experts, academics and many, many ordinary people from both East and West. To my shame, I began writing the article convinced that the Wall would come down within a year or two—and ended, persuaded by my largely West German sources, with an embrace of the conventional wisdom that it would be around for decades, if not forever.

Basic facts about the Wall are drawn from many sources, among them: The Wall, Press and Information, Office of Land Berlin, 2000/2001; Bilanz der Todesopfer, Checkpoint Charlie Museum, 1999; *Die Berliner Mauer*, Fleming/Koch, 1999; *Encyclopedia Britannica*, Berlin Wall; a variety of Web sites pertaining to the Berlin Wall. Other useful references include Frederick Taylor's fine history *The Berlin Wall: A World Divided, 1961–1989*, 2006; Peter Wyden's tour de force *Wall: The Inside Story of Divided Berlin*, 1989, which among other things is the source of the Allensbach data on West German attitudes toward the Wall and reunification; William F. Buckley Jr., *The Fall of the Berlin Wall*, 2004. One of the best travelogues of this genre ever written is Anthony Bailey's *The Edge of the Forest*, a reporter-at-large feature published in the June 27, 1983, *New Yorker*.

For the "butcher's bill" on the Cold War, great credit is owed to the

Brookings Institution and its comprehensive *Atomic Audit: The Costs and Consequences of U.S. Nuclear Weapons since 1940*, 1998, compiled by Stephen I. Schwartz and his research team. See also "The Hidden Costs of Our Nuclear Arsenal," Schwartz, June 30, 1998, Brookings Publications; "U.S. Military Spending in the Cold War Era," Robert Higgs, *Policy Analysis*, November 30, 1988; *We All Lost the Cold War*, Richard Lebow and Janice Stein, Princeton University Press, 1994; "Four Trillion Dollars and Counting," the *Journal of Atomic Scientists*, 1995; *The Cold War*, Martin Walker, 1993; *The Black Book of Communism*, 1997. Statistics on casualties in Cold War conflicts drawn from *Warfare and Armed Conflict*. President Dwight D. Eisenhower's "The Chance for Peace," a speech delivered to the American Society of Newspaper Editors on April 16, 1953, should be required reading for contemporary policymakers.

Anyone who traveled in the East bloc, and to East Berlin in particular, will be familiar with the phenomenon of "sticky" air and the gestalt of a communist police state. For those who are not, I recommend Anna Funder's *Stasiland*, 2003. A series of popular movies, growing out of what the Germans today call *Ostalgia*, or nostalgia for the old East, capture something of its spirit, among them *The Lives of Others*. I am grateful to Wikipedia and its wonderful link to GDR jokes. The DDR Museum, on Karl-Liebknecht Strasse in Berlin, offers a vivid evocation of daily life in the former East Germany.

As a final note, I should clarify my use of *socialism* and *communism*. The rulers of Eastern Europe employed the terms interchangeably. Needless to say, their "socialist" workers' states, ruled autocratically by themselves, bore little resemblance to modern Europe's socialist or social-welfare parties.

CHAPTER 3

Interviews with Nemeth, Kulcsar, Pozsgay and others, including many of the leaders of Hungary's future political parties, were conducted in Budapest in November and December as part of a *Newsweek International* cover story dated December 12, 1988. The interview with Karoly Grosz was in Budapest in July 1988.

The best book I've found on Hungary's break with communism is Rudolf L. Tokes's *Hungary's Negotiated Revolution: Economic Reform, Social Change and Political Succesion*, 1996. For additional background: Charles Gati, *The Bloc That Failed: Soviet–East European Relations in Transition*, 1990; "Reforming Communist Systems: Lessons from the Communist Experience," paper by Charles Gati, June 1988; Tabor Hajdu, "Setting the Points," *Hungarian Quarterly*, Winter 1999.

See also George Bush and Brent Scowcroft, *A World Transformed*, 1998.

Gorbachev's remarkable comments to President-elect George H. W. Bush can be found in *The Turn: From the Cold War to a New Era* by Don Oberdorfer, 1991, as well as Richard Rhodes's admirable case study in the perils of geopolitical blindness, *Arsenals of Folly*, 2007. See also CNN interview with George Bush and James Baker, October 1997.

CHAPTER 4

Reporting and interviews—with government officials, Solidarity activists and ordinary people—conducted during frequent trips to Poland for *Newsweek* beginning in September 1988 through June 1989. I am particularly indebted to Bronislaw Geremek and Janusz Onyszkiewicz, the Solidarity activists I visited most in Warsaw, as well as Andrzej Wiecko, *Newsweek*'s office manager and translator extraordinaire.

For further background, I recommend: speech by General Wojciech Jaruzelski, 105th Landon Lecture, Kent State University, March 11, 1996, in which the Polish leader likens himself to a geopolitical "Hamlet" caught between the rocks of Polish patriotism and what he considered the reality of Russian occupation. See transcript, Brezhnev-Jaruzelski telephone conversation, October 19, 1981, National Security Archive; text of oral message from Brezhnev to Jaruzelski dated November 21, 1981, the Cold War International History Project. For a vivid sketch of life in communist Poland, I refer to Janine Wedel, *The Private Poland*, 1986, as well as *The Haunted Land: Facing Europe's Ghosts after Communism*, Tina Rosenberg, 1996. Perhaps the best reportage on the breakup of the East bloc, including Poland, is Timothy Garton Ash's *The Revolutions of '89*, 1990.

General Jaruzelski's critics often accused him of misrepresenting the Soviet threat in 1981. Though not "quivering with desire for military intervention," as he put it in his speech at Kent State, the Russians nonetheless sent unmistakable signals. Under the pretext of holding maneuvers, they mobilized the Red Army on Poland's eastern border. Leonid Brezhnev, the Russian leader, telephoned Jaruzelski on October 19, urging him to "take the decisive measures you intend to use against the counterrevolution," according to the official transcript of the telephone call. On November 21, the Soviet ambassador demanded a private meeting and read out an oral message from Brezhnev, suggesting that Poland was "losing control of the situation" to the point that the very existence of socialism in Poland (and elsewhere) might be threatened. "Doesn't this suggest to you that a failure to take harsh measures will cost you?" Brezhnev asked, urging the Poles to increase their "combat readiness."

That letter, for all its threatening rhetoric, was a masterpiece of ambiguity. Never did it specifically direct Jaruzelski to use force; neither did it indicate whether the Soviets were prepared to intervene. Yet he had no doubt. "Brezhnev's message was very similar in tone to the notorious letters addressed to Alexander Dubcek in 1968," he later said. No less threatening, he added, was an ultimatum announcing a drastic cut in gas and energy deliveries, to take effect on January 1, 1982—a use of Russia's energy weapon that, in Poland's economic straits, would have proved devastating.

By early December, the pressures had apparently grown too great. At a meeting with the General Staff of the USSR Armed Forces, according to CIA documents, Jaruzelski ordered his generals meeting with their USSR counterparts to endorse a plan to admit into Poland, under the pretext of maneuvers, the Soviet Army, the National People's Army of the GDR and the Czechoslovak People's Army. Documents presented at the meeting showed that the Soviets were readying three armies consisting of eighteen divisions across Poland's borders. The invasion date was set for December 8. According to the Soviet plan, the Polish Army was to remain in its bases. Source: Wilson Center, Cold War History Project, document dated December 1, 1980. As Jaruzelski told it in his Kent State address, his only choice was the "lesser evil"—cracking down on Solidarity.

CHAPTER 5

The story of Nemeth's mission to Moscow in March 1989 is drawn from interviews with Nemeth in March 1995 and April 2008. Nemeth was absolutely right in fearing that Grosz would seek to undercut him. See "Memorandum of Conversation between M. S. Gorbachev and Karoly Grosz, General Secretary of the Hungarian Socialist Workers Party, Moscow, 23–24 March 1989," National Security Archive. According to the secret minutes, Hungary's communist leader briefed Gorbachev on events in Hungary and, while praising their general direction, suggested that "their pace is somewhat disconcerting." Ideally, Grosz said, the communist party would "retain power by political means, avoiding armed conflict." Gorbachev's response was revealing. "Democracy is needed," he agreed, yet he added that it was important to "clearly draw boundaries." The "limit," he suggested, should be "the safekeeping of socialism and the assurance of stability." He apparently did not recognize the degree to which those twin goals had grown incompatible.

It is interesting to note that (1) Nemeth first met Gorbachev in 1985, when the future Soviet leader visited Hungary for three weeks to study Hungarian agriculture. Excerpt from an unaired CNN interview dated October 1997: "That was the first time I [Nemeth] saw him in action, not like that sort of stupid old-guard representative from the Politburo, but someone who really asked real questions." Hence Nemeth's surprise at

Gorbachev's subsequent hard-line defense of socialism. (2) In the run-up to this phase (late 1987 and early 1988) Gorbachev asked working groups headed by Alexander Yakovlev and others to delve into the relationship of Leninism to perestroika and to investigate how and why classic socialism had gone wrong. He seemed to think that if communism could be put back on the right track, it could be saved and even become a model for egalitarian prosperity.

Sources for the material on the Bush transition include *A World Transformed*, George Bush and Brent Scowcroft, 1998; *Germany Unified and Europe Transformed*, Philip Zelikow and Condoleezza Rice, 1995; George Shultz, *Turmoil and Triumph: My Years as Secretary of State*, 1993; James Baker, *The Politics of Diplomacy*, 1995; *American Diplomacy and the End of the Cold War*, Robert L. Hutchings, 1997; Adam Michnik, *Sleepwalking through History*, 1999; Elizabeth Pond, *Beyond the Wall*, 1993; Harvey Sicherman, "The Rest of Reagan," *Orbis* 44, 2000. For an analysis of the CIA National Intelligence Estimates on the Soviet Union and Eastern Europe, in the original, few compilations are better than *At Cold War's End*, edited by Benjamin B. Fischer, available on the Internet at www.cia.gov/csi.

The quote from Cheney concerning Gorbachev's possible ouster comes from an interview with CNN on April 29, 1989, as cited by Hutchings. The astonishing admission by Rice that she "missed" the revocation of the Brezhnev Doctrine—one of the decisive moments of the century—comes from the *Bulletin of Atomic Scientists*, July/August 2004. Former U.S. ambassador to Moscow Jack Matlock describes his fruitless efforts to persuade the Bush transition team, and later the White house, of Gorbachev's bona fides in his memoir *Autopsy on an Empire*, 1995.

George H. W. Bush's inaugural address was rather like the man, decent but a bit wooden. He spoke about the passing of the totalitarian era, "its old ideas blown away like leaves from an ancient, lifeless tree," and about a new American engagement in the world, refreshed by its freedoms but circumspect in the use of power. "Some see leadership as high drama, and the sound of trumpets calling, and sometimes it is that," he said in one memorable passage of the speech, as personally revealing as it was wise. "But I see history as a book with many pages, and each day we fill a page with acts of hopefulness and meaning. The new breeze blows, a page turns, the story unfolds."

A former colleague of Condoleezza Rice recalled a discussion of Gorbachev and Soviet military capabilities from the time when she sat on the board of the Institute of East-West Strategic Studies in New York. Rice insisted that the Soviet leader's talk of peace and a "common house of Europe" was merely a facade for a dangerous Warsaw Pact military buildup. To her mind, it was a ruse to lull the West into complacency. She spoke forcefully of the money Moscow was spending on new weapons, and the prospect of Soviet tanks rolling through the Fulda Gap on the intra-German border and on toward Frankfurt and the heart of Western Europe.

"Condi," said the colleague, a former British diplomat and intelligence officer named Ian Cuthbertson, director of studies at the think tank, "this simply is not a true picture." He walked her through his particular specialty, the Soviet order of battle. His picture of the real Red Army was very different from the impressive force on paper. He essentially counted out which tank battalions had been cannibalized for spare parts, how badly trained Warsaw Pact forces had become, how low on supplies they were, from ammunition to petrol. (Of a typical eight-hundred-tank division, usually no more than a hundred tanks would be operational; a small fraction of that number could be considered combat-ready; and an even smaller number had crews well enough trained to do more than drive the tanks around a parade ground.) His bottom line, as he told Rice: "The Soviet army can barely roll out of its barracks, let alone through the Fulda Gap." Subsequent scholarship has borne him out. At the time that Rice was urging uncompromised vigilance against the Soviet threat, the enemy was essentially decomposing.

CHAPTER 6

Material for the May Day celebrations is based on a reporting trip to Budapest for *Newsweek*. The reconstruction of the critical events of May 1–3 and their aftermath is told by Miklos Nemeth and Gunter Schabowski, a member of the Politburo and party chief of Berlin who had formerly been editor in chief of East Germany's official newspaper, *Neues Deutschland*. Both Nemeth and Schabowski have been interviewed elsewhere concerning the exchange between Kessler and Karpati, including an exceptional BBC–Spiegel TV documentary *The Fall of the Wall*, by Brian Lapping Associates (under the direction of David Ash and Stephen Clark) in 1994, and CNN's 1998 series called *The Cold War Project*. All quotes either appear here for the first time or were confirmed with the original source.

A further word on Schabowski. Among the most powerful men in the country, he was at one point considered a possible successor to Erich Honecker. I met him in early 1999, just after his seventieth birthday. A genial and engaging man, he was remarkably straightforward (and startlingly critical) in discussing his central role in the events of 1989. It was long ago, but they remained vivid. No one who was immersed in them forgets. Unlike Schabowski, some never move on.

The material on Horst Teltschik's secret visits to Budapest and his relationship with Hungary's reformers, and Nemeth in particular, is drawn from a conversation in the spring of 1999 in Munich at the headquarters of BMW, where Teltschik was a member of the board of directors. Nemeth confirmed details of these meetings, saying that Kohl offered to ship "trains full of coal" to Hungary to counter a cutoff of Soviet energy supplies, should it occur. Kohl also promised to intervene with the International Monetary Fund in lightening the burden of Hungary's debt. "The Hungarian government had lied to the IMF, cheated them for years," Nemeth told me in April 2008. "I wanted to set the record straight—but also to protect ourselves in doing so." He stressed his desire to move toward what was then the European Community and away from the Soviet counterpart, COMECON. In all this, said Nemeth, "I got Kohl's very, very strong support."

Genscher's visit to Washington is described in his memoir, *Rebuilding a House Divided*, 1998. See also Zelikow and Rice, *Germany Unified and Europe Transformed*, 1995, for the insider reaction to Genscher's visit and to the subsequent flap over the Lance missiles. What made this diplomatic interlude so surreal was its almost complete geopolitical irrelevance. By April, nearly all aspects of military power had become open to negotiation, from intercontinental missiles to chemical weapons and conventional armaments. Following his agreement with Ronald Reagan to reduce ballistic warheads, initialed the previous year, Gorbachev had in December announced massive unilateral cuts in Russian forces in Eastern Europe—a move that the *New York Times* editorial board likened in global effect to the 1918 declaration of Woodrow Wilson's Fourteen Points, or Churchill and Roosevelt's Atlantic Charter of 1941. Adding insult to injury, many of the United States' other European allies had begun lining up with Germany. With the exception of British prime minister Margaret Thatcher, whom Kohl irritably referred to as "that woman," few saw the logic of pushing new weapons on Europe at the very moment that the threat was receding.

How vast was the gulf between the doyens of the Bush administration and someone such as Teltschik. In contrast to the American national security team, he saw events in the East as a "historic opportunity," as he put it to me at the time. His individual role was critical to events in Hungary, and therefore to the revolutions elsewhere in Eastern Europe. Yet it is almost entirely unknown, even in Germany. "No one has told this history," Teltschik told me in our meeting in Munich. "Not even me in my book, nor Kohl in his."

CHAPTER 7

I took a series of reporting trips to Poland during the election campaign and its aftermath, traveling and interviewing extensively around the country. I was repeatedly struck by the comparative innocence of both sides. Solidarity had no inkling of how well it would do. Lech Walesa, in particular, railed at being drawn into early elections, convinced they would favor the communists—who he assumed, mistakenly, would use their superior organizational power to stage an effective, all-out campaign.

Solidarity's spokesman Janusz Onyszkiewicz laughed when I asked him how he thought the vote would go. "We have no organization. We have no money. Poland is a complete political wilderness. No one has any idea what will happen." The communist party's chief political pollster and campaign strategist, Colonel Stanislaw Kwiatkowski, advised official candidates that their "personality," rather than their political affiliation would be what counts with voters. "We are confident," he told me, sharing his projections that the communist party would win anywhere from a quarter to half of the Senate, as well as a majority of the contested seats in the lower house. Other party leaders, however, did not share his optimism. Jerzy Urban, the information minister, who was running as an independent in Warsaw, grumbled that Solidarity looked unstoppable. What would he do if he lost? He joked about opening a porno magazine. At least, I took him to be joking. In fact, that's just what he did—and wound up making millions.

While Solidarity won the election decisively, it can be argued that both sides lost, as the eminent British historian Timothy Garton Ash notes with trademark irony in his account of 1989, *We the People*. Often forgotten in the hoopla accompanying Solidarity's victory was an important fact: only 62 percent of Poles voted in this most important election in the nation's history—far less than the 79 percent in the 1975 parliamentary elections, when only communists ran. Most Poles were too tired, too dispirited, too fed up with politics and politicians to bother. Those who did vote crossed out communists with the flair and vigor—*pfft, pfft, pfft*—bred of decades of anger, frustration and disappointment. But few thought Poland would much change with Solidarity in the government, or that their own lives would improve. Yes, June 4 marked the death of communism in Poland. But it died as much with a whimper as a bang.

I moved on to Budapest shortly after the Polish elections, meeting Erich Honecker in Berlin as a sort of geopolitical detour. The behind-the-scenes dimension comes from interviews with the principals, Pozsgay and Nemeth in particular, as well as members of the Committee for Historical Justice. Grosz's calumny against Nagy at that decisive meeting of the Central Committee in the days leading up the funeral come from an interview with Nemeth by the National Security Archive in Washington, backstopped by Tokes, who also chronicled the downfall of Karoly Grosz and the mass defections from the party that would seal his fate. I also relied on the NSA interview for the material on the death threats Nemeth received during this period, as well as a CNN interview undertaken as part of the network's 1997 Cold War History Project.

The interview with Honecker took place on June 7, 1989, with the *Washington Post* and *Newsweek*. For Honecker's visit to Cuba, see Charles S.

Maier's brilliant *Dissolution: The Crisis of Communism and the End of East Germany*, 1998. The segment on the Warsaw Pact summit in Bucharest and the genesis of the plot against Honecker is based on interviews with Schabowski and Nemeth as well as transcripts of Honecker's and Ceausescu's speeches of July 7, 1989. Honecker's mirror-image letters to Moscow, in 1980 and 1989, can be found online in the Woodrow Wilson Center's Cold War Archive. And, of course, Oskar Fischer should not be confused with Joschka Fischer, German foreign minister from 1998 to 2005.

Sources useful for the segment on America's awakening include, among others, *A World Transformed*, George Bush and Brent Scowcroft, 1998; *Germany Unified and Europe Transformed*, Zelikow and Rice, 1997; *American Diplomacy and the End of the Cold War*, Robert L. Hutchings, 1997; James A. Baker, *The Politics of Diplomacy*, 1995. Nemeth's account of his conversation with President Bush appears in an interview in the BBC–Spiegel Television documentary *The Fall of the Wall*, 1994.

It's worth noting, too, that if the White House was slow to fully appreciate the magnitude of changes under way in the East, the U.S. embassy in Warsaw was not. Declassified cables from the period show Ambassador John Davis and a senior political officer, Daniel Fried, to have been genuinely foresighted in predicting Solidarity's decisive victory in the elections and the general course of events on the ground. This cable traffic is available on the Web via the National Security Archive. U.S. reporting from Hungary was no less incisive, affirming once again that policymakers in Washington (as elsewhere) often hear only what they want to hear.

CHAPTERS 8–9

The saga of the Pan-European Picnic is chiefly based on interviews with Miklos Nemeth and the tenth-anniversary recollections of Laszlo Nagy, one of the key organizers. The bizarre tale of Frau Silvia Lux, an East German schoolteacher, and her children was told to West German television upon her arrival in Austria and reproduced in the documentary by BBC–Spiegel TV *The Fall of the Wall*, 1994. (Transcript 3/13, Liddell Hart Centre of Military Archives, King's College, London.) Two quotes from Imre Pozsgay ("This invitation gave me a chance . . ." and "nerve-racking . . .") come from the same source. (Transcript 3/25, Liddell Hart Centre.)

There is some confusion about the role of those "West German officials." Bonn's ambassador to Budapest at the time, Alexander Arnot, told me that his consular officers had no role in the Pan-European Picnic; yet on-scene accounts make clear reference to people who identified themselves as such. Nemeth said that roughly a dozen West German officials were involved in the plot, including Chancellery officials, members of the

BND (West Germany's intelligence service) and the Budapest chapter of the German Red Cross. Arnot was not informed, according to Nemeth, at least not directly. Genscher's reactions to Nemeth's visit to Bonn can be found in his memoir, *Rebuilding a House Divided*, 1998.

The related chapter, "The Great Escape," draws on the same interviews, including one with Michael Jansen, the German diplomat tasked with organizing shelter for the tens of thousands of East German "tourists" holed up in Hungary with no plans for returning home. He spoke specifically of secretly shuttling personally between Vienna and Budapest in preparation for the Great Escape. Jansen went on to assist East Germans in Prague to escape to the Federal Republic during the events of late September and October.

See Rice and Zelikow for Fischer's charge of "treason!" The statistics on the number of East Germans encamped around Lake Balaton and elsewhere come from Maier's *Dissolution*, while the numbers on those who fled during the first days and weeks of the exodus are drawn from Rice and Zelikow. Gunter Schabowski colorfully described the reaction of the East German Politburo, as well as the story of Erich Honecker's disastrous "Big Idea." The reactions of ordinary East and West Germans, as well as government officials, are drawn from a series of reporting trips in Berlin and other cities during September and October for *Newsweek*.

For the account of George H. W. Bush's July visit to Poland and Hungary, see *A World Transformed*, Bush and Scowcroft. The quote from Nemeth ("We both knew . . .") also comes from the BBC–Spiegel TV documentary. For the murmurings of German unification, beginning in earnest that September, see Zelikow and Rice as well as *American Diplomacy and the End of the Cold War* by Robert L. Hutchings, the unnamed NSC aide who counted himself among those "thrilled, not to say astonished, onlookers."

The interview with Ceausescu was the fruit of a play to his vanity. Recognizing his thirst to be noticed on the world's stage, I wrote through his ambassador in Bonn that Kenneth Auchincloss, my boss and the editor of *Newsweek International*, had always wanted to meet him. "Related to the Kennedys," I intimated, precipitating an invitation with all the pomp and circumstance normally accorded a visiting head of state. As part of the deal I was given two weeks' free run of the country in advance of the interview. It was an unprecedented license to go everywhere, largely uninhibited by the police, talking to peasants in their fields, townspeople, the few dissidents not in jail. If Ceausescu's handlers hoped I'd write a flattering portrait of his tyranny, they were mistaken. The final result—a cover story published in August—was officially classified as a state secret, according to intelligence authorities I met in Bucharest after Ceausescu's death.

One anecdote about the interview bears inclusion. Into the second hour of Ceausescu's monologue, Ken Auchincloss decided enough was enough is enough, even from the Danube of Thought. "Well, thank you, Mr. President," he said, hoping to end the show. Ceausescu stopped in midgesture, the torrent of his words suddenly arrested. A funny look, almost boyish, at once disappointed and disbelieving, crossed his face. He had probably never, ever been interrupted like this. His fist, momentarily frozen above his head, slowly came down. His eyes lost their manic intensity and seemed to slide back into the real world from somewhere in Outer Megalomania. "But . . . but . . . but," said the dictator plaintively. "I'm . . . I'm . . . not finished yet."

CHAPTER 10

The interval from early September through mid-October was a whirlwind of travel from one East European capital to another: Warsaw, Prague, Budapest, East Berlin, Bonn, Vienna and back again. I've confined the narrative to interviews with the principals in the drama: Nemeth, Pozsgay, Schabowski, Walesa, Mazowiecki, Havel. But many others played large roles in the events. Among them, in Poland: Bronislaw Geremek and Janusz Onyszkiewicz, a mathematician and alpinist who became Solidarity's spokesman (and had spent years in jail) and went on to become defense minister and eventually vice chairman of the European parliament. In Czechoslovakia, besides Havel, Jan Urban, a dissident signatory of Charter 77, and his best friend, Ivan Gabal, both future founders of Havel's Civic Forum movement, were very helpful, as was Jiri Dienstbier, also a Charter 77 signatory and future foreign minister, as well as others who figure in these pages and many more who do not. I still remember Milos Jakes with the greatest distaste.

Interviews in Budapest included U.S. ambassador Mark Palmer, various opposition-party leaders and foreign ministry officials. The scene featuring Imre Pozsgay was a great cameo moment of 1989, and highly ironic. By disbanding the Hungarian Socialist Workers Party when he did, disenfranchising hundreds of thousands of members in his anticommunist zeal, Pozsgay destroyed his own career. Had he found a way to hang on to them, he might well have realized his ambition to be a democratic Hungary's first president, according to Rudolf Tokes.

CHAPTER 11

I was in East Germany for most of the period covered in these final chapters. The insider's account of Gorbachev's visit on October 7 comes from

Schabowski. Gorbachev's aide was Anatoly Chernyaev; the story is excerpted from his diary in the Archive of the Gorbachev Foundation. Gorbachev had added, "I will not say a word of support for Honecker. But I will support the republic and the revolution." Chernyaev himself clearly saw this as a critical moment. Protests in Dresden that day drew twenty thousand people. The next day the Hungarian Socialist Workers Party planned to disband. Poland's communist party, he predicted, would not last past its next congress in February. "The dismantling of socialism as a world phenomenon has been proceeding. Perhaps it is inevitable and good. And a common fellow from Stavropol [Gorbachev] set this process in motion."

I was a witness to the riots in East Berlin on the night of October 7, of course, but relied for background on events in other cities, including Leipzig, Plauen and Dresden, on contemporary news reports as well as two indispensable histories: *Wir sind das Volk*, a painstaking and ultra-detailed chronicle from October 7 through December 17, 1989, published in 1990 by Hannes Bahrman and Christoph Links, and *Dissolution: The Crisis of Communism and the End of East Germany*, 1997, an autopsy of East Germany's final years by Charles S. Maier, a professor of history at Harvard University. The conversation between Egon Krenz and Milos Jakes, as well as the latter's aside concerning Gorbachev's behavior at the state dinner, is related in the BBC–Spiegel TV documentary, *The Fall of the Wall*. So is Jens Illing's frightening account of the security preparations for the night of October 9 in Leipzig.

Precisely who prevented that bloodbath, and how, remains unclear. I've reached the best judgment I could based on interviews with Schabowski, Krenz and other sources. Krenz's call to Soviet ambassador Vyacheslav Kochemasov is recounted by Maier as well as Zelikow and Rice, by way of the Russian envoy's autobiography, *Meine Letzte Mission*, 1994. See also Elizabeth Pond, *Beyond the Wall: Germany's Road to Unification*, 1993. The chilling directive announcing action against the "counter-revolutionaries . . . with weapons in the hand" can be found in *Wir sind das Volk*. The exchange between Helmut Hackenberg, the regional party chief, and Krenz comes from the BBC–Spiegel documentary. The eyewitness account of Erich Honecker's downfall on October 17 is told principally by Gunter Schabowski. Officially, Honecker's resignation would be for "health reasons."

Krenz recalled his increasingly desperate efforts to keep his government together in an interview with *Newsweek* in the spring of 1990, likening the experience to "riding a whirlwind." *Wir sind das Volk* documents how quickly and inexorably popular pressure built across the country during the interval between Honecker's ouster and the fall of the Wall on November 9. The conversation between Bush and Kohl is drawn from a declassified White House transcript dated October 23, 1989, 9:02–9:26 a.m. EST.

Concerning Krenz, the chancellor remarked, "I am not sure how courageous he is."

CHAPTER 12

The climax of the Fall is based almost entirely on firsthand reporting from East Berlin the night of November 9 and afterward. The reconstruction of the press conference, as noted in chapter 1, is based on interviews with Schabowski and Krenz, as well as the official GDR government transcript and original video clips of the event. The drama of that bitter, internecine summit of the Central Committee, presided over by Krenz and dominated by Gerhard Schurer's hair-raising portrayal of the country's economic crisis, is recorded in rich and authoritative detail in Maier's *Dissolution*. The dilemma of those who made the fateful decision to open the Wall—the commanders of the border crossings at Checkpoint Charlie and Bornholmerstrasse—is perfectly captured in the BBC–Spiegel TV documentary by the head of the East German visa office. He, too, had futilely been telephoning for instructions as the crowds built at the Wall. At the moment of the country's existential crisis, he said, "I couldn't find anyone to talk to."

The Wall is long gone. But for a reminder of how it all happened, and who ultimately deserves credit, I suggest a visit to the new Reichstag, refurbished and reopened in Berlin on April 19, 1999. Tucked away on the northeast corner of the building, oddly far from public view, is an unobtrusive bronze plaque, missed by almost all who visit:

> To the Hungarian people from the German people,
> To whom we owe thanks for a united Germany,
> A democratic Hungary, and a free Europe.

In Hungary, revolution came with little trace of popular upheaval. It would be too easy to suggest that knowledge of the people's unhappiness forced the country's reformers to act. It did not. They chose their own path, knowing that it did not necessarily bode well for themselves. "They are of historic importance," Horst Teltschik would tell me, speaking of Nemeth and those around him. "If you look at the history of mankind, there are very few examples where the leadership of a dictatorship became a leading force for democracy, knowing that in elections they would lose."

Years later, in a conversation with Teltschik, Hungary's Prime Minister Jozsef Antall referred disparagingly to those "old communists."

"Without those guys," Teltschik tartly responded, "you would never have come to power."

CHAPTERS 13 AND 14

The conversation between Bush and Kohl comes from a White House transcript dated November 10, 1989, 3:29–3:47 p.m. My guides to the Velvet Revolution were Vaclav Havel, Jan Urban, Ivan Gabal and his wife, Zdenka Gabalova. I will always be indebted to them for opening the door to one of the most moving experiences of my life.

My thanks to Hanns Schumacher, then an aide to Hans-Dietrich Genscher at the German foreign ministry, for getting me on that military transport to Bucharest. Videos of the Ceausescus' execution can be found on the Internet. *Videograms of a Revolution*, directed by Harun Farocki, captures the scene on Palace Square on December 21 and 22, 1989. The transcript of Ceausescu's "trial" makes far more compelling reading than might be captured in these brief excerpts. The transcript of his dressing down his generals over Timisoara, setting the stage for the massive killings in the city, is if anything even more telling about the man and his nature. Miklos Nemeth is the source of the reference to Hungarian intelligence helping Ceausescu's pursuers catch the fleeing dictator.

I am indebted to Richard Andrew Hall for his exceptionally researched reconstruction of the revolution-turned-coup in his Ph.D. thesis for the University of Michigan, "Rewriting the Revolution: Authoritarian Regime-State Relations and the Triumph of Securitate Revisionism in Post-Ceausescu Romania," 1997. One of the most exhaustive studies of the period is *The Romanian Revolution of December 1989*, 2005, by Peter Siani-Davies. Also useful was Edward Behr's *Kiss the Hand You Cannot Bite*, 1991, and *Modern Romania* by Tom Gallagher, 2005. Among the best compilations of academic writing on Romania and the events in Eastern Europe is *The Revolutions of 1989: Rewriting Histories*, edited by Vladimir Tismaneanu, 1999.

The closing remarks by Havel, Nemeth and Schabowski in the chapter entitled "Denouement" are all drawn from first-hand interviews.

EPILOGUE

The casualty figures come from *World War II: Combatants and Casualties, 1937–1945*. The Soviet Union lost 23 million soldiers and civilians; the toll for the United States was 418,000—a very considerable number, to be sure, but not commensurate with Soviet losses.

Charles Krauthammer's article "The Unipolar Moment" appeared in the Winter 1990–91 issue of *Foreign Affairs*. In 1993, Samuel P. Huntington published an essay in *Foreign Affairs* entitled "The Clash of Civilizations?"

He expanded it, eliding the question mark, in his book of 1996: *The Clash of Civilizations and the Remaking of World Order.* See also Ronald Steel, *Temptations of a Superpower,* 1996, and Robert W. Tucker, *The Imperial Temptation,* 1992, coauthored with David C. Hendrickson.

Robert Kagan's admirable essay in the Spring 2008 issue of *World Affairs,* "Neocon Nation," traces the bipartisan history of American idealism from 1776 to the present. Notably, it concludes (with a nod to David Halberstam) that U.S. foreign policy historically trends to excess—and trouble—when its leaders "fail to examine the assumptions of the era." The more absolutist the assumptions, the greater the ensuing troubles. This is very much the story of America's post–Cold War interlude, all the more so as time went on.

For an early and somewhat unnerving example of the White House's Manichaean vision, consider a speech by President Bush at Iowa Western Community College on January 21, 2000: "When I was coming up, it was a dangerous world, and you knew exactly who 'they' were. It was us versus them, and it was clear who 'them' was. Today we are not so sure who the 'they' are, but we know they're there." The conversation on faith-based foreign policy was reported by Ron Suskind in the *New York Times Magazine,* October 17, 2004, and amplified in his 2007 book, *One Percent Solution.* See also Mark Danner's "Iraq: The War of Imagination" in the December 21, 2006, issue of the *New York Review of Books.* The quote from Cheney is cited by former Treasury Secretary Paul O'Neill in his book with Ron Suskind, *The Price of Loyalty* (2004). The full citation reads: "You know, Paul, Reagan proved that deficits don't matter." O'Neill reports that the remark left him "speechless."

I've stressed the military aspect of the Reaganite myth of Cold War confrontation, mainly for brevity's sake, but there is also a strong economic component. The argument can be summed up fairly simply: by dramatically boosting American military spending in the 1980s, including the Star Wars missile defense, Reagan forced Moscow into an arms race it could not afford. The consequent economic pressures contributed to the collapse of the Soviet system. Intuitively, the case has a certain logic, for the Soviet Union did slide into economic crisis during the Reagan years. But while military expenditures were undoubtedly absorbing an ever-larger share of Soviet resources (again, chiefly because of falling oil revenues), it cannot be said this had much to do with the United States. If the Reagan administration substantially increased U.S. defense spending, the Soviet Union did not. Indeed, its defense budget was essentially unchanged through the 1980s, as Peter Scoblic notes in a thoroughly researched book, *Us vs. Them,* 2008. Mikhail Gorbachev, among others, long before he came to power and Reagan's military buildup had gotten under way, recognized that Moscow should *reduce* its military spending. Scoblic's conclusion, like that of other analysts: "The Soviet Union suffered no economic stress as a result of the Reagan buildup. Conservatives [who argue otherwise] are therefore retrofitting the Reagan administration—and themselves—with a degree of agency and optimism that they simply did not possess."

Blinded by the light of its triumphal march through the post–Cold War years, the United States failed to fully come to terms with the enormous changes in the world around it. Fareed Zakaria brilliantly sketches out the perils—and opportunities—of this new global landscape in *The Post-American World*, 2008. See also Leslie H. Gelb, *Power Rules: How Common Sense Can Rescue American Foreign Policy*, HarperCollins (2009). The quantitative backstopping for my brief discussion of this theme came partly from an article in the *Financial Times*, June 27, 2008, by Robert Hormats and Jim O'Neill at Goldman Sachs, "A New World for America's Next President." The caveat is this: The administration of George W. Bush did not create the myth of American triumphalism, even if his White House elevated it to cult status. Americans bear a collective responsibility, and no fresh start or clean slate is possible under a new president without that recognition. This is the point of Tony Judt's important essay, "What Have We Learned, If Anything?" in the May 1, 2008, *New York Review of Books*. Building on the theme in his book *Reappraisals*, 2008, he argues that the United States is locked in an "age of forgetting," such that it no longer knows where it came from, or what it stands for, with "calamitous" results and the prospect of worse to come.

INDEX